T0355819

INVEST LIKE AN INSTITUTION

PROFESSIONAL STRATEGIES FOR FUNDING A SUCCESSFUL RETIREMENT

Michael C. Schlachter

Apress·

Invest Like an Institution: Professional Strategies for Funding a Successful Retirement

Copyright © 2013 by **Michael C. Schlachter**

ISBN-13 (pbk): 978-1-4302-5059-3

ISBN-13 (electronic): 978-1-4302-5060-9

President and Publisher: Paul Manning
Acquisitions Editor: Morgan Ertel
Developmental Editor: Jeff Olson
Editorial Board: Steve Anglin, Mark Beckner, Ewan Buckingham, Gary Cornell,
    Louise Corrigan, Morgan Ertel, Jonathan Gennick, Jonathan Hassell,
    Robert Hutchinson, Michelle Lowman, James Markham, Matthew Moodie,
    Jeff Olson, Jeffrey Pepper, Douglas Pundick, Ben Renow-Clarke,
    Dominic Shakeshaft, Gwenan Spearing, Matt Wade, Tom Welsh
Coordinating Editor: Rita Fernando
Copy Editor: Deanna Hegle
Compositor: SPi Global
Indexer: SPi Global
Cover Designer: Anna Ishchenko

Distributed to the book trade worldwide by Springer Science+Business Media New York, 233 Spring Street, 6th Floor, New York, NY 10013. Phone 1-800-SPRINGER, fax (201) 348-4505, e-mail orders-ny@springer-sbm.com, or visit www.springeronline.com. Apress Media, LLC is a California LLC and the sole member (owner) is Springer Science + Business Media Finance Inc (SSBM Finance Inc). SSBM Finance Inc is a Delaware corporation.

For information on translations, please e-mail rights@apress.com, or visit www.apress.com.

Apress and friends of ED books may be purchased in bulk for academic, corporate, or promotional use. eBook versions and licenses are also available for most titles. For more information, reference our Special Bulk Sales–eBook Licensing web page at www.apress.com/bulk-sales.

Any source code or other supplementary materials referenced by the author in this text is available to readers at www.apress.com. For detailed information about how to locate your book's source code, go to www.apress.com/source-code/.

Apress Business: The Unbiased Source of Business Information

Apress business books provide essential information and practical advice, each written for practitioners by recognized experts. Busy managers and professionals in all areas of the business world—and at all levels of technical sophistication—look to our books for the actionable ideas and tools they need to solve problems, update and enhance their professional skills, make their work lives easier, and capitalize on opportunity.

Whatever the topic on the business spectrum—entrepreneurship, finance, sales, marketing, management, regulation, information technology, among others—Apress has been praised for providing the objective information and unbiased advice you need to excel in your daily work life. Our authors have no axes to grind; they understand they have one job only—to deliver up-to-date, accurate information simply, concisely, and with deep insight that addresses the real needs of our readers.

It is increasingly hard to find information—whether in the news media, on the Internet, and now all too often in books—that is even-handed and has your best interests at heart. We therefore hope that you enjoy this book, which has been carefully crafted to meet our standards of quality and unbiased coverage.

We are always interested in your feedback or ideas for new titles. Perhaps you'd even like to write a book yourself. Whatever the case, reach out to us at editorial@apress.com and an editor will respond swiftly. Incidentally, at the back of this book, you will find a list of useful related titles. Please visit us at www.apress.com to sign up for newsletters and discounts on future purchases.

The Apress Business Team

This book is dedicated to the clients with whom I have worked over the years. Without the experience I gained from working with you and from helping you resolve the issues you deal with every day, none of this would have been possible

Contents

Foreword

For more than 100 years, public and corporate defined-benefit pension plans have provided a secure retirement to tens of millions of people. Throughout stock market booms and busts, war and peace, and economic prosperity and famine, defined-benefit pension plans have provided a sense of security and stability to generations of workers and their dependents, playing a critical role in the social contract. Combined with personal savings and Social Security, pension plans have been a key part of the typical retirement model, commonly described as a "three-legged stool."

Today, that stool is gradually shifting across America to balance on only two of those legs: Social Security and private savings, often in the form of a 401(k) plan or its equivalent. Corporations across the country are shutting down or selling off their pension plans, and many state and local governments are considering ways to reduce benefits or shift to something like 401(k) plans for their workers. New companies, even some of America's most valuable and successful companies, have reached maturity during this period of decline in the pension industry and have chosen to offer their employees only defined-contribution retirement plans right from the very start. Accordingly, the fraction of American workers covered by a traditional defined-benefit pension plan has plummeted over the last few decades.

As a result of all of these changes, individual savings are more critical than ever before, since individual workers are now expected to take 100% of the responsibility for planning and saving for their own retirements. Unfortunately, however, most individuals lack the knowledge, tools, and resources to manage their retirement security as successfully as the professional investment experts employed at many pension plans. In most cases, individuals do not even have a clear idea of how much money they will need at retirement to provide for a secure future, leading them to delay or minimize their retirement contributions for years and exposing them and their families to the potential for severe hardship, sometimes only a few years after retirement. If those individuals had saved a moderate amount more money over their working careers and had been able to invest those savings even marginally more successfully, these poor outcomes could have been completely different.

Managed properly, the vast majority of the assets in any retirement plan, regardless of whether it is a defined-benefit pension plan or a personal defined-contribution plan, should result from a lifetime of investment returns.

My organization, for example, the California Public Employees Retirement System (CalPERS), the largest defined-benefit pension plan in the United States, has publicly reported over the last several years that approximately 60 to 70 cents out of every dollar paid to retirees has come from those investment earnings, not from taxpayer or employee contributions. This illustrates just how critical those investment returns can be. The difference in assets at the time of retirement between two people who saved identical amounts yet had radically different investment philosophies and strategies can be staggering. Often, those differences result not from an informed choice to save in poor-returning investments or to take on unnecessary levels of risk, but rather from a dearth of clear information in a sea of confusion. Far too often, people respond to the confusion and complexity of the investment industry by postponing the decision to start saving for retirement or by investing for a lifetime in nothing more than cash portfolios with terribly low interest rates.

The advice in this book is very similar to what I have observed Michael Schlachter delivering to clients over the years I have known him—clear and concise, with an emphasis first and foremost on risk reduction and cost savings, while keeping an eye toward the long-term horizon. Michael often tells his clients that while no decent return can be earned without taking some level of risk, not all risks are worth taking, and he repeats that advice in many ways throughout this book.

As Michael demonstrates in the pages that follow, the more that you as an individual can emulate the strategies, tools, and tricks of the trade that a pension fund employs, the better the chances that your retirement will be as comfortable as you have hoped it will be.

Henry Jones
Chair, California Public Employees Retirement System Investment Committee
Former CFO (retired), Los Angeles Unified School District

About the Author

Michael C. Schlachter, CFA, is a Managing Director and Principal at Wilshire Associates, a diversified financial services company, and the lead investment consultant to many of the largest pension plans in the United States. He and his team advise clients with more than $300 billion in assets. Previously, he worked for several years as an equity analyst and trader at Goldman Sachs. Michael's experience working as both a hands-on securities analyst/trader and a high-level investment consultant has given him an understanding of the investment industry that ranges from the 40,000-foot view right down to the weeds. He earned an MBA at the University of Chicago's Graduate School of Business and an undergraduate degree from Princeton University. Michael is also a Chartered Financial Analyst (CFA) and a member of the CFA Institute.

Michael lives in Boulder, Colorado, with his wife, their two sons, and their rescued retriever mix. When not writing or advising clients, Michael usually can be found skiing and running in the Rocky Mountains.

Acknowledgments

My thanks go out first and foremost to Henry Jones for contributing the foreword to this effort, as well as for all of your advice and counsel over the years. My sincerest thanks also go to Nate Morrow at eVestment Alliance for generating many of the manager universes and data series that appear in the charts in this book. You and your data were a lifesaver. I would also like to thank Julia Bonafede, Reena Lalji, and Benkai Bouey at Wilshire Associates for reviewing the content of this book, in some cases multiple times, as well as Michael Rush at Wilshire for directing me to Venture Economics for the venture capital fund and buyout fund data series; my parents, Jim and JoAnn Schlachter, for serving as my in-house Baby Boomer focus group; Morgan Ertel at Apress for believing in this effort; Rita Fernando at Apress for her editorial assistance; and Matt Wagner at Fresh Books for helping me to finally make this 7-year dream project a reality. Finally, I would like to express my heartfelt thanks to my beautiful wife, Christina, who worked so hard to keep this book balanced between confusing consultant-speak laced with industry jargon and something that was far too basic to be interesting. If you read this book and find that it is just at the right level of understanding for an individual investor trying to figure out how to plan their financial future, Christina is entirely to credit.

Introduction

The retirement world is generally on a steady march away from traditional pension plans and toward individual retirement responsibility in 401(k)s, Individual Retirement Accounts (IRAs), and the like. The fact of the matter is, however, that the average person, who is now responsible for their retirement security, often lacks the tools to manage their assets and future expectations as well as the professional managers of those pension plans are able to do.

A variety of studies have been published in recent years that indicate that traditional defined benefit pension plans on average have experienced annual returns that are 1% to 2% higher than defined contribution plans, like 401(k)s and IRAs.[1] Although a 1.5% improvement in the rate of return may not sound like much, $100,000 invested at the rate of 6.0% for a working career of 20 years would have grown by the time of retirement to $320,000; that same $100,000 invested at a rate of 7.5% would have grown by the time of retirement to $425,000. As you can see, that average 1.5% underperformance of a 401(k) or IRA versus a defined benefit pension plan may sound small, but it can make a very meaningful difference.

While some members of the financial press and some political leaders like to blame pension plans for every budgetary and societal ill in the history of the world, maybe this return advantage indicates that they actually do some things right. Plenty of arguments have been made over the last several years about the high cost of pension plans to corporations and public agencies. However, that cost is at least partially offset by the superior returns of pension plans. In addition, you can't argue about the cost of pension plans without considering the societal cost of replacing pension plans with individual responsibility.

This book is not intended, however, to engage in the ongoing political debate over the merits or failures of pension plans versus defined contributions plans (I merely will note that other studies have shown that pension plans are actually cheaper than defined contribution plans to reach the same benefit level).[2] I will leave that to the politicians, commentators, and political writers to work out among themselves. Instead, in this book, I will take it as a given

---

[1]"Defined Benefit vs. 401(k) Investment Returns: The 2006-2008 Update," Towers Watson; and, "Investment Returns: Defined Benefit vs. 401(k) Plans," Center for Retirement Research at Boston College.
[2]Beth Almeida and William B. Fornia, "A Better Bang for the Buck: The Economic Efficiencies of Defined Benefit Pension Plans," National Institute for Retirement Security, 2008.

that the average person is more responsible for their own retirement security than ever before, and I will try to teach that average person about what we as individuals can learn from pension plans. What do the biggest retirement savers and investors in the country do to generate superior returns at lower costs? Do the better results that pension plans exhibit come from superior asset allocation? Better managers? Lower fees? Alternative asset classes? Risk reduction?

Yes. All of the above.

Pension plans employ all of these tools to generate better returns than the average individual investor. However, as I will show, very few of these advantages are exclusive to pension plans. In fact, most of the strategies and approaches to investing that drive these superior results can be copied by individuals who understand their strengths and weaknesses, who understand where to take smart risks and avoid dumb ones, who have learned how to be disciplined when it comes to asset allocation and cash flow management, and who know how to reduce the greatest drain on assets: fees and expenses.

It is easy to make a small fortune in the investment world: Begin with a large fortune and start chasing the latest trends and "hot" advice.

If you are looking for investment advice that is guaranteed to make you rich overnight, put this book back on the shelf and look elsewhere. That's right, just put the book down and walk away. There are plenty of magazine articles, get-rich-quick seminars, and late night infomercials out there that will do a much better job of selling horrendously bad advice to you than I could ever do.

My goal with this book is just the opposite: to help you protect your wealth and grow it in a risk-controlled manner over time. The contents of this book will never make for great cocktail party chatter, as they won't lead to stories of huge successes with individual stocks or bonds. They will, however, help to ensure that your investments are properly positioned for whatever befalls the market: bubbles and busts, growth and recession, war and peace, predictability and surprises.

After working with large institutional investors (endowments; foundations; and the pension plans of states, cities, counties, and large corporations) for almost two decades, I have discovered a great divide between the advice that professionals provide to multibillion-dollar clients and that which financial planners,[3] stockbrokers, and television "experts" often provide to individuals.

---

[3]In my experience, there are some genuinely great financial planners out there, as I discuss in the chapter on fees and expenses. The secret to finding a terrific one, and avoiding the ones that will eat up your wealth, is all a matter of incentives. If they are paid to sell you stocks or funds, they will sell you all the stocks and funds you can buy. If they are paid to grow your wealth, then you may have found a winner. More on this in Chapter 9.

I often find myself yelling at the TV or crumpling up the offending newspaper or magazine, cursing the shortsightedness that pervades such "advice."

If an investment recommendation is right for the long-term interests of the pension plans of Pennsylvania or Oklahoma or Hawaii, why isn't the same advice right for somebody in their 40s or 50s? It certainly isn't a matter of time horizon because a 50-year-old in good health could expect to live for 30 to 50 more years. Given the pace of modern medicine, somebody in their 30s today might have at least 70 years to go. These long-term time horizons are no different from the long-range planning that pension plans must do. I think it is fair, therefore, to argue that the long-term view of a pension plan should be no different than it is for anybody in the fat part of their earning years, seeking to build wealth for their retirement, children, or grandchildren.

Sure, there are some small differences. Pension plans might invest 5% to 15% each in private equities (venture capital and leveraged buyouts), real estate, or hedge funds. Unless you have obscene amounts of money already, exactly replicating the set of investments available to, say, the South Dakota Teachers Retirement System probably isn't in the cards for you. Similarly, if you can afford to invest 8% of your net worth in a collection of office buildings around the country, as some pension plans might do, I doubt you are reading this sentence right now. (The people you pay to read this sentence for you should give me a call.)

However, as I will show in later chapters, there are ways to replicate the diversification advantages those exposures might bring through other investment vehicles. Moreover, although venture capital, real estate, and hedge fund investments tend to dominate the headlines, they are actually a small fraction of most institutions' investments. There are notable exceptions, like the endowments of Harvard, Yale, and some other large foundations, who often invest up to half of their money in such things; but most retirement-related institutional investors have 80% to 100% of their investments in stocks and bonds. With a little bit of thinking and hard work on your part, you could build a portfolio every bit as diversified and risk-controlled as most multibillion-dollar pension plans.

My goal is to give you the tools you need and the road map to get you there.

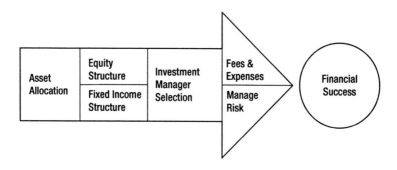

Throughout this book, I will use the graphic shown here, which I call the "Road Map to Financial Success," to move us through the entire investment process that pension funds employ to manage their assets. I will note, however, that while the graphic appears as though it is suggesting that there is a single trip toward wealth, in practice (and as we will discuss in this book), wealth building is a continuous process. You never get to spike the football and head back to the bench. Successfully managing your assets and growing your wealth is an ongoing process. As a result, you need to be able to continuously balance the long-term view with short-term steps.

I start this book in Chapter 1 with a discussion of the advantages and disadvantages that you have as an individual investor vis-à-vis the multibillion-dollar pension plans. Not surprisingly, there are things that pension plans can do with regard to fees, dedicated staff, and some types of asset classes that are largely impossible for regular people to copy exactly. However, with a little bit of creativity, you can use strategies that are "close enough" to generate returns that replicate the unavailable asset classes. You may not even miss having them in your portfolio! At the same time, individuals actually have a number of advantages over pension plans, including flexibility of action, lack of oversight and scrutiny, and a lack of political and outside pressures. While these advantages and disadvantages might prevent an individual from investing their assets as if they were building a perfect copy of, say, the State of Oregon Public Employees Retirement System, you would be surprised at just how close you can get.

Next, in Chapter 2, I will discuss asset allocation, which is the all-important task of determining how much of your money should be dedicated to various asset classes. Are you risk averse and want 80% of your portfolio invested in low-risk bonds? Do you have 40 years to retirement, little in assets, and an aggressive plan to save money and therefore want to take on high levels of risk in exchange for the prospect of superior returns? What should you do as life events change your plan? How does the process of simply growing older affect your investments over time? As I will show, determining the mix of assets that is appropriate to your needs dwarfs any other decision you make, including your selection of money managers or individual securities. If you decide to read only one chapter in this book, I recommend that this is the one you review.

In Chapters 3 through 6, I will lead you down the food chain from asset allocation to a discussion of the proper investment structure for both stocks and bonds. Studies have shown that the decisions you make regarding growth stocks versus value stocks, large capitalization stocks versus small capitalization stocks, core bonds (like Treasuries and investment-grade corporate bonds) versus high yield bonds, and so on, have the second-highest amount of impact on your portfolio. We will discuss ways to mitigate unwanted risks in your portfolio and show why chasing the latest "large cap growth" or "small cap value" trend can be hazardous to your financial health.

In Chapter 7 I get to the heart of what most people erroneously consider to be the most important element of investing: individual security and/or money manager (mutual funds, typically, for individual investors) selection. The vast majority of investors, including the multibillion-dollar pension plans that I work with, spend the lion's share of their time reviewing how their investment managers are doing relative to some index and the managers' peers; debating when to change to new managers; and then determining which investment managers are better than their current stable of partners. In reality, while these topics will take up more than 90% of your time, they will make maybe 5% of the difference in your returns. Selecting an investment manager is something that investors probably shouldn't even waste their time on at all—except that investment managers are the only thing most investors can actually try to control on a short-term basis. Stay tuned.

In Chapter 8, I will discuss one of the true differentiators between individual investors and pension plans: "alternative" investments, a broad term that generally includes anything other than plain old stocks, bonds, and cash. Some alternative investments that you most likely have heard of include private equity, real estate, hedge funds, commodities, timberland, agricultural land, and some types of distressed debt, among others, and most have regulatory or practical hurdles that may be impossible for individual investors to surmount. Do you really need to invest in these types of assets? Why do pension plans do it? Are there proxies that can be used in place of these asset classes if they are not accessible to individuals? Do the cons outweigh the pros of these types of investments for individuals? What about for pension plans?

Although this book is designed to present you with a road map to financial success, you may need to rely on the services of financial institutions or qualified advisors to fill in the blanks that are particular to your situation. That's why, in Chapter 9, I will discuss how to determine if these partners are in the business of helping your best interests—or their own. Of course, when you seek the help of a money manager to help guide your investment decisions, you will necessarily incur fees and expenses. However, you don't have to pay an arm and a leg to achieve the returns you desire. In fact, choosing investment options that are the most cost effective is the single best way of improving performance and often can have an even greater impact on your results than selecting the right manager for your portfolio. As you'll learn in this chapter, given two identical investment options, the one with the lower fees will serve you better over a long period of time.

Since I will be getting near the end of the book, in Chapter 10 I will provide some dessert for this meal of advice and regale you with the real-world experiences—both good and bad—of some of the plans and investment management products discussed in this book. This section is not meant simply to entertain, although you are certainly welcome to laugh all you want to. Rather, the goal of this chapter is to show you that even $100 billion plans that have 50 staff members and the Treasury Secretary on speed dial can get things wrong once in a while. Understanding how some of these things can go wrong might help to prepare you for avoiding, or at least understanding, the worst case scenario: suffering a loss or major setback that imperils your financial future. In addition, if the moral of any of these stories helps you to avoid similar mistakes, everyone wins.

Finally, in Chapter 11, I will summarize the major lessons learned and the final advice that I have to give to you after you have absorbed all that I have shared.

Welcome to the first steps on your journey to financial success!

How You Compare to the Big Funds

Advantages and Disadvantages of Individual Investors

Large pension plans are the rock stars of the investment world. Everyone in the industry wants to manage a piece of their portfolio, and every industry publication wants to interview their people and discuss their latest move. When the trustees or investment staff at one of these plans makes an asset allocation change or replaces an investment manager, hundreds of millions (or even billions) of dollars can change hands rapidly, potentially making or breaking the careers of individuals working across the financial industry who sell or manage the kinds of portfolios in which large pension plans will invest.

Not only are large pension plans revered within the financial industry, but they also have significant advantages over their fellow market competitors, including individuals like you. First, because pension plans generally have huge economies of scale, they are able to negotiate fees that are well below "market" rates. Because it costs a money manager virtually the same amount in operational expenses to invest $100 million that it does to invest $500 million (just buy five times as many shares, in the latter case), it's not uncommon for money managers to be very flexible about the fees they charge pension plans for managing very large portfolios. Second, some money managers will custom-tailor investment portfolios to the needs of the largest plans, and they may even dedicate sales or client service staff to their biggest investors. Some of the very largest pension plans have recently started forming "strategic partnerships" with investment management firms where they have exclusive access to a firm's research and personnel, enabling them to incorporate these unique insights into the pension plan's decision-making process.

How can you or I or any individual investor compete against 800-pound gorillas like that in the marketplace? Don't they have all the contacts and information? It sure seems that way when you read the articles in the financial press that glow about the strategies employed by some of the nation's largest pension plans that are unavailable to the average individual.

Is there anything the individual can do to level that playing field? At first glance, it may seem like individuals have little chance of competing against these behemoths. However, although it may not be readily apparent at first, there are plenty of opportunities out there for all investors, if they are willing to look for them. In this chapter I address the question of whether there is anything that the major pension plans do that the little investor can replicate—even if he or she must do so on a different scale and with the aid of an off-the-shelf source. In addition, I will identify some possible advantages that individual investors surprisingly have versus these giants.

Although it is important to recognize that the individual investor is very clearly playing the role of David in the battle of David versus Goliath, David can still compete and sometimes can even win, just as he did in the fable. Yes, many advantages flow to the largest players in the investment marketplace, but there are still lots of things you and I can do to level the playing field for ourselves.

Advantages of the Individual Investor

Advantage 1: Freedom from External Pressure Regarding Your Amount of Contributions into Your Retirement Plan

Your largest advantage as an individual investor is that you are free from having to decide in conjunction with external parties how much or how little should be contributed into your retirement savings. If you find that your current savings or your projection of how much you will have saved by a given future date is not sufficient, you can make the decision on your own (or in conjunction with your spouse or heirs) about how to fix that. Do you need to reduce your future expectations of how lavishly you will live in retirement? Maybe downsize the boat or RV you plan to buy someday? Or do you want to double your monthly savings? Any or all of these are reasonable ways to get back on track. Ultimately, the decision over which one to choose is yours, and it can be made relatively quickly and painlessly.

For a pension plan, the decision to modify contributions into the investment portfolio is not nearly that simple. The benefits (the future retirement commitments to employees) are often collectively bargained and contractual, making them extremely hard to change—witness the outrage in 2011 by teachers and others when a newly elected governor reduced pension benefits. Additional funding for a public plan, if needed, comes from the taxpayers, and you are guaranteed that a large fraction of the members of the press, public, and political classes will always object if tax rates or government spending needs to increase, especially in the current economic environment where it seems like every public agency is being asked to do more with less. Although these battles over contributions and benefits can be fought and sometimes won by the powers that rule pension plans, it is far more pleasant to decide with your spouse over dinner one night to find an extra $500 a month to sock away than it is to wage a multiyear war in the courts and press for an additional $5 billion a year of taxpayer money.

Advantage 2: Freedom from Inflated Expectations

Although I don't want to say that pension plans are unrealistic about the future, given that most of their forward-looking return expectations are roughly in line with the 100-year history of market returns, they are uniformly "highly optimistic" that strong markets and returns will persist in the future—which is the second biggest advantage that you have as an individual investor over pension plans. When public pension plans budget over the long term how much the city or state needs to contribute to the plan every year, the calculation is based at least in part on their long-term return expectation, which often ranges between 7% to 9% (one city plan even has a 10% return expectation). The higher the pension plan assumes their future returns will be, after all, the less the taxpayers need to contribute to the plan each year since a higher return assumption means that more of the future benefit payments are expected to come from investment returns, not contributions. A reduction of that discount rate by even as little as 0.25% or 0.50% can mean hundreds of millions of dollars, or even billions of dollars, in required additional annual contributions of taxpayer money to the largest plans to maintain the same level of benefit security. As a result, even though many public pension plan trustees would love to reduce return expectations to better ensure that the fund earns a return at least as good as what is expected of it, the pressure to keep assumptions where they are to minimize increases in required contributions is typically overwhelming from the city or state that sponsors the plan and is facing its own budget squeeze. A rule of thumb that I have observed over the years is that for every 0.25% to 0.50% reduction in the expected future rate of return, a pension plan needs to increase contributions by about 10%. In today's budget environment, that kind of increase in spending by almost any government can be a very difficult proposition, no matter how much it increases the stability and security of the pension plan in the future by decreasing the chance that the long-term returns will underperform that optimistic goal. Instead, cash-strapped plan sponsors often need to maintain aggressive expectations of future returns, resulting in a level of risk required to reach these lofty targets that can lead to significant losses from time to time.

This presents a huge advantage for the individual investor over pension plans as far as reaching stated goals is concerned. You get to be as realistic, or even as pessimistic, as you want to be! Do you want to reduce risk in your portfolio and increase your bond holdings? Your return expectation might fall from 7% to 4%, and you will have to save more and spend less in retirement, but no one is stopping you from doing that. If you follow the most optimistic set of assumptions around and plan as if you will always earn 9% per year, and then miss that target most of the time, at retirement you will be short of the level of assets that you had hoped to accumulate, making for a tough retirement. On the other hand, even if you still believe deep in your heart that returns will be 9%, but you contribute and budget as if you will earn only 5%, there is a very good chance that you and your heirs might have a pleasant surprise when you reach retirement.

In the next chapter, I will discuss how to develop the asset allocation mix, as well as the resulting return and risk expectations, that is right for your needs. For now, as well as in that chapter and throughout this book, I will encourage my readers to be as conservative with their investments as possible. If you plan for weak returns or relatively large risks and losses, and you contribute to your savings as if you have not saved enough, there is a far better chance that you will enter retirement in a strong financial situation than when you merely wish upon a star for high returns to compensate for weak savings.

Advantage 3: Size

We often don't think of small size as an advantage in the investment arena, and I outlined earlier in this chapter the many advantages that can flow to a very large investor. However, if you understand how your smaller size can work in your favor, it can be instrumental to your success. As I will discuss in the next section in this chapter regarding the disadvantages the individual faces, and as I alluded to in the introduction to this chapter, pension plans have tremendous advantages in access to well-performing investment funds, alternative asset classes (more on this in Chapter 8), and lower fees due to economies of scale. Unfortunately, they also can find themselves resembling a sailing oil tanker, unable to turn on a dime. Smaller investors, by definition, are more nimble in the marketplace than very large investors, because an individual's decision to move tens of thousands or even hundreds of thousands of dollars between investment managers or asset classes can be accomplished far more quickly and easily, and at a lower relative cost, than a pension plan's decision to move billions of dollars. Although I will discourage using this nimbleness to chase trends or time the markets later in this book, it is important to recognize than when a change does need to be made, an individual can do it far more cheaply and easily than a large institution.

Another advantage that stems from your smaller size is the ability to take advantage of opportunities that would not make a meaningful difference to a large pension plan. An investment with a limited capacity could have a tremendous impact on your portfolio but may not even amount to a rounding error for a large pension plan. In many cases, the largest plans find themselves having to dismiss investing in what could turn out to be great ideas simply because the potential gain is so small in relation to the total assets that they simply do not have the available staff or interest to pursue it.

Advantage 4: Freedom from Distracting External Pressures

Managing a pension plan, especially a large one that draws a lot of attention or scrutiny, can be a very difficult job. The staffs of these plans and their boards of trustees have tremendous pressure on them to satisfy a wide variety of external and internal constituents. By and large, the public pension plans with which I have worked over the years have strived as hard as they can to balance all these external pressures, but no one would argue with the fact that many of the investment decisions made by these boards, like most decisions made by practically any committee, are often compromises among these competing pressures. In contrast to those pension Trustees who have the unenviable job of trying to navigate this minefield of external interests, the final advantage that you bring to the table in the creation of your own retirement plan is the fact that you get to design an investment portfolio that is 100% right for your needs, without compromise. You don't have constituents or employees watching and dissecting your every move. The press doesn't report on everything you do. No members of the public show up at your meetings, berating you for making money off of something that might have externalities.[1]

As an individual investor, you also do not necessarily have to conform with the requirements of socially responsible investing (SRI), which increasingly is a factor that some large pension plans and many major endowments and foundations need to address. Investment managers at many institutional investors, especially those affiliated with a religious order or university, typically must follow guidelines that prohibit them from investing in companies whose lines of business are objectionable to the organization. Catholic organizations, for example, often limit investments in defense contractors or manufacturers of certain reproduction-related pharmaceuticals. Other religiously affiliated groups may object to investments in alcohol or gaming companies (the latter of which is the industry euphemism for casino gambling). Similarly, the pension plans of health care providers may prohibit investment in tobacco companies by their investment managers, while Middle Eastern clients may pass over investments in financial institutions that make money from lending and interest income in violation of Sharia Law.

Such restrictions are a way for investors to avoid profiting from activities or businesses that they find objectionable and to make a public statement of their beliefs. If an investor wishes to pursue such a strategy, such as avoiding all investments in oil companies because he or she finds pollution objectionable, then that investor should invest accordingly. I would never argue that SRI strategies should not be pursued if it is meaningful to the client and the client understands the potential impact on investment returns, and a large number of my institutional clients over the years have had one or more of these restrictions on their portfolios. After all, it is their money, and they need to sleep comfortably at night with the decisions they have made and the sources of their investment profits.

---

[1] An externality refers to a typically negative implication of an action to some other party that doesn't directly affect you. For example, investing in a real estate fund that makes money by evicting low-income tenants and raising rents, an oil company that isn't perfectly clean with its industrial wastes, a tobacco stock that makes its money selling addictive carcinogens, or a private equity company that improves profits by closing down factories and shipping jobs to China are all perfectly legal, potentially highly profitable, and very common investment strategies. However, all of these investments result in ill effects for other people. If you choose not to invest in one or all of these, someone else who isn't guided by the same compass will gladly take your place. If you do choose to invest in them, though, it is highly unlikely that the people affected by these investments will show up at your door, protesting how your money ruined their lives. With a large public pension plan or a major college endowment, angry constituents frequently appear at public meetings to protest the actions the fund has taken when they have these external consequences.

However, investors should be aware that these types of strategies can come at a cost to their investment returns. Any type of limited or restricted portfolio will underperform a more diverse portfolio over the long term. If two active investment managers are managing similar portfolios and one can choose among all 500 stocks in the S&P 500 index while the other can only pick from 450, the 500-stock manager will most likely outperform in the long run. Sure, I can find a year (or maybe even a decade) where a tobacco and alcohol-free portfolio underperforms a non-restricted portfolio. But over one hundred years, the manager with more options available should do better by exploiting every option in the opportunity set.

When avoiding an industry in protest of its products or past actions, it is important to understand that while that might make a very important moral difference to you, it is unlikely that your decision to avoid investing in a particular company will make much of an impact on that industry's returns. If there are profits to be made, someone else will gladly buy the stocks you refuse to buy. For example, many of the largest pension and health care plans in the country refuse to buy tobacco stocks, since these plans are responsible for their members' health care costs and do not want to invest in an industry that costs them so much money and does so much damage to their members' health—a completely understandable objection to profiting from a product or supporting an industry that directly hurts their membership. Still, despite the large number of institutional and individual investors who refuse to buy their stocks, tobacco companies just keep on ticking year after year after year. True, smoking and lung cancer deaths are on the downturn in the United States—but this is more due to a public education campaign about the ills of smoking than it is to the decision by the State of XYZ or the ABC Healthcare Company to sell its shares in Philip Morris. Elsewhere in the world, where prevention efforts are less common, Philip Morris and its competitors are doing a fine job replacing customers more quickly than they kill them. So, whereas the divestment of tobacco stocks from many portfolios is completely reasonable as a statement of principle, it has not caused tobacco companies to go out of business.

In fact, despite the divestment activities of so many large investors, some of these "sin stocks," as they are known, actually have done very well. For example, in a study that I undertook for a pension plan client, I found that from 2001 to 2012, excluding tobacco stocks hurt the performance of their equity portfolio against a broad market benchmark that includes tobacco companies in 11 of those 12 years. By the end of the 12-year period, choosing to avoid profiting from tobacco had cost the system more than 3% of their equity assets in aggregate. Despite this mounting evidence of the opportunity cost of the decision, the client decided to continue to exclude tobacco out of a continuing objection to the industry, its products, and the health impacts on its membership.

The one main exception to this rule that divestment does not directly force change was South Africa in the 1980s. The vast majority of institutional investors (and many governments and individuals) locked arms and refused to invest in any company that did business with the apartheid regime. It took years of trade and investment restrictions, as well as government pressure, athletic competition blockades, travel limitations, and more, but the regime finally fell. Although the effectiveness of the apartheid investment embargo was certainly impressive, keep in mind that this situation represents a rare case that happened on a scale that dwarfs your personal refusal to invest in something—or even the refusal by a handful of state pension plans whose assets might total hundreds of billions of dollars—and constituted far more than a mere ban on stock investment. In most normal cases, unless everyone refuses to play ball, there are plenty of other parties who are still willing to invest when the opportunity is right, despite any moral reservations about a company or an industry.

If we as a society agree that certain businesses, industries, or countries need to be isolated for the welfare of all, divestment can work as a strategy if it is as widespread as was the effort against South Africa. On the other hand, if divestment is done piecemeal, with each individual or organization expressing a limited and mutually exclusive view of objectionable practices or industries, the conscience of each investor may be improved—but it is unlikely to impact society as a whole.

In my experience, most pension plan boards understand all of this. They know that divesting from something may cost them money over the long term. However, the pressure from the membership, public, media, or others to divest from certain stocks or industries can be too much to bear. Sometimes, despite this cost, the Trustees of the plan divest because they simply believe it is the right thing to do. In other cases, the path of least resistance is to simply give in to the pressure being exerted on them and divest. Regardless of the reason for agreeing to divest, the plan may need to replace the profits they just gave up with higher contributions from the taxpayers. If avoiding a number of stocks or bonds costs the fund 1% per year, then an increase in contributions or a decrease in future benefits will have to make up the difference.

What is the bottom line of this discussion for you, the individual investor? I intended this section to explain that one of the major advantages you have as an individual investor over pension plans is that you get to do what is right for you without compromise. If you want to invest in something, you can. No one is watching. No one is pressuring you. If you want to invest in British Petroleum 5 minutes after an oil well blows up, a huge body of water is polluted, 300,000 sea birds die, and the stock drops 60%, you can do it—precisely at the same time a major university is being forced to sell its stock at the bottom by students outraged by the company's conduct. You can keep the long view in mind and seek profits wherever you can find them without worrying about picketers on your front lawn. As much as they wish they could keep as objective an outlook as possible in mind, many large institutional investors recognize that they must answer to constituent groups that might prevent them from taking such an action, yielding a huge advantage to individuals able to act without the same level of scrutiny.

Remember, your greatest advantage is that you (and your spouse and family) are your one and only constituency. No one else's needs have to be balanced with your own. There are no private equity CEOs whose favor needs to be courted in exchange for access to a future fund, no unions to serve, no elected officials to please, no taxpayers to appeal to. The impact of all of these external influences varies from pension fund to pension fund, but there is no arguing that investment returns would be better in an environment removed from all of these non-investment pressures—which, fortunately, is exactly what you have in your favor.

Disadvantages of the Individual Investor

I don't want to paint too perfect of a picture, however. If investing was as simple as I have made it out to be thus far in this chapter, pension funds wouldn't have staffs of dozens or even hundreds of people, boards of trustees, and external investment consultants. If pension plans consistently outperform individual investors by 1% or 2%, as I discussed in the Introduction to this book, there must be some clear reasons for their success. Otherwise, all the problems outlined previously that pension plans face would render the opposite result, and individual investors historically would have achieved better performance.

So, what disadvantages do you have versus the large funds? I will discuss them in the following section and then spend many other sections in this book, including the chapters on investment structure (Chapter 3 through Chapter 6), manager selection (Chapter 7), and cost reduction (Chapter 9), helping to find you ways to mitigate their impact.

Disadvantage 1: You Only Live Once

First and foremost, you only have one work career to build a sufficient pool of assets by retirement, and if you outlive your assets, you lack the recourse available to most pension funds. Public pension funds rely on taxpayers as their ultimate financial backstop, and corporate plans can turn to the company for additional contributions, if necessary, or to the federal pension insurance company, the Pension Benefit Guarantee Corporation, should the company face bankruptcy. Endowments and foundations can turn to grateful alumni or charitable contributors when times are tough to help bring the value of the investment portfolio back to the needed level.

Unless you are one of the declining number of people covered at least in part by a traditional defined benefit pension plan, you have none of these supports, except for a social security benefit. If you invest in something that is too risky and suffer major losses—or if you spend from your savings after you retire as if you plan to live for 10 years and instead end up living for 40—you have no sponsoring entity like taxpayers, corporate income, or university alumni to make additional contributions to keep your retirement account solvent.

As a result, you need to maintain dual goals in mind at all times: (1) solid growth of the contributions you make and the assets you already hold (the same as a pension plan) and (2) a far greater focus on downside protection than even most pension plans entertain. While a 50% drop in value will significantly impact a pension plan and the plan sponsor, resulting in far higher contributions by the government entity backing the plan and likely higher taxes on individuals under its jurisdiction, or a reduction in corporate earnings due to the need to divert more of the company's income into the pension plan, the public or corporate pension plan will likely live to fight another day and will eventually recover. For individuals, that type of decline in the value of the portfolio could be fiscally fatal to an individual near retirement because there is no backstop to turn to for that individual to make up the newfound shortfall.

Disadvantage 2: Uncertain Time Frame

As alluded to previously, your time frame is uncertain: Will you live to be 70 or 100? While family history may be some guide (if every recent female ancestor made it to 95, for example, and you are female and in good health, you have a higher probability of a long retirement than other people whose ancestors typically do not survive past age 70), nothing is certain. The continued improvement in medical care compounds this issue. If your family has a history of heart disease in men, for example, leading to early death, simply taking a daily dose of Lipitor or Zocor might give you decades more than those that came before you. For someone only in their 20s or 30s, there exists the very real possibility that major afflictions like heart disease, cancer, stroke, and other ailments could be cured by the time you are 80, resulting in extended life spans previously never thought to be possible. Or you might be one of those lucky people who smokes, eats bacon, never works out, and yet lives to 110. The problem that individuals face is the uncertainty of how much money they will need in retirement, because we simply have no way of projecting how long any given person might live.

Although most people would probably be happy to spend an extra decade or more on earth, the possibility that you may live longer than you expect to poses the real risk that your assets may not be sufficient to your needs in retirement. It also is a risk that pension plans do not need to consider as strongly as you do. While no one can predict how long a given individual will live with any precision, predicting the average age and distribution of ages at death for a population of 100,000 can be done fairly precisely, thanks to advances in modern actuarial science. As a result, a pension plan can calculate how much money is needed to support 100,000 people in retirement as a whole, even though we cannot precisely predict how much any single one of them will need or how long any individual will live.

As a result, downside mitigation (protecting your investments from large losses, especially when you are close to retirement) and over-saving are the best defenses against outliving your assets. If you expect to live for 15 years after retirement, there is no harm in saving throughout your working career as if you expect to live for 25 years, or in reducing spending once you retire to stretch the savings you have accumulated over 15 years into enough to last for 20 years or more. The worst outcome of such an approach to asset conservation would be that you leave your heirs, alma mater, or favorite charity something after you are gone—which is a far better outcome than spending an unexpected final 8 years in poverty.

Disadvantage 3: Lack of Time to Dedicate to Investing

Managing your assets is most likely not your full-time job. Major pension plans and the largest endowments can employ dozens or even hundreds of financial professionals whose primary responsibility it is to manage the plan's assets, and there are real benefits to having talented and qualified individuals reviewing and evaluating a variety of investment opportunities on a constant basis.

While I will discuss throughout this book the many benefits of maintaining a long-term investment approach with minimal day-to-day tinkering, there is obviously some merit to having professionals watch and manage the assets of a pension plan on an ongoing basis. They can do more research into the latest strategies than you have time to do, know their investment managers far better than you ever will, and employ the most advanced tools to understand the real risks underlying their portfolios. Bear in mind, though, that the flip side to this is that your lack of dedicated staff prevents constant change and micromanagement of your investments, which might be an advantage in disguise. As I will discuss in Chapter 9 on fees and expenses, reducing transactions costs and the drag on assets from making frequent changes can be as great a benefit to returns as finding an investment that actually makes you money! After all, as Ben Franklin once put it, a penny saved is a penny earned.

Disadvantage 4: Fewer Investment Options

As an individual investor, many of the investment options available to large pension funds will simply not be open to you. Investment managers that offer products in private equity investments, real estate investments, and hedge funds may have limited lists of desired clients or minimum investment sizes that exceed your means. In addition, building your own portfolio of direct investments in real estate (your own portfolio of office buildings, for example) or private equities also may be well beyond the means of most private investors. In Chapter 8, I will discuss alternatives to these types of direct investments through liquid, publicly traded vehicles that can work as the nearest available proxy. They aren't a perfect fit, but they may be better than nothing. Or, you may conclude, they simply are not worth the cost. Frankly, there are even some large pension plans that have come to the same conclusion about alternative investments and have limited their portfolios to a combination of stocks and bonds.

Disadvantage 5: Inadequate Access to Information

The largest investors have a myriad of sources of independent, accurate, and complete data and information. Large pension plans retain the services of investment consultants (or armies of consultants, in some cases) and purchase or otherwise have access to vast databases of information about potential investments, their returns, their holdings, their personnel, their organizations, and the inner workings of their investment process. What do you have? Access to Yahoo! Finance, the *Wall Street Journal*, *Barron's*, and a variety of other publications and internet data sources that every other investor gets to share. These are neither unique nor complete sources of information and can leave you with far less data about your investment options than a pension fund may have. However, as we will discuss in Chapter 7, the selection of active managers is far less important than popular opinion holds. While there is no question you are at a disadvantage versus pension plans when it comes to obtaining complete and accurate information about all your investment options, I again will show you ways to mitigate the damage that might be done by that disadvantage.

Disadvantage 6: The Problems with Mutual Funds

Mutual funds are not perfect replications of the types of portfolios in which pension plans invest. Mutual funds have looser guidelines, more cash holdings, and greater turnover than the "institutional quality" portfolios that the same investment managers might offer to pension plans. As I will show in Chapters 5 through 7, the selection of funds that minimize these negatives is paramount to success.

Disadvantage 7: Fees, Fees, Fees

Finally, on an apples-to-apples basis, individual investors will pay higher investment management fees than will pension plans. If you give a money manager $10,000 in some strategy and a pension plan gives them $100,000,000 in that same strategy, the pension plan will pay less in fees than you will, since the fees charged for large institutional portfolios are normally less than those for retail mutual funds. Even if you were able to precisely match the investment managers and asset allocation used by a given pension plan, you will tend to underperform the investments made by that large plan based solely on the difference between their fees and yours. At the same time, however, that pension plan will have to pay custodial bank fees, overhead operational expenses, and the salaries of its dedicated staff—all of which you can avoid, assuming that managing your portfolio is not your full-time job. Given that fees and expenses can be the largest drain on investment performance over long periods of time, I will dedicate Chapter 9 to a discussion of what you can do to mitigate their impact.

As I said previously, precisely emulating the asset allocation, manager lineup, and returns of your favorite large public pension plan is impossible. Far too many hurdles exist along your investment path. However, once you understand both your advantages and disadvantages as an individual investor versus your larger investment brethren, you can seek ways to reduce your disadvantages and increase the payoffs from your advantages. Even if you can only close the gap a little between your returns and those of a pension plan, every little bit helps! As I will show in Chapter 9, even a reduction in expenses of as little as 0.10% a year can have a tremendous impact over a 40-year career and a subsequent 30-year retirement.

Summary

It can be done. If you follow the plan laid out in this book, focusing your attention on asset allocation and a steady, disciplined investment and contribution schedule over time, your retirement assets can grow as you need them to. By minimizing unwanted "dumb" risks and maximizing your chances to profit from "smart" risks, which will be discussed in Chapters 3 through 6 and again in Chapter 10, your path to success becomes even clearer.

Yes, you do not have a staff of experts assisting you every day with every investment decision you make. Although I will discuss in both Chapter 2 and Chapter 9 how some outside advisors can be useful to an individual investor, they are not your permanent assistants in the same way as the staff is to a large pension plan. You and your family are generally on your own, which can be both a blessing and a curse.

As I will say time and time again throughout this book, the ability to be disciplined in your contributions and realistic in planning for your retirement spending plans is the single greatest secret to financial success. It also happens to be your greatest advantage versus large pension plans, which need to take into account the interests of a myriad of affected and interested parties in every investment decision that they make.

Thinking that you can have investment returns that approximate those of a $100 billion, market moving, major investor seems like a daunting proposition. Indeed, it is. However, much like the prospect of climbing a mountain or running a marathon might be intimidating to the average person but entirely achievable with the right training and planning, generating investment returns that fulfill your needs can be done with a steady approach like the one outlined in the pages that follow.

Asset Allocation

The Largest Determinant of a Retirement Plan's Return

In the beginning of this book, I introduced the following graphic, the Road Map to Financial Success, which shows the flow chart to get you on your way to a healthy portfolio.

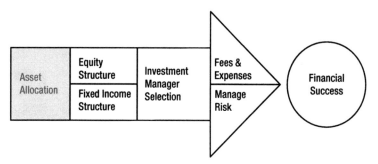

The first step in building any financial plan is asset allocation. "Asset allocation" is the technical name for the process within which an investor determines how much of his or her assets should be put into stocks, bonds, cash, real estate, or any other asset class. This process should not be a shot in the dark or taken lightly, nor should it be subject to constant fluctuation or the whims of an investor's reaction to market movements.

Rather, asset allocation should be consistent with an individual's financial goals, savings rate, and required rate of return. Most important, asset allocation should be based heavily on an individual's risk tolerance as well as the combination of asset classes that will produce the optimal expected return and risk characteristics for his or her needs. For example, most academic research and practical industry experience says that a long-term investor who has a long time horizon until his or her assets will need to be drawn down should tend to invest heavily in riskier assets that will generate superior returns over a long period of time. On the other hand, an individual nearing retirement should be far more concerned about the possibility of significant losses that will impact the quality of his or her retirement than the prospect of continued asset growth and will therefore invest more heavily in low risk, income-generating assets.

If you're worried about how to establish a proper asset allocation mix, fear not. In this chapter, I will walk you through a straightforward process for determining the right asset allocation for your needs. I will also discuss the various online tools and in-person advice you can leverage to simplify the process for you. Before I begin, however, I'd like you to consider a statistic that floats around the pension industry like a "Golden Rule." Various studies have confirmed that 90% to 100% of the difference in return among pension plans, endowments, or any other types of investors comes from asset allocation.

Think about how meaningful that is for a minute: 90%.

While the headlines in the magazines trumpet the performance of great mutual funds versus the S&P 500 Index, and the ads on TV during golf events tout how well those mutual funds have performed against their "Lipper Peer Group Averages",[1] the performance advantage that comes from a superior mutual fund contributes less than 10% to the total return of your portfolio. Granted, 10% is meaningful, and it is important to pick the right funds once you have established your investment structure. However, most individual investors spend a lot more than 10% of their limited investment time figuring out which mutual fund to invest in.

Generally speaking, institutional investors have made the same mistake. If most businesses have the 80/20 rule, whereby 20% of a company's clients or revenues requires 80% of the employees' time, then the investment industry should have the 90/10 rule. More than 90% of most investors' time is spent picking money managers that generate less than 10% of their results. Although you should never alter your asset allocation on a whim or on a daily basis, as I will discuss later in this chapter, you need to recognize the important role that asset allocation plays in determining your financial outcome and periodically review your plan to make sure that it fits your long-term needs. In this next section, I illustrate the large differences in return that asset allocation can make.

---

[1] More on peer groups and the problems they present in Chapter 7.

Example: Three Individuals and Their Differing Asset Allocations

Let's consider the example of three individual investors with markedly different asset allocation plans. In this first example, I will assume that each of them invests solely in index funds:

1. Bob has a high risk tolerance and, at age 30, is many years until retirement. He is investing from every paycheck and can live with a few years of poor performance because he doesn't mind buying stocks when the market is down. In fact, whenever he gets a chance to buy after a decline, he calls it "bottom feasting." For the period of our study, Bob has a portfolio that is comprised of 80% US stocks/20% bonds.

2. Susan is in her early 40s and has both a slightly shorter time horizon than Bob and a lower risk tolerance. In addition, with three kids approaching college age, Susan is uncertain as to how much she will be able to invest over the next several years while she and her husband pay for tuition. While she still wants to grow her assets, she is also concerned about taking a big loss in any one year that will set her off course. With the help of her advisor, Susan determined that a 60% stock (half US, half non-US)/40% bond portfolio is best for her.

3. John recently retired and is in good enough health that he expects to live for many years. He also has been fortunate enough to amass enough wealth that he will probably be able to pass something on to his heirs when he is gone. Whereas his advisor suggested that most retirees prefer a portfolio exclusively in income investments, John preferred a 25% US stock/75% bond portfolio to allow a decent fraction of his portfolio to continue to grow over time.

Take a look at the year-by-year performance of each of the three investors[2] in Table 2-1. What should be readily apparent are the huge differences in performance each investor achieved on an annual basis, yet they all ended up in roughly the same place.[3] Given the highly volatile performance of a number

---

[2]All calculations assume annual rebalancing at year end to target portfolio weights.
[3]This is due in part to the exceptionally strong bond market over the last decade, which had results that rivaled equities in some years. That past performance is unlikely to persist, given that rates cannot fall much more, and will lead to a far stronger argument for a diversified portfolio in the future, when asset classes begin to diverge again.

of stock and bond markets over the last two-plus decades, the differences among them in total are far smaller than one might have guessed. Still, that 1.4% advantage Bob had over John equates roughly to the advantage the average defined-benefit plan has had over a defined-contribution plan. That small difference can add up.

Table 2-1. Annual Performance of Three Individual Investors

	Wilshire 5000 Index	MSCI - All Country World Index (excl USA)	Barclays Aggregate Bond Index	Bob	Susan	John
1991	34.20	13.97	16.01	30.56	20.86	20.56
1992	8.97	-10.98	7.41	8.66	2.36	7.80
1993	11.29	34.89	9.76	10.98	17.76	10.14
1994	-0.07	6.62	-2.92	-0.64	0.80	-2.21
1995	36.46	9.94	18.47	32.86	21.31	22.97
1996	21.22	6.68	3.62	17.70	9.82	8.02
1997	31.30	2.04	9.68	26.98	13.87	15.09
1998	23.43	14.47	8.68	20.48	14.84	12.37
1999	23.56	30.92	-0.83	18.68	16.01	5.27
2000	-10.89	-15.09	11.63	-6.39	-3.14	6.00
2001	-10.96	-19.50	8.44	-7.08	-5.76	3.59
2002	-20.86	-14.67	10.27	-14.63	-6.55	2.49
2003	31.63	41.40	4.11	26.13	23.55	10.99
2004	12.48	21.35	4.34	10.85	11.89	6.38
2005	6.38	17.11	2.43	5.59	8.02	3.42
2006	15.77	27.15	4.33	13.48	14.61	7.19
2007	5.62	17.12	6.96	5.89	9.61	6.63
2008	-37.23	-45.24	5.24	-28.74	-22.65	-5.38
2009	28.30	42.14	5.93	23.83	23.50	11.52
2010	17.16	11.60	6.54	15.04	11.24	9.20
2011	0.98	-13.32	7.84	2.35	-0.57	6.13
2012	16.06	17.39	4.22	13.69	11.72	7.18
Average Annual Return	9.39%	6.55%	6.81%	9.18%	8.15%	7.79%

Data courtesy of Wilshire Associates, MSCI, and Barclays Indexes.

There are four themes to remember from this chart.

First, the long-term cycle of the financial markets averages out investor performance, if you can stomach the ride. In the mid-to-late 1990s, when stocks roared ahead, Bob outperformed Susan and John due to his aggressive stance in that asset class. Similarly, when stocks collapsed after the Internet bubble burst in 2000 and the credit crisis of 2007–2008 began, his losses far exceeded those of his peers. However, in the long run, he "won." Just as the typical "invest for the long term" advice predicted, Bob's higher risk asset allocation generated higher returns over this 22-year period.

The second theme is to keep your investing time frame appropriate to your needs if you even want to try to stomach the ride of a long-term market cycle. If Bob had been planning to retire in 2002, for example, his high-risk 80%/20% allocation mix would have been completely inappropriate because he would have found himself beginning to liquidate his investments to fund his retirement at the very bottom of the market cycle. After all, given the kinds of losses that can be incurred in any particular year with an 80/20 mix, there simply would not have been time for Bob to bounce back if his retirement was looming.

The third theme is simple: stay with it. If you are investing long term and you have the long term in mind, keep the long term in mind. If Bob had gotten scared in 2002 or 2008 and pulled out of the market, he would have missed the recoveries in 2003 and 2009. When you select your asset allocation, you should anticipate that for every few great years, there will be a few lousy years. The great years will offset the impact of the lousy years—as long as the lousy years do not lead you to move to a completely cash portfolio when you see your asset value drop 25%.

In Bob's case, his assets grew by 77.3% from the beginning of 2003 through the end of 2007 and had recovered to his 1999 asset level by the end of 2004. If he had gotten scared by the market decline and retreated to cash after the end of the tech bust, he would have missed some spectacular returns, especially in 2003.

Fourth, there are other ways to diversify a portfolio beyond simply investing in stocks and bonds. For Susan, her decision to pursue a different asset allocation mix from Bob and John and invest outside the United States helped her greatly in 1993, 2002, 2004, and 2005, when she performed as well as, or better than, Bob, despite his 20% greater allocation to stocks. However, before we all run out and buy exclusively non-US stock funds, notice 1992, 2001, 2011, and 2012. Despite her more conservative investment style, Susan got burned relative to Bob's investments when the international stock markets tanked. Had Susan invested her 60% in stocks solely in the United States, her return would have been 8.81% per year on average, indicating that the international diversification, at least in this example, mitigated her annual volatility but also held down her total return for the period relative to the other two investors.

Despite the apparent negative performance implication in Susan's example, I present many more reasons why diversifying your stock portfolio outside the United States makes sense in Chapter 4, when I discuss the rationale for a global equity portfolio.

Getting on a steady path to success takes time and patience, but it all starts with one step. As the old adage goes, "A journey of a thousand miles begins with a single step." From an investment perspective, the equivalent of this saying is, "A retirement plan with a million dollars begins with a single dollar." But it does not stop there. A retirement plan with a million dollars starts with a single dollar, regular contributions, strong earnings, and the discipline to stick with it until you reach your goal. There are few stories of overnight riches when it comes to investing. Without the next Cisco or Google starting up in your garage, reaching your financial goals will take years and years of work, discipline, and continuous planning.

Asset Allocation and You

In asset allocation, there is planning—and then there is OVERplanning. Although I cannot overstate the value in creating an investment plan and sticking to it (more on this later on in this chapter, when I discuss the value of regular contributions), investors also have to be careful to avoid tinkering with their portfolios too much.

Most institutional investors take a long-term view of asset allocation, and so should you. They do not attempt to "time" the markets, shifting in and out of stocks and bonds based on the latest economic data. Instead, pension plans commonly pick an asset allocation that is designed to fit their needs for the next decade or more. Based on the demographics of the population of contributing and retired members within their plan, they can predict roughly how much they will need in assets and cash flow for benefits in the future. As a result, they can determine how aggressive or conservative their investments need to be to achieve the returns that they need to fund those benefits. They can also estimate how much they need to contribute to the pension plan on an annual basis.

Large plans have an advantage in this respect over the individual investor, in that they know when their members are going to die and will invest accordingly. That may be overstating the point very slightly. They don't know precisely how long any given member of the plan will live, but they do know how long each member will live on average. Based on the laws of large numbers, actuaries can predict that X members of the pension plan will die this year and that the average 38-year-old plan member, for example, will live for 41 more years.[4] Sure, some will beat the odds and live to 100, but others will succumb to disease or car crashes in the next few years. On average, the demographic behavior of a population of 1,000 or 10,000 or 100,000 people in a pension plan is fairly predictable.

In planning for retirement, it is safe to assume the worst, and in the world of retirement planning, the "worst" is that we live forever. You may have heard people say, "I want to live long enough (or have my money last long enough) that my check for my funeral bounces." Whereas many individual investors want to leave something for their children, grandchildren, and charity, the principle of having exactly enough for what you want for the exact amount of

---

[4]That is an example only. Please consult a current actuarial table to see how long a 38-year-old is really expected to live.

time that you will live holds true in a case of an investor picking the perfect asset allocation.

Because it is almost impossible to predict the exact date someone will write a check for their own funeral, however, the most practical alternative is to invest your assets as though that day will never come. Spending some of the value in a retirement account over time is fine, but you cannot draw down a great deal of it and still expect to have enough to last. A general rule of thumb is to plan to spend about 5% of your assets each year in retirement, but, like any rule of thumb, it may not be perfectly applicable to all people. If you have a 4% gain in your investments in a given year and inflation is 2%, then spending 5% results in a decrease of 3% in the value of your assets after inflation. If you retire very young (lucky you), that 3% annual decline may be too much to bear because your assets could run out before you do. If you retire at 80, a more generous spending plan may be in order.

Table 2-2 demonstrates how quickly assets can disappear if you spend too aggressively.

Table 2-2. Longevity of Assets Under Different Spending Scenarios

Age	Annual Spending		
	$50,000	$75,000	$100,000
65	$1,000,000	$1,000,000	$1,000,000
66	$990,000	$965,000	$940,000
67	$978,600	$927,100	$875,600
68	$965,724	$886,154	$806,584
69	$951,293	$842,010	$732,727
70	$935,223	$794,508	$653,792
71	$917,428	$743,482	$569,536
72	$897,817	$688,759	$479,701
73	$876,295	$630,158	$384,021
74	$852,764	$567,490	$282,216
75	$827,120	$500,557	$173,995
76	$799,255	$429,155	$59,055
77	$769,056	$353,068	
78	$736,406	$272,073	
79	$701,182	$185,935	
80	$663,256	$94,412	
81	$622,492		
82	$578,753		
83	$531,891		
84	$481,754		
85	$428,184		
86	$371,014		
87	$310,071		
88	$245,175		
89	$176,137		
90	$102,760		

Table 2-2 imagines a hypothetical retiree who starts with $1 million in savings. We assume that the portfolio is invested after retirement in a fixed income-heavy portfolio that earns 4% per year. Whereas a spending rate of $50,000 per year, increasing by 2% per year for inflation, maintains some value of savings past age 90, the higher spending rates of $75,000 or $100,000 per year will deplete the entire retirement account in 10 to 15 years. If this individual has a reasonably long life expectancy, is married to a younger spouse who plans to live off this portfolio, or wishes to leave something for his or her children and grandchildren, some adjustments must be made. The three options available are that the retiree must save more while he or she can, retire later, or plan to spend less in retirement. If we are realistic today about what spending limits we have in retirement, we can make those adjustments to our plan sufficiently far enough ahead of the game to change the outcome.

Be a Long-Term Investor

What all of this means is that you, just like institutional investors, must think and act with the long term in mind. Pension plans design their asset allocation with their eye on at least the next ten years, not current market trends. As a result, the first steps that you need to take include figuring out how much growth you need in your assets and how much risk you are willing to bear. In most cases, someone at 35 should be far more aggressive than someone at 70, but circumstances might be different for different individuals. There may be the occasional 35-year-old with a huge trust fund that needs to be protected, and conservatism is the right solution. There may also be the occasional 70-year-old who has $100,000,000 from the sale of his company and only needs a very small fraction of that wealth to live. Unlike the normal 70-year-old who is concerned with finding income-generating assets to provide safety in retirement, he can afford to invest 100% in stocks with the goal of creating a huge estate for his children.

Whatever your investment goal and long-term plan is, it should be created with a clear head and mind. If at all possible, engage the services of an accountant or planner at least for this part of your retirement plan. I'll discuss how to utilize this kind of external advice this later in this chapter.

After you have picked the retirement plan that best suits you and your needs comes the hardest part: You have to stick with it. Make sure that whatever plan you come up with is a plan that you like and can afford to stick with. A plan you will want to change in six months is a recipe for disaster, not riches.

Pension plans typically review and, if necessary, change their asset allocations every three to five years. In the interim, they normally leave it alone, despite up markets or down markets. They also rebalance their assets back to that target on a very regular basis, especially when the investments move away from their proportionate targets by more than a few percentage points.

I said earlier this is the "hardest part" because humans are tempted to second-guess themselves. When stocks outperform bonds, it can be terribly hard to stay the course and rebalance back to your target asset allocation, selling part of those terrific-performing stock funds to buy more of the bond funds that seem to be treading water. Every time you see a friend who made a boat-load of money on a stock and bought a new car with the proceeds, you may second-guess your plan that tells you to sell every time those stocks go up to buy more of the stable (or boring) bond funds.

On the other side, in a market correction, when stocks fall 30% or 40% in only a few months, it can be incredibly painful to sell relatively stable fixed income investments and buy stocks to get back to target, only to see stocks fall another 10% or more as the "bear" market continues. It feels like you are throwing good money down an endless hole: right up to the point that it works and you find yourself rebalancing into stocks and other risky assets when the market finally begins to recover.

Every cycle eventually ends, and every market correction finds a bottom. When the trend ends, the reversal can be quick and violent. Following the October 2007 to March 2009 market decline, when most equity markets fell by 45% to 50%, stocks rose 30% in a matter of weeks after bottoming on March 9, 2009. Investors who had run for the hills and "capitulated" near the bottom, throwing in the towel after months and months of bad news and moving their assets to cash or bonds, missed that recovery. Sure, they could reinvest once they felt like things were back on track, but because they rode their stock investments all the way down and then gave up in early 2009 and moved to other types of assets, the fact that they missed that initial 30% recovery will cost them forever. When an individual who missed that initial recovery retires, this could mean the difference between retiring with $3 million in total assets and $4 million.

In the spirit of full disclosure, even institutional investors fall into this trap. By the middle part of the last decade, a hospital company had made many capital improvements over the years and had taken out loans to pay for the improvements. As collateral for the loans, the hospital pledged the portfolio for their foundation. Some of the loans had covenants attached that mandated a minimum value of the hospital's charitable foundation (the bank wanted to protect its collateral) and gave the bank the option of demanding full payment on the loans in the event the value of the foundation declined too much. As the markets fell and fell in 2007–2009, the foundation value began to approach the levels at which these covenants would be triggered. As a defensive move, the hospital company sold large portions of its stock portfolio and moved the assets into money market funds, thus protecting a floor value of the assets. In all fairness, the foundation trustees never really wanted to throw in the towel like that, but the bank that held their debt really forced them into a corner. This decision to de-risk after the market decline was driven more by that external pressure than by a fear amongst the trustees that markets would never recover. However, the end result was the same as if they had merely decided to reduce equity risk at the wrong time. I'm not exaggerating when I say that they mistimed the market almost exactly perfectly. Four days after they sent the orders to their external money managers to start selling on March 5, 2009, the stock market hit the bottom. The next two weeks saw an increase of almost 15%. In the interest of protecting its principal in the event this nascent recovery was not for real, the hospital waited several months before fully investing back to its long-term target, missing a 40% recovery on its assets in the process.

That 40% missed opportunity will reduce the hospital's ability to conduct research and make other capital improvements forever. In a competitive market for health care, the hospital has had to tighten its belt and lean more heavily than ever on charitable donors to recover its asset levels and avoid being left farther behind its peers who were able to remain fully invested throughout the market cycle.

Is a Three to Five Year Review Cycle for Asset Allocation Always Appropriate?

Are there any exceptions to the rule of standing by your targets without fail? Yes, as seen in the example of the health care company previously, there are circumstances in which you might need to revisit your asset allocation before the full three to five year planning period has elapsed.

To determine the right time to take a fresh look at their asset allocation plan, pension plans, endowments, and other institutional investors normally use the general rule of every three years *or whenever circumstances significantly change*, whichever comes first. If a corporation buys another company and merges the two entities' pension plans together; a pension plan is frozen to new entrants (a common occurrence these days, sadly); the benefits are increased or reduced; the plan sponsor makes an extraordinary contribution into the plan; or anything else that renders moot the assumptions that were used at the time the target was developed, most pension plans will review their asset allocation mix before they reach that magic three-year anniversary. After all, the asset allocation mix selected was for a given liability in the pension plan and a given amount of assets that has now significantly changed.

Remember, though, upswings or downswings in the markets do not count as reasons to revisit the asset allocation plan. When the plan's asset allocation targets were determined less than three years ago, some degree of volatility was anticipated. The long-term target that was chosen was one that the plan sponsor was comfortable with for all environments and for years into the future. An interim change before the three years is up should therefore always be due to a change in circumstances, not market values.

How does this translate to individual investors? The same logic applies: keep your plan for the duration of the target period unless the situation changes. What are allowable triggers for a change? The same as those for a pension plan:

1. Population change: The number of people in your plan changes (marriage, divorce, children are born, a deadbeat brother moves into the space above the garage).

2. Liability change: How much money you will need in retirement changes (you take or leave a job that offers a pension plan, thereby changing how much of your own savings you will need to live off of; you and your spouse decide to spend five years in the Peace Corps after retirement, decreasing future cash needs for those years you are overseas).

3. Funding ability change: How much money you are able to contribute changes (you or your spouse get a large raise or pay cut, someone enters or leaves the workforce, and/ or there is a one-time contribution to your savings in the form of a severance package or inheritance).

The basic inputs into the calculation are simple, regardless of whether you are a $100 billion pension plan or an individual just starting a career. How much do you need at retirement? How much can you expect to earn on what you have already saved? How much can you save each year? When—and only when—one of these circumstances changes significantly can an interim target change be made to the long-term targets. When one of these triggers does hit, though, you should reset the three-year clock. Take a fresh look at your circumstances just like you did the first time around and work from a blank sheet of paper to design a plan that fits you today. Then put it aside and spend the next three years implementing that new plan before you examine it thoroughly again.

How Early You Start Determines How Much Your Assets Can Grow

Imagine five people who start investing at different ages, all with the common goal of retiring at 65 years old. Due to differing life events and circumstances, each is able to start investing at a different age and can contribute a different amount each year. For the sake of simplicity, we will assume that all have the same asset allocation and money managers and will earn 7.0% per year.[5]

Our first individual investor, John, has been unable to save for most of his life. With kids, a homemaker wife, troubles at work, and a boat, John was not able to start consistently saving until he reached age 50. He has $50,000 in the bank, which he converts into investments, and then takes the $10,000 he is no longer paying in college tuition, as his last child has just graduated, and plows them into his portfolio. At age 60, he realizes that he may not have enough to retire, cuts his spending to the bone, and increases contributions to $25,000 per year.

Second, Leslie and her husband are able to save a little earlier. At age 40, with $25,000 previously saved, Leslie gets a promotion and a raise, which enables them to begin to save $10,000 per year. When Leslie turns 47, her only child enters college, and she and her husband take a four-year break from making contributions, deciding to start contributing again when Leslie is 51. Like with John, after tuition payments (and soccer uniforms and dance classes) are over, Leslie and her husband increase their annual contributions to $15,000 each year until they turn 65.

Mark completes college at 24 (the best six or seven years of his life) and starts contributing $2,500 the next year to a savings plan. On his 30th and 40th birthdays, he celebrates by increasing the annual contribution to $5,000 and $7,500, respectively. From 45 to 52, Mark's kids are in college and he, too, makes no contributions. With the last graduation, contributions increase to $10,000 until age 65.

Julie's parents decide when she is born to set her off on the right track, so they contribute $2,000 per year into an IRA in her name. As she gets older, income from summer jobs and babysitting replaces Mom and Dad's contribution. On graduation from college at 22, she resumes the $2,000 contributions after a four-year break while she was in school. At 25, to keep this simple, she matches the plan laid out for Mark that increases savings at each major birthday.

In addition to our four hypothetical individuals, in Table 2-3 I have also shown the results for "Julie Jr." Julie Jr. is Julie's alter ego who invests in precisely the same pattern as Julie, but who is lucky enough to work for a company from ages 22 to 65 that offers a match on retirement contributions of $0.50 per dollar,[6] up to a maximum of $3,000 per year.[7]

---

[5]For the mathematicians out there who want to replicate my calculations, I will assume that the annual contributions occur on June 30, and therefore earn one-half of a year's worth of investment gains in the remaining six months of the year.

[6]This assumes the match starts at age 22.

[7]According to *Vanguard's* 2012 "How America Saves" report, 91% of all American companies offer a match. If your company does not, you can see in Table 2-3 how the impact on your retirement savings might be sufficient to make you seek one that does, even for lower pay.

Table 2-3. Results of Various Lifetime Savings Plans

	John	Leslie	Mark	Julie	Julie Jr.
Age Started Investing	50	40	25	0	0
Maximum Annual Contribution	$25,000	$15,000	$10,000	$10,000	$10,000
Total Amount Contributed	$275,000	$305,000	$260,000	$295,500	$295,500
Assets at Age 65	$487,317	$788,520	$1,170,272	$2,815,747	$3,378,596

Take a look first at the amounts contributed by each individual. They really aren't that different, ranging from a total of $260,000 to $305,000, yet the end results vary by a factor of 6 (or even a factor of 7, if you include the benefit of finding an employer with a moderate match). Taking two of these individuals as an example, over a lifetime, John and Mark have contributed almost the same amount. However, despite the far larger amounts plowed into savings by John later in life when he can afford to do so, he simply cannot overcome the tremendous advantage that Mark gained by investing smaller amounts earlier in life, which resulted in a total asset level more than twice as large as John's.

If I still haven't convinced you of the advantage of investing as early as you can, here are two more examples: If Julie had not stopped making $2,000 annual contributions during college, her final value would have been $3,022,286, which amounts to $206,539 more at retirement just for making a total of $8,000 more in contributions. If Mark had been able to make even a $2,500 contribution during the seven years his kids were in college, that $17,500 total would have meant a retirement value that was $66,106 higher.

"But I'm already 46!" you say. "I have had a lot of fun, but saved nothing. What do I do now?"

I am sorry to have to tell you this, but according to Einstein's theories, time travel is not possible. Unfortunately, if you have been unable or unwilling to commit to a plan until now, you cannot go back and make up for 20 years' worth of missed contributions, obviously.

What you can do, though, is start now. In addition to determining that time travel isn't possible, Albert Einstein once said that the most powerful force in the universe in compound interest—a contention that is clearly demonstrated by Table 2-3, which shows vast differences in ending asset values as a result of the amount of time interest was allowed to compound. With our previous sample investors, John contributed more per year than did Leslie, but he ended up with about half her assets at retirement. If you are 46 already, start now, and front-load as much as you can. Don't wait until you are 50 to really start "socking it away." Those four years can be incredibly meaningful!

As an example, if you start saving $10,000 per year at 46, you would have $507,000 by 65. If you wait just two years to read this book, think it over, develop a plan, and write the first check, your savings at 65 would only be

$424,000. Two years of delays and $20,000 in lower contributions results in an ultimate difference of $83,000 at retirement.

Time is NOT on your side. If you wait just two more years until you are 50 to start saving, the $40,000 of foregone contributions and four years of missed returns results in a retirement value of $352,000, $155,000 less than if you just started now at age 46.

What on Earth Does This Have to Do with Pension Plans?

I know, this book is supposed to be about the lessons we can learn from pension plans, not simply a rehashing of the classes we took in high school math on the benefits of compound interest. So, how is this relevant?

It's simple: Very generally speaking, many of the pension plans that have had trouble or failed over the last decade did not have the savings discipline of any of the individuals discussed previously. Many plans benefited from the outstanding market performance of the 1990s and, due to a combination of income statement padding and some arcane and shortsighted IRS rules that prevented corporate plans from making normal contributions when they reached certain "overfunded" levels, they stopped making contributions into their plans. When the Internet bubble burst in 2001, many plans had not made a contribution in several years and had not built up sufficient assets to ride out the market downturn. Had they chosen to (or been allowed to) continue to contribute each year in a conservative manner, the potentially greater "surplus" in such plans by 1999 would have meant much more of a cushion as the stock market plunged.

As we have seen, the markets will rise and the markets will fall. What is important is for investors to maintain their discipline of investing and contributing to their retirement assets, despite the external market.

The other reason that pension plans failed to meet their targets is due to another lack of discipline: spending discipline. Many plans, especially public pension plans, that did continue to contribute throughout the 1990s[8] often converted their paper "surpluses" into higher benefits for plan members without a corresponding increase in contributions to make up for what was essentially a retroactive increase in costs. That asset "surplus" wasn't intended to be spent but to be saved for a rainy day.

---

[8]Public pension plans are driven by a different set of rules than are corporate plans (ahhhhh, the benefits of being a nontaxable entity and avoiding IRS rules) and therefore were able (required, in many cases) to continue to contribute throughout the 1990s, despite the fact that their funding statuses appeared to be quite solid.

For individual investors, this example again demonstrates the value of sticking to plans. If your ultimate goal is to retire to a small house on a golf course in Arizona, you will need $X in assets when you retire. If your goal is to buy a dive boat on Cozumel, you will need $Y. If your goal is to buy a winery in Napa, you will need $Z. Don't get halfway to the target and then change your goal without making a corresponding change in your savings plans.

Although everyone has the right to change their minds over time, an individual needs to make sure that the plan changes when the end goal changes. Just because the markets are soaring and your $2,000 annual savings appears to be enough to buy the RV in 20 years, you need to be sure to build a sufficient "surplus" so that when the rainy day hits (and it will, as markets will periodically fall), the assets are sufficient to ride out the storm.

When Good Plans Go Bad

When times are good, it is very tempting for a pension plan to fall into this trap. If assets are ahead of where they need to be at a given point in time, it is far too easy for elected officials, trustees, or plan sponsors to reduce contributions or raise benefits (often without making additional contributions). In practice, however, these changes simply cause the plan to spend its surplus.

As mentioned earlier, in the 1990s, many corporate plans were prevented from making any contributions into their plans at all due to their significantly overfunded statuses and the desire under tax laws to prevent corporations from shielding excess earnings from taxation by making "unnecessary" pension contributions. When asset levels in these plans fell with the market declines during the bursting of the NASDAQ bubble, many plans suddenly found themselves significantly underfunded, resulting in large "catch-up" contributions that haven't yet done the job. Some companies were even forced into bankruptcy or restructuring due to the enormous nature of the new contribution requirements. Had these companies been allowed to make steady annual contributions, instead of being barred from contributing by the IRS, even when the contributions weren't viewed as necessary, the additional "rainy day" savings would have helped them weather the storm that followed.

Two Different Approaches Toward Benefit Levels Results in Very Different Financial Situations

The following is a real-world example of two pension plans that took two very different approaches toward contribution and spending discipline. These two public pension plans are located in geographic regions that happen to neighbor each other in the same South Eastern state. Both have a similar amount of total assets, similar political leanings, and similar demographics. I refer to one fund as "Plan A" and the other as "Fund B."

Despite significant pressure from various mayors and other city officials over the years, Plan A has not raised benefits for its members nor reduced contribution rates in the pension plan since the early 1990s, choosing instead to provide additional defined-contribution plan benefits for employees who have long tenures with the system and have reached the maximum benefit under the pension plan. Despite the twin market declines in 2001–2003 and 2008, Plan A remains significantly overfunded today, with assets worth more than 115% of the accrued pension liability.

Fund B, in contrast, has not been nearly so careful. During the 1990s, when returns were routinely 10% or better for several years in a row, the local board of elected officials made a few decisions that would impact the future health of the system.

First, as assets began piling up, the board decided to spend some of the plan's excess returns. Every year that returns exceeded the expected rate of return (around 8%), half of the excess returns would be set aside into a special account that would be used to provide a supplemental benefit to retirees. When the retirees saw the assets growing well and placed pressure on the (elected) board to share some of that wealth, they were more than happy to accommodate them by providing the membership with that additional benefit.

Second, the board decided to spend some of the surplus for the community, too, by reducing the local authority's[9] required contribution into the plan when things were good. Whenever the annual return outperformed that same 8% hurdle, a quarter of the outperformance was set aside into an account that would be used to offset the required contribution—in other words, whenever returns were better than expected, not only did the required contribution fall (because the above-expectation growth in assets helped to close the underfunded gap), but the above-average gains were used to offset even more of the community's contribution into the plan. On the other hand, if the fund underperformed the 8% target in a year, that was it: no extra contribution or no return of any funds from those two set-aside accounts.

This may be getting a little confusing, so I will stop to sum up the situation for anyone who didn't follow what was going on. If the fund returned 8% in a year (the expected return for any given year, which is used to calculate the present value of the liability), all was well. The assets grew 8%, the liability was assumed to grow 8%, and all was good in the world. If the assets grew 3%

---

[9]For example, this could include the city, county, or state that funded the plan.

(a mediocre return) or fell 5% in a poor year, both of which were assumed to occur from time to time under a normal distribution of outcomes, a little bit of ground was lost in trying to keep up with liability growth, but that's life. Some years are good and some are bad. Remember from the example of our individual investor, Bob, that remaining invested after a bad year lets your assets recover in a good year.

Here's the problem: All those decisions the board made meant that there were no more "good" years. If the fund returned 16%, 8% better than expected, 4% (half the outperformance) would go to that supplemental benefit and 2% (another quarter of the outperformance) would reduce future contributions, leaving only a 10% return for the assets in the fund. In practice, therefore, every time the fund outperformed, most of the outperformance went somewhere else. Every time the fund underperformed, the loss was the pension fund's to keep. How can anyone keep pace with that 8% expectation under these circumstances?

Third, in May 2003, luckily right at the bottom of the market, the community issued a Pension Obligation Bond. This is a public debt issuance where the proceeds from the bond sale are used to bring up the value of an underfunded pension, with bond service to be covered by future tax revenues. When rates are low, you tend to lock in a low financing rate, hopefully well below your expected return. However, tax increases, especially in a politically conservative area, are never really welcome. So, to keep people happy, the board coupled the bond issuance with a significant increase in benefits to future retirees, thereby negating much of the financial benefit of the "catch-up" from the proceeds of the bord because an increase in benefits means an increase in liabilities.

Fourth, in early 2007, the markets were in the midst of their fourth good year in a row. A new bubble was forming in real estate, but everything else was doing well, too. Few realized that the debt markets were about to come crashing down. So, what did the board do? Well, because things were going so well over the last few years, they raised benefits again! Shortly thereafter, of course, we experienced the dual fun of the "Credit Crisis" and the "Great Recession," leading most risky assets to fall in value by 50% or more.

Today, Fund B, the community fund that did not accumulate any rainy day surplus is now less than 70% funded. In other words, for every dollar it has promised to retirees in present value terms, the fund has less than 70 cents on hand. Plan A, thanks to its diligence and conservatism, has $1.15.

What lessons can we as individuals draw from this? Although the differences between these funds have impacts in the hundreds of millions of dollars, the behaviors exhibited by these two sets of professionals behind the funds are replicated every day by individual investors. On one hand, we have a group (Plan A) that is committed to a disciplined, austere, long-term plan and continues to maintain that conservative discipline and commitment to steady contributions through thick and through thin. On the other hand, we have a group (Fund B) that was less careful with its funds, deviated from its investment plan, raised benefits, decreased contributions, and ignored the long-term implications of doing so.

A personal investor that exemplifies the same behavior as Plan A would save every week or month up to the point that it started to hurt, and maybe even beyond that point—$1,000 per pay period, say. Every pay period without exception. This person would also have a clear goal in mind, maybe a modest retirement, and would stay focused on that plan like a laser.

Conversely, a personal investor that mimics Fund B would contribute $10,000 one month and then skip four months to pay for a lavish vacation to reward himself for making that big contribution that first month. Then, after a month in which stocks happened to have a great run, the individual's end goal would shift from a modest retirement to a castle in Tuscany with a winery, to which he makes a nonrefundable down payment equal to half his life's savings, with his current house and cars pledged against some extra debt. After all, if stocks keep going up 5% a month forever, like they did for him last month, he will be a billionaire soon enough, and the debt doesn't matter! Then, when stocks naturally fall in subsequent months, as they tend to do, he stops making savings contributions and takes out another loan against his wife's 401(K) to service the debt on the Tuscan property, finding himself radically underfunded versus his financial goals and in need of large savings contributions just to tread water.

Sure, the second individual is a bit of an exaggeration. However, Figure 2-1 illustrates that at least a little of this reckless behavior among individuals is fairly common.

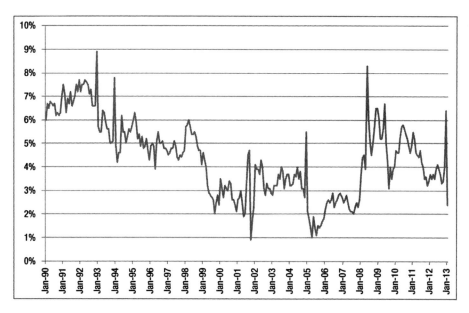

Figure 2-1. US Personal Savings Rate. Federal Reserve Bank of St. Louis—Federal Reserve Economic Data

As Figure 2-1 shows, the savings rate among individuals as a percentage of income was fairly level for a few years after the negative effects of the technology bubble began to wear off, and then, as the housing market and stock market really began to take off, people felt like they were wealthier due to their growing assets and believed that they needed to save less. In 2008, the financial crisis hit, and suddenly people felt poorer again. Investment balances and savings were down significantly, and people as a whole began to save more to make up the difference.

The point of all of this is that although we can bemoan the behavior of governments and plans like Fund B, which save less when times are good and then feel the need to raise contribution levels and taxes to pay for them when times are bad, we can see that the population is just as guilty of the exact same behavior—saving less than is needed and spending more than is prudent. I'm here to help you, as an individual investor, break that cycle in your own investment plan. Let's keep our investment levels constant over time to take advantage of both good times and bad.

Dollar Cost Averaging

I've said it before and I'll say it again: Markets will go up and they will go down. Unless your Magic 8 Ball is way more accurate than mine, there really is no way to predict swings in price from month to month to month. If you wait to buy until you think prices have bottomed, you will probably miss the bottom. If you think prices are too high and hold off on buying more shares, you may very well be underinvested in the next bull market.

So, what is an individual investor to do in lieu of finding a mythical market price predictor? The best strategy is just to keep buying a given dollar amount periodically over time, no matter what—which is also known as "dollar cost averaging." In fact, even if you could get your hands on a mythical market price predictor, dollar cost averaging is probably a better bet. Why? Believe it or not, using this strategy, you actually will end up purchasing your investments at a lower average price than you probably would have paid if you had some small ability to time the markets. Here is why: If you invest the same dollar amount every period, when prices are high, you buy fewer shares. When prices are low, you buy more shares. As a result, your weighted average buying price automatically falls below the average market price.

Here is an example. Mary invests $300 every month. She logs onto her brokerage's web site on the last day of the month and simply buys $300 worth of her favorite mutual fund. Over the next three months, the prices at which she transacts are $20, $15, and $25 (this is a very volatile fund).

Over those three months, the simple average market price is $20. But Mary doesn't get exactly that average. In the first month, when the price is $20 per share, Mary buys 15 shares. At the end of the second month, the price is $15 per share, and Mary buys 20 shares. At the end of the third month, the price is $25 per share, and Mary buys 12 shares. Overall, she has spent $900 for 47 shares at an average price of $19.15. That is 85 cents per share better than the average price of $20 per share for that time period.

At this point, you are probably thinking that I spent all day long trying to find some combination of prices to make that example work out the way it did. Honestly, I didn't. I just picked three prices out of thin air that I knew were evenly divisible into $300 per month.

Here is more proof. Table 2-4 shows month-ending prices for Microsoft[10] stock for each of the last 12 months up to the time of this writing, as well as the dollar cost averaged transaction schedule for an investor buying $500

---

[10] I know, Microsoft is pretty "old school" as an example. I was going to be trendier and use Apple as an example, but given that my $500 would buy less than 1 share each month, the math wasn't very exciting.

worth of the stock every month. To make this example fair, I'm assuming that the investor can buy fractional shares.[11]

Table 2-4. Effects of Monthly Dollar
Cost Averaging

Date	Closing Price	Shares Purchased
10/31/2011	$26.63	18.78
11/30/2011	$25.58	19.55
12/31/2011	$25.96	19.26
1/31/2012	$29.53	16.93
2/29/2012	$31.74	15.75
3/31/2012	$32.26	15.50
4/30/2012	$32.02	15.62
5/31/2012	$29.19	17.13
6/30/2012	$30.59	16.35
7/31/2012	$29.47	16.97
8/31/2012	$30.82	16.22
9/30/2012	$29.76	16.80
Average Closing Price:	$29.46	
Average Purchase Price:	$29.29	
Savings Per Share:	$0.17	

Data courtesy of Yahoo Finance.

Dollar cost averaging would have saved you $0.17 per share over just the past year. That comes to $35.30 for the 204 shares purchased, or a little more than one of those shares for free. Imagine if you dollar cost averaged your monthly purchases over a decade, or even over a career. Given enough time, the discipline of steady contributions will really add up to some significant benefits.

Picking Your Asset Allocation

Now for the fun part. By now you understand the need for a disciplined commitment to savings, and we are all agreed that we will pick a plan and stay with it through thick and thin, right?

---

[11]In reality, most investors cannot buy fractional shares of a stock like Microsoft. Rounding off to the nearest whole share each month might generate a different result. However, given that mutual funds trade in three-digit decimal share amounts, the math will hold for most investors in 401(k) plans or other accounts where they buy mutual funds. I also used decimal shares because my $500 amount was arbitrary. Someone saving $10,000 a month cares a lot less about decimals than someone saving $500 a month, and I don't want the $500 amount to disprove the example.

Great!

What's the plan?

It depends. The "right" asset allocation plan is defined as the one that is right for you. You need to sit down with your significant other(s) and determine what your retirement goals are. What are your current assets? How much can you afford to save? How much risk can you tolerate? These are the types of factors that will determine if a portfolio of 80% stocks and 20% bonds is right for your needs or if you are better off with 20% stocks and 80% bonds, or some other combination entirely.

Unfortunately, without sitting side by side with you and understanding your complete financial picture, I cannot tell you exactly what your asset allocation should be. What I can do is offer you guidance in where to get some direction to build your plan.

Assumptions

The first step that any pension plan takes in determining its asset allocation is to develop a set of assumptions for the expected return and risk of every asset class it is investing in or considering. In the same way, you need to first figure out what you expect your investment options will return. If your financial plan will require you to achieve a 6% return on average every year, does that mean you need to invest 100% or 40% in stocks?

Pension plans typically adopt these assumptions from their investment consultants, enlist economists to help them determine their assumptions, or use internal macroeconomic models to develop their own assumptions. All of these custom solutions are probably unavailable to help you specifically. That doesn't mean that you cannot use these resources to your advantage at all, however. For example, most public pension plans typically publish their assumptions online in their meeting agendas, meeting minutes, or annual reports.

If your local pension plan doesn't publish its own assumptions, it would be pretty easy to check what the major plans—like CalPERS, CalSTRS, Florida Retirement System, Texas Teachers, and the rest—use in their models simply by referencing their meeting minutes or annual reports online. You could even survey a few to see if there is any consensus.

Another option would be to do some digging and check what the major investment banks and commercial banks are predicting. Although most macroeconomic research by banks is reserved for their major clients, you might be able to find a few sets of assumptions from some credible sources with a quick Google search. Typing "asset class assumptions" into a search engine just gave me a number of links to assumptions published by several investment management companies, consulting firms, and economics research organizations. If you don't want to rely on any one particular source, you can also use the *Wall Street Journal*, which periodically publishes a survey of a large population of economists' expected returns for stocks and bonds. It doesn't cover all the other asset classes you might consider, but at least it gives you a general indication of overall expectations for some of the largest asset classes, like stocks and bonds.

Although in practice the math is a little more complicated, you now have at least a general guide as to what you should expect for returns from a given asset allocation mix. If you see a consensus that stocks are expected to return 8% and bonds 4%, you know that a 50/50 mix of both might get you a return that is somewhere around 6%. I'm discounting the importance of correlations in returns among asset classes here, which is very important in calculating risk estimates, because we really do not expect to be exact for this kind of planning exercise. Your goal is to find a reasonable return expectation that you can use in your calculations of how much you need to save to get to your retirement savings target and how to get there. Ridiculous levels of precision are unnecessary, given that reality will never perfectly reflect your expectations anyway.

Developing Your Plan

The next step is to put all these pieces together and see if the plan fits the goals.

Let's say you just turned 48 years old; can afford to save, say, $1,500 per month; you expect to earn 6% per year; you have already saved $225,000; you have 17 years until retirement; and you want to have $1.2 million in total savings at retirement to allow for $50,000 in annual postretirement income, you need to see if all these numbers add up into a credible plan that you can live with.

There are a lot of resources out there to help you build and test your plan.

The easiest to use, in my opinion, are the retirement planning tools on the web sites of most commercial banks, brokerages, and mutual fund companies—especially the companies that tend to provide 401(k) services. These web sites typically have a bunch of blanks that you can fill in with data—like how much you have saved, how much can you save, and how much you expect to earn—and then will give you an estimate of whether your retirement goal is realistic or not. Most of them now have "sliders" where you can easily adjust the assumptions in these models with your mouse and immediately see the long-term benefit of saving an extra $100 a month or deferring your retirement from 65 to 68.

The results that you get from these web sites are often quite eye-opening, and I recommend that anyone who seriously wants to plan for their future play with one of these for at least a few minutes. Socking away a mere $200 a month from your paycheck for your entire career may very well leave you broke after four years of retirement. Retiring with a balance of $1 million sounds like a huge amount of money today, until you realize that if you spend $75,000 of that balance every year, the money won't last forever. Be as conservative as you dare on your return expectations and as aggressive as you can be on the amount you think you will need at retirement. It is always better to err on the side of too much money at retirement than too little.

After you think you have a plan, show it to someone else. Your spouse might take one look at it and declare that your return expectation is unrealistic, or that the savings number is impossible, or maybe even that you can save more if the family makes certain sacrifices to increase your chances of reaching your goals.

Then, if you can, show it to an expert. Most commercial bank branches and some discount brokerage branches employ on-site professionals who can help with retirement planning, and they often do so for free if you have an account with the company. Typically these experts will invite you to walk through retirement-specific software programs, like the online sliders I mentioned, with them to help you get a better understanding of your needs. Like your spouse, an expert might help you find the flaws or unrealistic expectations in your plan so that you can avoid an unpleasant surprise later. These experts may also help you find better ways to build your plan by, for example, adding other asset classes or types of investments that you had not considered. Although I will discuss in Chapter 9 on fees and expenses how to make sure that you are not taken for a ride, listen to the advice for now and see if you think it is intended to benefit you or the bank. If it really helps your plan, this meeting could have been a great use of your time.

If All Else Fails, Trust the Experts

So the sliders on your company's 401(k) web site told you one thing, and the IRA guy at your local branch told you the exact opposite. You think that you can get 7% per year, and your spouse thinks you are crazy to be so optimistic. What are you to do?

There are two more sources of information or ideas that might help you to confirm or disprove your approach.

First, I previously suggested using the asset class return and risk assumptions from a large pension plan as a starting point. Why not use their target asset allocation, too? Unless you are very close to retirement, you should have a long-term focus in mind, just like the pension plan does. After much consultation with experts, the city pension plan or your state's pension plan might have changed its asset allocation to a new mix of X% stocks, Y% bonds, and Z% alternatives, resulting in an expected return of 7.2% per year. Although that might not be an exact match for your situation, it is one very credible determination of what a long-term plan should look like and how much it should earn per year. It will also provide a great starting point for your own work or a confirmation of your own estimates.

Second, target-date funds, which are mutual funds that invest in a wide variety of asset classes—including stocks, bonds, real estate, and cash, among others—can provide some great information about how experts are looking at asset allocation. These funds are offered by almost 200 mutual fund companies and are frequently included in 401(k) plans as an investment option, sometimes even the default option.

Target-date funds typically are offered in an investment family that includes a variety of retirement dates, each with a different asset allocation mix that changes over time, and incorporate an expected retirement year in the name of the fund. For example, a given mutual fund company might offer the TargetDate 2040 fund, intended for people who will be turning 65 within a few years of the year 2040. This fund today (in 2013) will be predominantly invested in stocks and other risky assets because people who buy this fund are expected to have more than 25 years until retirement. The TargetDate 2015 fund, in contrast, might be far more conservative, with large investments in bonds and other lower risk assets because participants in this fund are expected to be very close to retirement. Over the next 25 years, the portfolio manager for the 2040 fund will slowly change the asset allocation to one with a lower risk as the participants get closer to retirement; and the fund company will add 2050, 2055, 2060, 2065, and 2070 funds to its lineup as new workers enter the workforce in the decades to come.

Given that each of these companies publishes the underlying asset allocation mix in their prospectuses, on their web sites, and on industry web sites like Morningstar.com, a person who expects to retire in 2035 could look up the asset allocation for the 2035 funds offered by several mutual fund companies to see how closely the average asset allocation fits the plan that she or he has come up with. Alternatively, the individual could just invest in that target-date fund and call it quits. In a perfect world, the fund that matches the individual's expected retirement year has an appropriate asset allocation for an average person of the same age, eliminates many of the investment structure risks and complexities that I outline in Chapters 3 through 6, and takes care of the selection of the underlying investment funds on behalf of the investor. Frankly, individuals could put 100% of their assets into one of these funds, spend all their spare time thinking about how to come up with extra contributions to their savings, and use the rest of this book as a doorstop if they really wanted to. That is, after all, the entire reason target-date funds were created in the first place. They serve as one-stop solutions for people who don't have the time, knowledge, resources, interest, or confidence to make their own investment decisions and want someone to hand them a solution that does all the work for them. This doesn't mean that target-date funds are perfect, but they very well might be good enough for people who don't have the time, knowledge, or resources to do better. Target-date funds often will charge higher fees for the total portfolio than an individual could find on his or her own by building his or her own portfolio, especially if an individual makes liberal use of index funds. Nevertheless, that incremental cost may be worth it for the peace of mind that these funds provide to their participants about their asset allocation. Be aware, however, that target-date funds are designed for a generic investor of a given age. Because every investor has a unique risk tolerance, time frame, and asset value, the asset allocation that might work for one individual, or for the generic 32-year-old investor, may not be a perfect fit with every potential client.

Summary

If you take nothing else from this book, understand that a disciplined approach to making continuous contributions into a portfolio with an appropriate level of risk is the single most successful way to achieve your financial goals.

When you are ahead of plan after a bull market, stay on plan. Keep contributing. Don't take a rest and trust that you are done. When the market falls in value, don't panic. Save more if you can, sure, but do not make radical changes to your plan that prevent your assets from recovering over time, assuming you have time to recover. Most important, be realistic and be conservative. Be realistic and conservative in how you think you need and want to live after retirement to make sure that you save enough to get there. Be realistic and conservative about your annual return expectation. Be realistic and conservative about how much you can contribute, erring on the side of too many contributions whenever it is possible to do so.

Whereas you have a lifetime to save and invest, you only turn 65 once, and you only get the results of one retirement plan when you do. If your asset balance at retirement isn't exactly what you and your planner projected when you were 28, would you rather discover that you will retire with too much money or too little? Oversaving and outperforming your return expectations will likely lead to a far more comfortable retirement than would be the case if the chips do not fall in your favor. By picking a conservative asset allocation that is right for you, coupled with a disciplined plan of aggressive contributions, you can greatly increase your chances of building a retirement reserve sufficient to your needs.

Investment Structure for Stocks, Part I

Basic Domestic Equity Considerations

In Chapter 2, I discussed the importance of selecting an asset allocation plan that is appropriate to your needs. Now that you have determined what percentage of your assets should be invested in stocks, the next step is to determine how those equity investments should be structured. Studies have shown that if asset allocation drives 90% of the returns of a total portfolio, structure decisions, the next part of our arrow-shaped Road Map to Financial Success, determine more than 5% of the results. In this chapter and the one after it, I will guide you through the major considerations that both pension plans and individual investors face when it comes to constructing an equity portfolio.

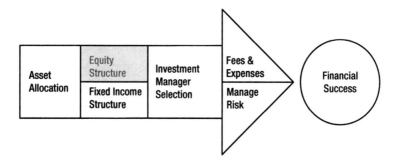

When they are tasked with buying individual stocks or mutual funds that invest in stocks, many investors get too caught up in chasing the latest trends, like investing in growth stocks after a technology boom has dominated the market for years or entering a foreign market based on recent results. However, these types of decisions do little to improve an investor's long-term results because chasing yesterday's trend is never a safe investment and often will dramatically increase the level of risk in his or her portfolio. That's why, in this chapter, I will discuss some basic elements of each of the many types of biases that investors fall prey to when constructing their portfolios and demonstrate why most pension plans avoid them and their resultant risks wherever they can. In addition, I will review the merits or unnecessary risks that come from an overreliance on only growth or value investing, or on an imbalance to large cap, mid cap, or small cap stocks (an explanation of what these mean will follow for the uninitiated). I will start, however, with the most fundamental debate that every investor must wrestle with—whether to invest actively or passively.

Active versus Passive Investing

If you want to invest in the stock market index simply to reap the gains of the overall market returns year after year, you are, by definition, a passive investor. A variety of money management companies offer index funds, or mutual fund products that simply buy shares in every company in a given index (the S&P 500 is the most common example) in the proportions in which they are weighted in the index. Let's say that Apple Computer and ExxonMobil each comprised about 4% of the benchmark and Microsoft comprised about 2%. An index fund manager who has invested $10 billion of aggregated client money would therefore hold $400 million each of Apple and ExxonMobil stock, $200 million worth of Microsoft stock, and $9 billion in the other 497 companies in the S&P 500 in proportions that are determined by the index publisher and roughly equate to the relative size of the outstanding market capitalization (the total value of a company's stock) of each company.

As client money is added to or removed from the index fund, adjustments are made to make sure that as close to a perfect match as possible is made with the index constitution. If Apple grows to comprise 5% of the index, the existing positions will have grown in value correspondingly. As a result, any new cash that is invested in the index fund will now be 5% invested in Apple and 1% less in something else (most likely a very small amount less spread across most of the other 499 companies in the index).

Indexed mutual funds and exchange traded funds (essentially mutual funds that trade throughout the day like individual stocks and often carry slightly lower fees than mutual funds that use similar strategies) are among the cheapest ways to invest in stocks, thanks to fierce competition among mutual fund managers, which has brought the cost of these vehicles down dramatically over the last decade. To demonstrate how easy it can be to run an index fund, and therefore how little it should cost the individual investor, one state pension plan that I used to work with employed one single worker to manage a 500 million dollar S&P 500 index fund. This employee was tasked with tracking the plan's holdings in an Excel spreadsheet, comparing these holdings with the published weights in the index on a daily basis, and trading the portfolio when necessary to rebalance back to target weights—as a part-time job! Index funds require no stock analysts to develop forecasts for earnings or growth prospects for companies because they make no decisions about adding or deleting stocks based on the perceived merits of each company as an investment. As much as the portfolio manager may love or hate a stock, if S&P says that XYZ Corporation comprises 0.32% of the S&P 500 index, the index fund manager will attempt to hold precisely 0.32% of his assets in shares of that company without any independent judgment. If the S&P 500 index returns 4.23% in a given month, a fund that is intended to track that index as closely as possible will return for its clients very close to that same 4.23%, less some minor deviations for small misweights, client cash flows, recent dividend payments, and the fees that the manager charges the investors.

On the other side of the spectrum are actively managed mutual funds and other investment products. In these funds, a portfolio manager (or, in some cases, a group of portfolio managers and/or analysts) will decide which companies to buy and sell whenever they deem it appropriate. Teams of analysts for the money management company will spend their days talking to customers, competitors, and suppliers, trying to determine which companies will have better returns than their peers in the near future. The portfolio manager and his team will crisscross the country, visiting factories and meeting with CEOs to try to determine firsthand which are the best investment opportunities. Then, the portfolio manager might build a portfolio with investments in his favorite, say, 75 of the companies in the S&P 500, leaving out the other 425 companies. Every day, small adjustments will be made to the portfolios, with new companies being added or old companies being sold completely every few weeks or months. Over the course of a year, a typical actively managed mutual fund might buy and sell 50% to 150% of the portfolio, holding any individual position anywhere from a few months to a few years. As a result, rather than returning the results of the S&P 500 stock index when it is up 4.23% in that same month, the hypothetical portfolio manager mentioned previously will return the sum of his 75 company subset. If the active manager is up 7% or down 3% in the same month that the index is up 4.23%, his disassociation from the benchmark would be completely expected, given that the manager is not trying to replicate the index returns. Instead, the active manager is trying to add value from the selection of superior stock investments above the benchmark as consistently as possible so that over longer periods of time, clients earn a better rate of return than they would have received in the index fund.

That better rate of return is, of course, the *goal* of the actively managed fund, not a promise. Keep in mind that the sum of the returns of all investors in the stocks of the S&P 500 index is basically equal to the market return, less transaction costs and investment manager fees. Let's say that we are both portfolio managers and I like IBM and you don't, so I buy it and you don't. You like GM and I don't, so you buy it and I don't. At the end of the day, our individual portfolios, and the portfolios of all of our peers, all the investment managers in the world, and all the mutual funds, will add up to have roughly the same performance as the overall index, less our average management fee. As a result, in aggregate, all investors in those stocks will earn the S&P 500 return, less transaction costs (the costs of trading, like commissions, market impacts, etc.) and any fees that the investment managers charge to their clients.

Choosing an active manager is, therefore, never a guarantee that you will outperform the benchmark. In fact, the vast majority of large cap core mutual funds (those that would be measured against the S&P 500) have a rather hard time consistently beating the benchmark.

Take a look at Figure 3-1, which plots the returns of 992 large cap core mutual funds against the S&P 500 index on a rolling three-year basis back to December 1989. Every point on this chart indicates how the returns of the S&P 500 for the preceding three years compared to the entire opportunity set (commonly referred to as the "universe") of large cap core mutual funds at that point in time. For example, the cluster of dots in the valley around 2002 indicate that for the three years ending on December 31, 2002 (December 31, 2000, to December 31, 2002), you would have been quite happy investing in actively managed funds because the index falls on the vertical scale around the 90 mark, indicating that about 90% of large cap core investment managers were outperforming the S&P 500 on a medium-term basis.

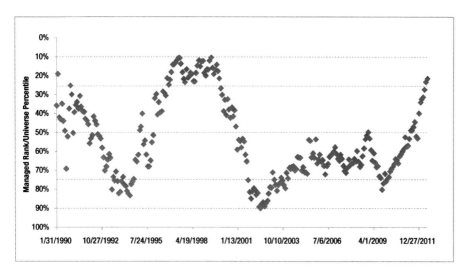

Figure 3-1. Performance of S&P 500 versus All Large Cap Core Funds
Data courtesy of eVestment Alliance

In contrast, in August 1996, the dots peak at around 10%, indicating that only 10% of large cap core mutual funds had better three-year returns than the S&P 500 index. In other words, 90% of large cap core mutual funds *underperformed* the index for the 1994–1996 period.

Since 2002, the index has made steady gains against the universe of actively managed funds, with roughly median performance from 2003 to 2008 (half of the mutual funds outperformed the index, half of the mutual funds underperformed). Most recently, the index ranked around 20%, meaning that approximately 90% of large cap core mutual funds have underperformed the S&P 500.

Over the entire history of Figure 3-1, you can see that the index has generally remained in the top half, with two short exceptions around 1994 and 2002. This means that there has been generally a better than 50–50 chance that any fund you pick will underperform the benchmark. In some periods, as I have previously mentioned, the odds of picking a "losing" fund have been between 80% to 90%.

I will discuss manager selection (how to actually go about picking investment managers) in Chapter 7, but, until then, understand that the deck in large cap core investing has been largely stacked against you!

Is this effect limited to only large cap core stocks? Let's take a look at large cap value managers.

The 600 large cap value mutual funds in Figure 3-2 tell a similar story to that which was told in Figure 3-1. Although there have been periods of decent relative manager performance over the course of the past 20 years, there is clear evidence that investing in large cap value mutual funds is a tough slog. From December 1989 until late 2008, the Wilshire Large Cap Value Index has pretty consistently ranked above the median manager, again indicating that more than half (and, again, at times as many as 90%) of managers have underperformed the benchmark.

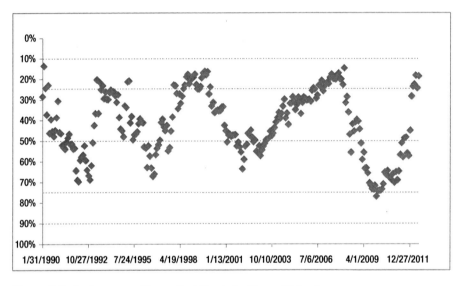

Figure 3-2. Performance of Large Cap Value Index Versus All Funds
Data courtesy of eVestment Alliance

The 2008–2010 Credit Crisis and the resulting recession was really the only exception to this rule, as evidenced by the extended period of below-median ranks by the index in Figure 3-2. Based on my personal observations, many managers became very conservative in their approaches to the market and their willingness to take risk during this time period. When clients began to withdraw money during the worst of the crisis, many investment managers raised more cash than was needed to protect themselves from future redemptions. Given how hard it was for managers to find any liquidity whatsoever in the market, many raised cash every time they got the chance. When a market is falling, holding 10% of your assets in cash instead of stocks can provide a great buffer against losses and make you look very good by comparison because only 90% of your portfolio continues to fall day after day, while the index sees 100% of its exposure remain in falling stock prices.

In March 2009, global stock markets bottomed and began a rapid recovery. Those managers who still had cash on their balance sheets instead of 100% stocks now saw that cash act like an anchor in a strong current, holding them back from going with the flow. The index had an almost vertical improvement relative to the universe, especially in 2011.

The evidence in Figure 3-2 about the performance of large cap value managers therefore indicates to me that the large cap core chart was not an anomaly; large cap investing in general is a difficult thing to do properly. There are literally thousands of analysts at Wall Street banks, money managers, and hedge funds—plus potentially tens of thousands of individual investors—looking at, for example, General Electric (or any other large cap company) every single day. The odds that the majority of them have superior information to the few others and can act on that information in a legal manner that provides superior returns to the population as a whole are very slim. Although there are certainly some large cap core and value managers that can provide consistently superior performance, as we will discuss in the chapter on investment manager selection, Chapter 7, finding them is a hard task.

Figure 3-3, which shows the distribution of returns of 351 small cap core mutual funds plotted against the Russell 2000 index, tells a slightly different story than Figures 3-1 and 3-2 did. Small cap investing is characterized by less information widely available to investors, fewer investment analysts poring over the same data, and, as will be discussed later in this chapter, widespread "cheating" by small cap managers (buying microcap or midcap stocks that are not contained in the benchmark).

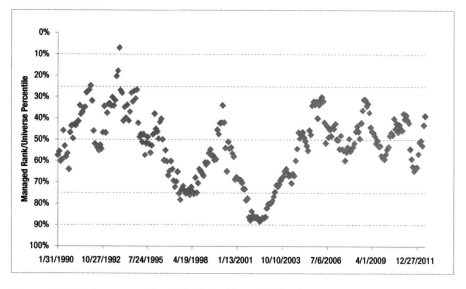

Figure 3-3. Performance of Small Cap Index Versus All Funds
Data courtesy of eVestment Alliance

From 1989 to about 2005, Figure 3-3 is almost an exact copy of the large cap core and large cap value charts, with extended periods of outperformance by the population of managers above the benchmark. In 2002, for example, more than 90% of small cap managers were outperforming the benchmark. The last five years, however, have seen more of a mixed bag, with the index oscillating from the 50th percentile to the top 25%, and most recently it has been hovering right around the median. I wouldn't say that Figure 3-3 is conclusive because the index does bounce around quite a bit, but you could certainly make the case that there is a better chance that you might pick an investment manager capable of outperformance when you select small cap active managers than there is for some of the large cap categories discussed previously. Although there is still plenty of opportunity for underperformance, this is an asset class in which the evidence at least begins to support the premise that you could find consistent outperformance in small cap core investing. This is the main reason why pension plans that tend to index most or all of their large cap allocations will hire active managers for small cap stocks—greater evidence that small cap stock managers might add some consistent value to their portfolios.

In Chapter 4, I will discuss the benefits of investing in a global portfolio for stocks, rather than investing in a predominantly domestic portfolio, as many investors tend to do. For now, Figure 3-4 clearly supports the premise that markets and capital are becoming more global. Whereas the 671 managers who invest in developed markets (generally, the first-world economies) outside the United States experienced some wild volatility relative to the index in the 1990s,[1] the path since has shown a smooth and steady transition. With each passing year, non-US markets have become more "information efficient,"[2] and the MSCI EAFE+C Index (Morgan Stanley Capital International—Europe, Australia, Far East, plus Canada Index) has moved up to around the 25% level. Over at least the last half decade, about a quarter of investment managers have outperformed the benchmark, while three-quarters have failed to do so.

---

[1] The main explanation for the last place rank for the index in 1991–1993 and the first place rank in 1989 and 1995 is due largely to Japan. Japan at the time had a total market capitalization that started to rival the United States. Investment managers almost to a one were afraid of committing that much to a single market and universally underweighted Japan. When Japan did well, the index looked fantastic. When Japan did poorly, all managers who kept a lower-than-market weight in the country (almost all of them) outperformed the benchmark.

[2] Meaning that information about any company that might affect the stock price is more quickly disseminated to the marketplace and is rapidly reflected in the stock price. With openness and transparency come more rapid market reaction and less time for any individual piece of information to be used for personal gain.

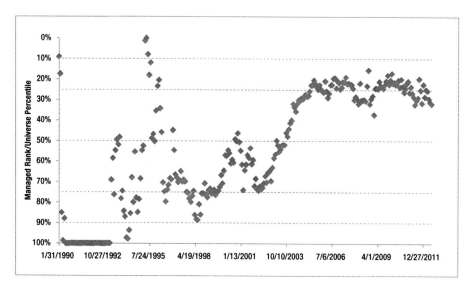

Figure 3-4. Performance of Non-US Equity Index Versus All Non-US Funds
Data courtesy of eVestment Alliance

For all you emerging markets fans out there, I saved the best for last for you in Figure 3-5. Emerging markets are countries that would have been considered as belonging to the Third World a few decades ago. Today, many of these countries have created world-class companies that can compete against their Western competitors very successfully, yet the countries still have smaller and less liquid stock markets, poorer legal controls, and limits on capital flows in and out of the country, thereby posing additional risks to investors beyond simply market returns. As these countries develop, they can progress from "emerging" to "developed" and move from market index to index. Consequently, after the index publishers give their stamp of approval to a country and pronounce it to now be "developed," they become available for investments from many more investors.

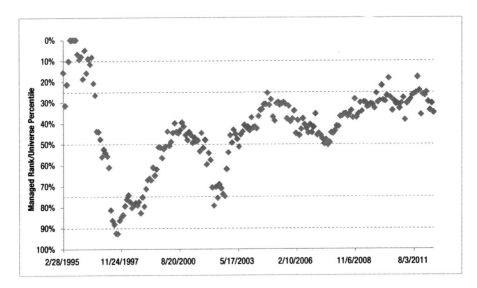

Figure 3-5. Performance of Emerging Markets Index Versus All Fund
Data courtesy of eVestment Alliance

Whereas recent evidence shows that only a quarter of the 463 emerging markets mutual funds in this data set have outperformed the MSCI Emerging Markets Index, the longer-term track record for this population of managers is far better, with the majority of investment managers having achieved extended periods of outperformance in the past. Like with developed markets, continued improvements in regulatory oversight, liquidity, and corporate transparency will likely lead to greater market efficiency for emerging markets—and that trend is obvious in the steady upward movement of the index in Figure 3-5, which indicates that emerging markets seem to be on a path to an environment in which it is far harder to add consistent value. Although there has been at least some evidence of the historic ability of investment managers to outperform, that may not be the case going forward.

Value versus Growth Investing

At this point, let's shift the discussion to "style bias" within portfolios. Value and growth investing are two very different styles of stock selection that can generate divergent returns for long periods of time. Value investors are considered the bargain hunters of the investment world, looking for stocks that are cheaper than average, usually with a high dividend. Some value stocks have low prices because they have fallen on hard times, like financial stocks did after the 2008 credit crisis, while others are simply companies that grow slowly and generate high cash yields, like utilities. Growth stock investors, on the other hand, are the optimists of the stock world, always looking for the Next Big Thing that will change the world. They are not buying stocks based just on the price today relative to the value of the underlying assets, but rather the potential value of those assets three or five years or more into the future, when the company's brilliant new invention has hit it big.

In 1999, I was asked by a potential client: "Is value investing dead?" The question was intriguing. At the time, technology and growth stocks were riding high on the unbelievable, and soon-to-crash, dot-com bubble. I'll go into more detail on this concept later in this chapter, but for the purposes of this example, academic theory says that growth and value investing should generally balance each other out over a period of many years, and neither growth nor value investing should have a systematic long-term performance advantage. However, one of these two "styles" can persistently outperform the other for several years at a time before it reverts—and, as seen in 2001, when the dot-com bubble finally burst, that reversion often can be violent.

You may be wondering what my response was to the prospective client's question. Unfortunately, I do not have a crystal ball. At the time, I gave the best answer any consultant could and proceeded to tell that prospective client and a few existing clients that I thought this bubble was overdone, that cycles will mean-revert at some point, and that they should avoid chasing returns. However, like many in the industry, I didn't make any major changes to what I was recommending to my clients at the time, nor did I flee away from growth stocks like one might from a tidal wave. Of course, hindsight is always 20/20. If only everyone could have known that the technology bubble was going to burst. Perhaps in hindsight the mere fact that someone was asking that question was a sign to run from growth stocks screaming for the hills.

In practice, most pension plans do not bias their portfolios toward a growth or value style but remain "style neutral" over time, with equal positions in both styles. Any investor looking to control overall risk in his or her portfolio should do the same.

In Figure 3-6, I have plotted the rolling three-year performance of the Russell 1000 Value Index less the performance of the Russell 1000 Growth Index since the inception of both indices more than 40 years ago. When the moving line is above the 0 point in the middle, value stocks are outperforming growth stocks on a medium-term basis. When the jagged line dips below the 0 line, the markets are in a period where growth stocks are outperforming value stocks.

Figure 3-6. Rolling Performance of Large Cap Value Versus Growth
Data courtesy of Russell Indices

Some experts believe value investing is the One True Way to Wealth because, like people who love to clip coupons or look for bargains at garage sales, buying something for less than it is really worth tends to reap strong results. However, the bad news is that you can see that there are meaningful periods of time where growth investing dramatically outperforms value investing. Fortunately for value investing aficionados, though, over the very long term, the cumulative track record has historically favored investing above growth investing. Figure 3-7 shows this outperformance.

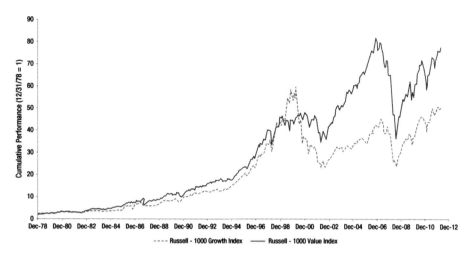

Figure 3-7. Cumulative Performance of Large Cap Value and Growth Indices
Data courtesy of Russell Indexes

From the inception of the Russell 1000 Growth and Value indexes to the present day, value investing has indeed generated more cumulative performance than growth investing. However, you can see that the two lines in Figure 3-7 have crossed in the past, when the cumulative record of one starts to exceed the other, such as in 1998 and 2000. Although the markets have been in an extended value cycle since the bursting of the dot-com bubble in 2000, the historical record indicates that this will not persist forever. Growth and value styles will revert again in the future, as they did in Figure 3-6 every time growth stocks jumped ahead and as happened in the early and late 1990s and from 2007 to 2012.

Furthermore, for those who believe in the long-term track record of value over growth, even if you had bought into the value-investing concept years ago, could you have lived with the volatility between these styles, as seen in Figure 3-7? Look at the tremendous outperformance of growth over value in the period from 1994 to 2000. Are you absolutely positive that you would have never thrown in the towel during one of those go-go growth periods, where all the press attention was about the latest world-changing technology stock? In all likelihood, unless you had a clear discipline to value invest through thick and through thin, it would have been very, very difficult to stay that course through some of the periods of strong growth performance. Figure 3-8 shows the two styles again with the addition of the S&P 500 Index.

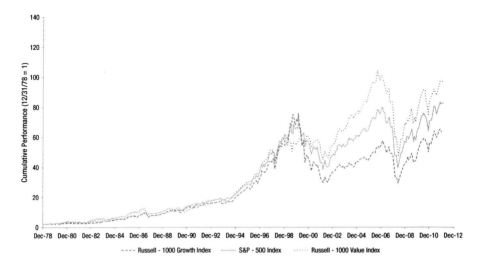

Figure 3-8. Cumulative Performance of Large Cap Value, Growth, and Core Indices
Data courtesy of Russell Indexes and Standard & Poor's

As shown by the S&P 500 index in Figure 3-8, a style-neutral approach gets you to roughly the same place as growth and value investing do after 34 years—and it does so with far less interim volatility by balancing the two style indices year in and year out.

What does this mean? Do pension plans never invest in growth or value managers? Of course they do. Many plans that understand the benefits of avoiding an overall style bias will still choose individual managers of all types (some plans do hire only core managers or broad index funds). However, instead of picking just one style or the other, plans with an eye on risk controls pick the best of breed of both kinds and try to keep their assets relatively even between them.

For every superstar value investor like Warren Buffett, who is out there looking for underpriced stocks forgotten by the market, there exists an equally great growth investor who is prescient about what technological advances will generate big returns tomorrow. Most of the fame and fortune acquired by Capital Guardian/American Funds and Janus came from a proclivity toward, and some very real skill in, growth investing, whereas firms like Sanford Bernstein (now part of AllianceBernstein) and Dimensional Fund Advisors (DFA) have had great success with value. Keep in mind that value investing and growth investing are two very different skill sets, and I have heard many reasonable arguments for why some special talent that can generate returns above the market over the long term might exist in either field. However, when you do pick your favorite value fund (or two or three for diversification), just make sure that you also have a meaningful investment in growth funds that offsets your exposure. This combination will help to ensure that your returns come from the real skill of both sets of investment managers and not simply from the incremental volatility of a subsection of the stock market.

If you believe that one style of investing holds more promise than the other for active management (e.g., you really believe that value pickers like Warren Buffett can beat the market while growth managers cannot really predict technology cycles), you don't have to pick active managers for both growth and value. Plenty of growth and value index funds and ETFs exist that can offset the incremental market risk of the style you like. Lists of these are available through every bank or brokerage's mutual fund screening tools or through industry web sites like Morningstar.com. Buy all the active value funds you like, if that is your preference, but offset that resulting bias with a low-cost growth stock index fund that protects you against being too wedded to the periodic bumps in the road that either style can experience.

Large and Small Capitalization Investing

A similar argument to that which I made for growth and value investing can be made for the merits of investing in large versus small companies. The world of active investors can be divided into two more camps: those that prefer large capitalization (large cap) companies, or the companies with the largest total stock market values, and those that prefer small capitalization (small cap) companies, or companies with a relatively small total value of their outstanding stock. The breathless reporting in 2011 and 2012 about how Apple was progressively the eighth biggest company on Earth, then bigger than Microsoft, then Exxon, then the GDP of Poland,[3] then the sum total of all the goodness and light and puppies in the universe,[4] and so on, is an example of, in this case, the media's obsession with large cap stocks.

Plenty of investors are equally obsessed with small cap stocks, always looking for some diamond in the rough that has technology that will eclipse anything else known to man but is not yet reflected in the price of the stock. If you know a stockbroker, chances are he has plenty of these to sell you. All it takes is one or two to quadruple in value to prove to him that small caps are the best way to go, even if 90% of his picks never pan out. We always remember our winners.

---

[3]This is a real example. Yes, I know that market capitalization is a measure of worth and GDP is a measure of income and the two are not comparable. Please explain this to the news web site (which shall go nameless) that published this story or otherwise just feel free to share my frustration with the financial mass media.
[4]This is not a real example.

In my experience, both types of people can be right. And both can be wrong, too. Dominant large cap companies tend to rule the roost for a decade or a century, generating great cash flow for their investors. On the flip side, there is always some start-up company (or "fallen angel," like wnen Apple was trading for $7 a share in 2003) that will prove to be a game changer five years later, when the stock is selling for $500.

The problem is that while I can think of plenty of individual examples of large and small companies that have done well, exactly as described previously, there are thousands of start-ups that languished or failed and hundreds of examples of leading large cap companies that missed the next wave and were eclipsed by a smaller competitor. As the evidence demonstrates, neither has a categorical advantage over the other. Figure 3-9 shows the cumulative returns of large capitalization stocks (represented by the S&P 500 Index) versus small capitalization stocks (represented by the Russell 2000 Index) since the inception of that small cap benchmark.

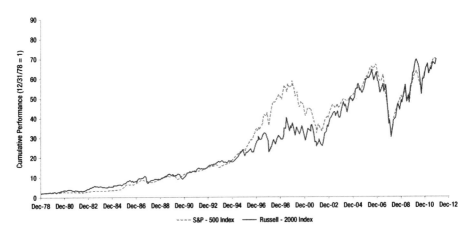

Figure 3-9. Cumulative Performance of Large and Small Capitalization Core Indices
Data courtesy of Russell Indexes and Standard & Poor's

As with growth versus value investing, periods of large and small cap stock outperformance repeat market cycle after market cycle. Over the course of 34 years, the complete history of the Russell 2000 small cap stock index, Figure 3-9 shows that neither has any advantage, with the three-plus decade cumulative returns for both the S&P500 Index and the Russell 2000 Index at almost the exact same level. As with the historical cumulative performance of value and growth investing styles, it is clear that the additional volatility of investing in just one size group of stocks dwarfs any potential performance advantage. The dramatic cumulative outperformance of large cap stocks by the end of 1999, followed by the return to almost identical historical performance by 2005, indicates how much rougher the path is for someone with either a large cap or small cap size bias in their portfolio to reach the same endpoint.

Academic studies[5] have generally concluded that small cap stocks outperform large cap stocks over long periods of time, due to the facts that there are more small cap stocks among which winners can emerge and the biggest companies have nowhere to go but down. Many of these results, however, have been questioned by practitioners, who rely more on real-world practical observation than just a database of returns. Maybe the small cap index does outperform the large cap index over some time periods (as some academic research has shown, unlike what is shown in Figure 3-9), but transactions costs like commissions can be higher among small cap stocks and eat into any performance advantage they might have. Furthermore, stock exchange liquidity and the markt impact of trading is far greater among small cap stocks, and management fees charged by mutual funds and other professional investment portfolios tend to be 50% to 100% higher for small cap stocks than for large cap. Once you include all of these effects, as well as the aforementioned increase in volatility from picking just one size group of stocks, I'm not convinced that pure small cap investing is worth the incremental risk that a size-biased portfolio can create. And, as shown in Figure 3-9, the 2000 stocks in the Russell 2000 seem to have generated the same returns as the S&P 500 since the inception of the Russell 2000.

As a result of the apparent lack of systematic biases to any particular size or style of investments, the vast majority of pension plans tend to maintain "size neutrality," which is similar to the "style neutrality" discussed previously. If the Wilshire 5000 Index[6] contains about 80% of its value in the 500 or 1,000 largest stocks and 20% in the rest, most pension plans will allocate 80% of their money in US equities to large cap managers and 20% to mid cap and small cap managers to eliminate any systematic bias to one particular market capitalization group over another.

Middle Capitalization Investing (Mid Cap Stocks)

The number of stocks on the US stock market has varied in my career from 3,500 to 9,000, and we are currently around the low end, with a little more than 3,900 tradable, liquid stocks available on today's market. Of all those public

---

[5]Many, including "Small Cap Opportunity, Too Big to Ignore?," Financial Advisor Magazine, June 19, 2012.
[6]The name of the Wilshire 5000 Index is a bit of a misnomer. Whereas the S&P 500 Index normally contains 500 stocks (sometimes a few drop out due to mergers or bankruptcies and are not replaced for a few weeks), the Wilshire 5000 Index simply contains ALL stocks in the United States and has ranged from 3,500 to 9,000 stocks over time, depending on how many are actually trading on exchanges. As a result, the Wilshire 5000 is generally considered to be the best measure of the entire US stock market.

companies, large capitalization stocks (sometimes called "large cap stocks") generally encompass the largest 500 to 1,000 companies in the United States, rank ordered by pure market capitalization (the total value of all their shares at current prices). The S&P 500 index, for example, is generally the most broadly followed large cap benchmark and includes 500 of the largest (but not necessarily the *actual* 500 largest) stocks in the United States. The Russell 1000 Index, meanwhile, generally includes the 1,000 largest stocks in the United States. Other vendors use different counts (Wilshire includes the largest 750 companies, for example), but they all get to generally the same place and represent the returns of most of the largest companies. In contrast, the Russell 2000 Index, the most commonly used small cap index, contains stocks 1,001 through 3,000, in a rank order listing of all US stocks by market cap.[7] But what about middle capitalization companies?

Middle capitalization companies—or "mid cap" stocks, for short—fall into that nebulous donut hole between large and small cap stocks. If your investment managers are using the S&P 500 and Russell 2000 as their large and small benchmarks, for example, stocks 501 through 1,000 (allowing for the fact that the S&P 500 is not comprised of precisely the 500 largest companies) aren't covered by their benchmarks. If they use the Russell 1000 (which is a pretty rare occurrence) and Russell 2000, though, the problem is defined away. But if they use the Wilshire Large Cap 750 (rarer still) and the FTSE small cap benchmark (impossibly rare), the donut hole comes back.

At the end of the day, does all this matter? In short, probably not. If you invest in a large cap index fund and a small cap index fund, the hole might still be there, since the most common large and small cap index funds try their best to match the S&P 500 and Russell 2000 indexes. As a result, I would suggest that index-oriented investors are better served by just using a total US market index fund and reducing their portfolio's complexity. However, if you use active managers for either the large or small cap portfolios, or both, this problem is smaller than it might appear to be.

Why is this so? Because, in reality, active investment managers color outside the lines a little. Large cap managers who try to beat the S&P 500 will buy stocks outside of the 500 companies in the index, usually reaching down into the next few hundred by size rank to find some companies that are a little less researched by Wall Street analysts or their peers. Small cap managers, meanwhile, will hang onto many of their great performing positions even as they climb in value firmly into the mid cap range. At the end of the day, both the large and small cap managers will pick over the best of that mid cap opportunity set so much that it really isn't as big of a chasm as you might guess.

---

[7]Neither Russell benchmark is adjusted on a daily basis. Stocks are added and deleted periodically as events warrant. As a result, some stocks in either benchmark may not necessarily be among the largest 1,000 or precisely the next 2,000 at any particular point in time.

There is even a name for such small cap managers that hang onto their winners as they creep into the mid-cap arena while still looking for new investments among the smallest companies: "SMid"—an amalgamation of "small" and "mid" to indicate a blending of the two styles of investment.

From Small to Small-Middle to Mid Cap Investing

Most small cap managers worth their salt will resist managing infinitely large amounts of money. In my experience, good small cap managers will normally cap or limit their assets under management to $1.5 billion to $2.5 billion for all clients. Small cap stocks, as commonly defined, tend to have market capitalizations of around $2 billion or less. When investing in these companies, investment managers usually want to hold very small fractions (at most, usually a few percentage points of the total stock) of the outstanding shares of a given company—especially when the stocks of the companies are as illiquid as small cap companies are for trading. In addition, investment managers normally will hold between 50 and 200 stocks in most actively managed small cap portfolios. If you add up those factors—small allocations to maybe 100 companies, none of which are bigger than $2 billion—you simply can't end up with a huge portfolio that holds tens of billions of dollars. What's more, compounding these factors are the buyers of these portfolios, the large institutional investors who dictate many of the terms in the marketplace. Most of these clients will tend to shun small cap investment managers who lack the discipline to close their portfolios to additional client contributions or new clients above a certain reasonable level of assets.

On the other hand, like many people, asset managers like to make money, and they know that the more client assets they manage, the more fees they collect, and the more money they can make. In addition, they like to add staff to their teams to expand their capabilities, creating more opportunity to add value for their clients. Unlike large cap investing or core fixed income, though, which are virtually infinitely scalable (more than one well-known core fixed income portfolio manager now has well over $500 billion in assets) given the size of those respective markets, the resources for small cap managers are limited by the size of the portfolios. Adding a needed sixth or seventh company research analyst to the team, a back-up trader, or a new client service person simply may not be feasible because the amount of fees the investment manager can earn on a size-limited portfolio is, as the adjective implies, limited. A $2 billion small cap portfolio that charges 0.75% a year in fees will generate $15 million in income. By the time the firm pays all of its investment and client service people, as well as all of its overhead and travel expenses, the cost of adding more analysts may not be affordable if the firm plans to limit its total assets to something close to that current $2 billion level.

What's a growth-minded investment manager to do? Pressures from clients to bring fees down are unrelenting, as are the pressures from corporate management or company ownership to deliver better results every year. As a result, investment managers will offer Mid-Cap or SMid portfolios as a way to leverage their current resources in a slightly larger market. ("SMid" cap investing, by the way, is the nickname for small-middle capitalization investing.)

Because the portfolio manager's most successful company investments have typically grown from a small capitalization size into several billion dollars or more, the argument could be made that the team already understands many of the companies in this new sector. If the portfolio manager has demonstrated the ability to consistently add value over the benchmark for stocks worth less than $2 billion, it follows logically that companies that have reached $5 billion are not especially dissimilar, and the portfolio team's investment acumen should generate similar results.

I don't necessarily disagree with that premise, and I have generally observed that SMid and Mid-Cap managers who have performed well generally have decent small cap products to offer to clients. And vice versa. My objection to SMid and Mid Cap, however, stems more from the overlap issues. If you have a small cap manager that is doing well—and is probably cheating a little by delving into mid cap stocks—as well as a large cap manager who is also dropping into the upper range of mid cap stocks with some of his investments, adding a dedicated mid cap manager usually leads to a significant amount of overlap with the large and small cap managers. A SMid portfolio has even greater overlap with small cap stocks, leading to the significant overweighting of this investment style. While I see nothing wrong in concept with the idea of mid cap or SMid investing, the overlap with the other managers and funds in the portfolio leads to unwanted duplication of some positions and a general overallocation to mid cap stocks.

So, why not just abandon small cap and find only a SMid manager? Great question. In concept, this should work perfectly: find a one-size-fits-all solution to your entire less-than-large-cap portfolio needs. In practice, though, it doesn't quite turn out the way you might expect. Remember the reason behind offering the SMid portfolio in the first place? The manager had reached the maximum manageable portfolio size for small cap investing and needed to move up the capitalization spectrum to continue to grow capacity and maximize corporate or personal income. For a manager who has both a small and a SMid portfolio, ask yourself, "If the small cap portfolio has reached its maximum, how many of those beloved small cap stocks are really in the SMid portfolio? Is the SMid portfolio just a way of disguising a mid cap portfolio as a small cap surrogate while continuing to charge (generally higher) small cap fees?" I usually find that the latter part of that question is the correct answer. The manager might throw a bone to small cap investing and include a handful of small cap stocks in a SMid portfolio. However, these stocks are usually the largest and most liquid companies in the small cap market, and their weight in the portfolio is dwarfed by the mid cap (and larger) companies.

Let's explore this with a little math to understand the reality of this type of investing. If a SMid portfolio has $10 billion under management and the investment manager likes to hold 100 stocks, even a position as small as 0.50% of that portfolio (not all positions in a 100 stock portfolio may be of identical size) leads to an allocation of $50 million to a given company. In the case of a true small cap company with an $800 million market cap, $50 million is equivalent to more than 6% of all the stock in the company. If the manager has a parallel position in the same company within a small cap portfolio, he could be approaching 10% of the entire value of the company between those two portfolios, or more than 10% of the outstanding, tradable stock if some of the company is privately held by founders or executives. Although allocations of this size are not unheard of, they certainly are very uncommon and present a variety of risks to the portfolios, including the limited ability of the investment manager to liquidate that position in a timely and cost-effective manner when appropriate. Instead of buying stock in that $800 million company, therefore, it is far more likely that the SMid portfolio simply will not hold shares in this company and will gravitate toward larger companies. In the end, what is marketed as a small-middle capitalization focus is really a middle-middle capitalization portfolio, with small cap stocks all but abandoned.

Summary

Investors, including large pension plans, like to take risks—as long as they understand the risks they are taking—and expect to be rewarded for taking them. After all, to earn any decent return, taking risks are necessary. However, when an investor takes risks, the return potential should be both apparent and proportionate to compensate him or her for the risks taken.

In this section, I have outlined the pros and cons of taking risk in active management versus passive management. I leave it to you, the individual investor, to assess whether you are smarter (or just luckier) than others and can select actively managed investment products that can consistently outperform the broader stock market.

More important, I have shown that although one should take risk to earn reward, there are many risks that are simply not worth taking. Significant size and style biases within portfolios add a tremendous amount of excess volatility over time, but they do very little to improve returns. If you wish to invest in an active manager who you think will outperform in some market segment, like small cap growth or large cap value, I wish you all the luck in the world. At the same time, however, I admonish you to offset that unrewarded style-based risk with another active or passive investment manager that brings all your investments on balance back to a broad market exposure.

Investment Structure for Stocks, Part II

Global Investing and Other Types of Active Management

In Chapter 3, I explained the basics of size and style biases (and the uncompensated risk that can result from adding a bias to your portfolio), and I also shed some light on the question of active versus passive management in equities. In this chapter, I will discuss two more major topics that investors should consider when determining how to structure an equity portfolio. First, I will address the question of how large pension plans think about how to allocate among US and non-US stock investments. Later in this chapter, I will expand the active versus passive management discussion from Chapter 3 into a wider review of the variety of products available to investors within the equity market and some of the more unique investment philosophies that are offered.

In the recurrent Road Map to Financial Success, we will stay in the second box on our path because this chapter continues the discussion of the proper structure for your equity portfolio. It also expands the discussion in Chapter 3 to topics beyond simple domestic structure considerations.

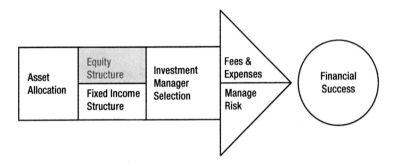

Global Portfolio versus Home Country Bias

Before the mid-2000s, it was common for the non-US portions of a pension plan's stock investments to constitute a quarter or a third of all its stocks. In other words, the typical plan had a ratio of three or four dollars invested in US stocks for every dollar invested overseas—and this wasn't just a US phenomenon. As shown in Figure 4-1, even as late as 2007, pension plans in the UK invested 50% of their equity money in UK stocks despite the fact that UK stocks were less than 10% of the global opportunity set. Continental European stocks made up only 21% of the global equity benchmark, yet German plans on average had 70% of their equity assets invested in Europe, French pension plans bought 75% of their stocks in Europe, and Italian pension plans found 88% of their stock investments in Europe.

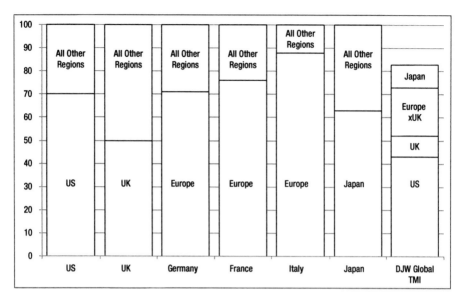

Figure 4-1. Home Country Biases Around the World, 2007[1]

Lately, however, there has been a seismic shift away from this "home country bias," especially among large institutional US plans, toward a more global approach to investing. The US markets comprise roughly 45% of global stock market capitalization, and clients have been moving toward an investment structure that mimics that reality. Not everyone has gone to a 55% non-US / 45% US position, but even a 50/50 split is a big step in the right direction.

To illustrate the fallacy of maintaining a home country-biased portfolio, what if I told you that my stock portfolio arbitrarily underweighted companies based in Washington, Florida, Arizona, and Minnesota just because I wanted to? Or, as discussed in Chapter 1, what if I significantly underweighted certain industries or countries not as part of a legitimate protest statement against them but just because I thought it would make no difference? You would think I was crazy. What if I asserted that there is no reason why a company based in Minnesota should have better or worse operational prospects and future market returns than a similar company that was based in Wisconsin and therefore doesn't need to be part of my portfolio? Would you also scoff at my logic if I increased my position in a company that moved its headquarters from Washington to Illinois (like Boeing did in 2000) just because that is where the CEO now calls home?

---

[1] Greenwich Associates, 2007.

Well, the same logic, or lack thereof, applies to US and non-US investing. Here a few examples of how the companies in which you invest actually operate. Toyota makes roughly the same share of their cars in the US as does Ford. Coca-Cola makes far more of its revenues and profits outside the US than within it, as do Apple and Microsoft. SAP (a German software company) and Daimler Benz (the German parent of the Mercedes car company) make far more money outside Germany than within it. What makes Toyota Japanese; Ford, Microsoft, Apple, and Coca-Cola American; and SAP and Daimler Benz German? Not their sales, not their profits, not their competitors. Merely the location of their headquarters.

An August 2011 study released by S&P Dow Jones Indices reported that 46.1% of the sales by companies in the S&P 500 were from operations outside the United States. This number was virtually unchanged from 46.3% of sales in 2010, 46.6% in 2009, and 47.9% in 2008, indicating that non-US operations are consistently a very large part of major companies' ongoing and future plans. Those numbers were an average for all 500 of the companies in the stock index, and of course some American companies will derive a significantly higher or lower fraction of their sales outside the United States. Coca-Cola, for example, earns 80% of its operating income outside the United States,[2] whereas a power utility like Duke Energy will receive the vast majority of its income from US operations because it is impossible to bundle up its main product (electricity) and put it in a shipping container or FedEx it overseas. Does that make Coca-Cola less of an "American" company than Duke? Frankly, I am hard pressed to think of a more quintessentially American company than Coke, even if the lion's share of their current operations and presumably almost all of their future growth will come from outside the US.

At the end of the day, GM, Ford, Chrysler, BMW, Daimler, Volkswagen Group, Fiat, Honda, Toyota, Mazda, and many others compete against each other on a global basis. Although some consumers might pick a car because of its perceived "Made in America" connotation (even if that car was actually assembled by a US company in South Korea or Canada), the vast majority of new car shoppers decide based on features and price, or the concept of Japanese manufacturing quality, or German or Italian performance. Why should your portfolio be any less open minded than your personal shopping preferences? Shouldn't the relative weights for BMW and GM in your portfolio be based on how well the companies will compete, profit, and grow over the next few years, not where the company's lawyers file their paperwork?

The same can be said for a myriad of other industries. GE competes against Siemens in a wide variety of products. American drug manufacturers compete

---

[2] Bloomberg.com, Sept. 11, 2012: "Coca-Cola Masala Gets $5 Billion to Catch Pepsi in India: Retail."

predominantly against their Swiss counterparts. As it moves away from desktop computers and into mobile devices like phones and tablets, Apple competes much more against Samsung (Korean) and Nokia (Finnish) than it does against fellow American companies IBM and Microsoft. Let's look at an absurd, but 100% true, example, just to make the point. Imagine that you have a stock portfolio that is weighted 3 parts US stocks to 1 part non-US stocks—the typical mix that many pension plans held ten years ago and a weighting similar to what was shown in Figure 4-1 as a normal European home country bias just a few years ago. In this portfolio, you bought 100 shares of US automaker Chrysler in 1997. In 1998, when Chrysler became part of Daimler Chrysler, you had to reduce your position to 25 shares, not because you thought the company had changed and wasn't a good investment for so much of your money, but because the headquarters was now in Germany and your 3:1 US to non-US weighting scheme dictated that you reduce your position. In 2007, Chrysler was bought by an American private equity company and became American again. As a result of its return to the United States, and had you been able to buy the (now privately held) stock, you would have bought 75 shares to get back to your original US-first position. Then, when Chrysler merged with Fiat in 2011, an Italian company, you would have sold those 75 shares again to get back to the proper weight in your portfolio because Chrysler, once more, became a foreign corporation. Do all those changes in your portfolio based on nothing other than the location of the corporate headquarters make any sense? Were any of those buys and sells based on how you thought Chysler would perform in the future? Wouldn't you rather make rational investment decisions based on a company's prospects for growth and profits than something as seemingly insignificant as the country the senior executives call home?

But, you may ask, what about the fact that China is booming or Italy and Greece are in the midst of an extended financial crisis? Does Japan's demographic problem cause an investment problem? Don't any of these considerations extend beyond the "invest in global competitors" argument posed above? Well, yes. In fact, pension funds have had concerns with investing directly in some countries for years, due to controls on capital flows (moving money into or out of the country), intellectual and other property rights, transparent and fair regulatory environments, liquid capital markets, human rights and freedoms, and a variety of other issues. As a result, the mantra among pension plans has often been, "Don't invest in China/Russia/Venezuela/Fill In The Blank, and instead invest in companies *doing business in* China/Russia/Venezuela/Fill In The Blank." You can still benefit from the inherent growth in these countries without many of the country-specific legal and other risks.

Today, partly as a result of pressure by some large pension plans and partly due simply to the forward momentum of history and progress, the specific fears about investing in some of these countries have dissipated. However, you don't necessarily have to invest in country X to get exposure to country X, just like investing in BMW isn't really a pure investment in German equities anymore. As a result, many large pension funds have simply abandoned the concept of allocating separately to US and non-US stocks and have simply treated all stocks as one big asset class. As you design your portfolio, I encourage the reader to take an equally enlightened view of how capital markets have evolved over the last several years and embrace a global outlook just like so many large investors have done.

In the end, the advantages of a global portfolio versus a home country biased portfolio really boil down to risk reduction more than return enhancement. Maintaining a home-country-first approach to investing keeps a higher weight on Oracle over SAP, CitiBank over Barclays, GM over Toyota, and Boeing over Airbus. If my arguments are right, none of those positions should generate a systematic advantage over time and will serve only to increase the risk in your portfolio, just as a portfolio of any 20 stocks is more risky than one with 100 stocks. Because markets for products are global, and capital flows are global, the only way to really embrace the opportunity set for stocks is to invest globally.

Other Types of Active and Quasi-Passive Equity Investment Management

In Chapter 3, I discussed some of the relative merits and demerits of active and passive investing, and when some investors might want to consider one over the other. In addition to these two traditional types of investment styles, pension plans and other institutional investors make widespread use of other types of equity strategies, including enhanced indexation and "alternative indexation" managers. Individual investors should be aware of these kinds of investments when they build out their portfolios.

Enhanced Indexation

Enhanced indexation is a broad title for two main types of portfolios but generally encompasses managers who seek to add small to medium amounts of value above the benchmark to their portfolios in a more consistent manner than a truly active portfolio does.

Pension plans who are fed up with the inconsistent performance of active managers and the higher fees demanded for that inconsistency have often turned to enhanced index managers as an alternative to both true active management and to just throwing in the towel and putting everything in an index fund. These managers will use highly risk-controlled portfolios, often driven by computer-based automated systems, to add half a percent or maybe a full percentage point of value above the benchmark as consistently as possible.

In good markets and in bad, a great enhanced index manager should always be just a little bit better than the index it is tracking.

The main downside to this approach is evidenced by Figure 3-2 from the previous chapter, which showed how active large cap core managers actually performed fairly well during the credit crisis in 2008. By turning to cash, managers were able to at least get a little bit of the portfolio out of the way of the market decline and protect some value for clients. Like fully passive index funds, enhanced index managers, on the other hand, would have remained as close to 100% invested as possible and ridden the rollercoaster straight down. When the market bounced in 2009, however, and those cash-hording active managers found themselves scrambling to catch up, enhanced index managers would have taken off with the market. So, once again, there is no free lunch. Active managers can protect value in a crash by shifting assets en masse to cash, but that can often come back to bite them later when they are not fully invested in a rising market. Passive managers and enhanced index managers, in contrast, will decrease your fees but capture all up and down market movements. Which way you choose to go is really a function of your risk tolerance and how well you can stomach the day-to-day and year-to-year market gyrations.

So, after that preamble, what are these managers, and what do they do?

Stock Selection Strategies

The more common type of enhanced index managers employed by pension funds essentially are computer-automated actively managed portfolios. When stock analysts try to figure out which stocks they think are best for their funds to invest in, they typically have a number of qualitative metrics that they might apply when they screen the database of all stocks or analyze an individual stock for investment. These metrics might be things like the ratio of price to earnings, the ratio of price to book value, the annual dividend growth rate, the growth rate of revenues, the length of tenure of senior management, and so on. The portfolio manager could, for example, prefer to buy shares of companies that have higher growth rates than the company's peers and a lower price/book ratio.

Instead of hiring an army of analysts to fly around the country to meet with companies, build models, and simply reflect the public information that everyone already knows, what if we could distill all that human decision making into a computerized stock picking process that uses the same tools as human analysts would to determine which stocks are underpriced and which are overpriced? Although you might need a team of mathematicians and computer programmers to get the process rolling and to refine your models over time, a highly disciplined system of computer stock selection might remove the emotional aspects of "falling in love with a stock" from the investment management process.

To live up to the "enhanced index" name, the portfolio managers (or, more commonly, a portfolio construction software package) take the stocks that the models like and dislike and apply that information to the model portfolio. Let's say that Apple is 4% of the S&P 500, Hewlett Packard is 1%, and IBM is 1.5% at some particular time. The computer models think that HP is under-priced and is a "buy," Apple has an inflated price and is worth less than the market thinks, and IBM is about right. As a result, the portfolio construction process might buy 1.5% of the portfolio in HP (a very small overweight vs. the index) and buy 3.5% in Apple (a very small underweight). Note that even though the models say that Apple is overpriced,[3] the portfolio will still hold a fairly large position in the company. Why? Because it comprises such a large share of the index that not holding the stock at all would add too much risk to the portfolio.

The index has a total of 6.5% in these three technology stocks, and so does the portfolio, resulting in no sector bias for or against technology stocks. In a similar vein, the portfolio could also slightly overweight Bank of America and underweight CitiGroup by the same amounts, and overweight GM at the expense of Ford. In all of these positions, the only difference from the index is that the securities weights in each sector vary from the index weight. Meanwhile, the weight of the total positions for the technology, finance, and transportation industries remains equal to that in the index.

If the automated stock selection and analysis process is right, the stock picks add a small amount of value relative to the index. If they are completely wrong, the losses won't be all that great since the positions only differ from the index marginally. If one particular industrial sector skyrockets to the moon (see technology, circa 1998) or falls to Earth (see technology, circa 2001, or financials, circa 2008), the portfolio will not be affected relative to the index. Instead, it will rise or fall in value accordingly because the portfolio as a whole matches the index's sector weights.

The point isn't to knock the cover off the ball and realize tremendous gains. Rather, the point is to recognize that in some sectors—especially large cap core US equities, where enhanced indexation is most prevalent—stock selection is extraordinarily hard due to the efficiency of information. Consequently, investors should be happy with roughly the market returns plus a tiny bit of value-added.

---

[3]This is a purely hypothetical example to demonstrate how these models work. I am not passing judgment on the relative valuations of these or any other companies in this book, and I do not recommend that you buy or sell any of these stocks based on these hypothetical examples.

"Synthetic Equity" Strategies

Beware: this is the part where I will probably lose half my audience. Feel free to skip to the next section if this part gets to be a little complicated for your tastes.

The other type of enhanced index strategy commonly used by pension plans is called a "synthetic equity" portfolio. This type of portfolio never actually buys stocks at all, but rather relies on a variety of other securities to replicate stock market returns plus a little bit of value-added. In this type of product, the portfolio manager will buy stock index futures, which are very common derivatives contracts that trade on major exchanges and replicate the returns of an index very closely. These securities typically require that the buyer pay a small amount, typically 5% to 10% of the value of the security up front. The other 90% to 95% of the synthetic equity manager's cash is available to settle daily mark-to-markets[4] in the value of the futures and are priced so that the buyer pays a short-term, overnight interest rate in exchange for the privilege of only paying 5% of the value up front. In this kind of strategy, instead of investing in low-risk T-bills or other cash-like securities, this remaining cash typically is invested in short-term fixed income securities, like corporate bonds or mortgage bonds, which should earn a slightly higher yield than the cash interest rate.

Generally speaking, these portfolios deliver fairly consistently small positive returns above the benchmark. For example, if the manager can buy one-year debt that earns 1.00% and is paying 0.25% as a financing rate for the futures, the net return to the portfolio is 0.75% above the S&P 500, with a minimum of risk in normal markets. However, if the interest rate spreads (the amount of additional yield earned by investments in assets riskier than government bonds) spike upward and/or the corporate investments default, you can expect to incur losses in the bond portfolio because you are holding one-year debt that will fall in value during periods of rapid upward rate movement. For a great example of how interest rate spreads can grow dramatically in a very short period of time, causing widespread underperformance in these types of investments, look to 2008, when rapid movements in interest rates severely impacted investors. In contrast, though, investors with a long-time horizon who stayed with these kinds of investments earned back those losses and then some when rates returned to more normal levels in 2009 and 2010.

How have enhanced index managers done?

---

[4] If the index rises 1% in a day, the holder of a stock index futures contract will receive that 1% in cash at the end of that day. Similarly, if the index falls, the contract holder needs to provide the cash value of that daily loss. Some or all of the other 90% to 95% held in cash is usually kept fairly liquid to enable these types of daily settlements.

Not all that badly. Figure 4-2 shows that at least half of all enhanced index managers have outperformed the benchmark in virtually all time periods dating back to the 1980s. Over the last five years, the index has ranked between 50% and 80% vs. the managers, indicating that there is a pretty good chance that many managers might actually generate consistent value for clients.

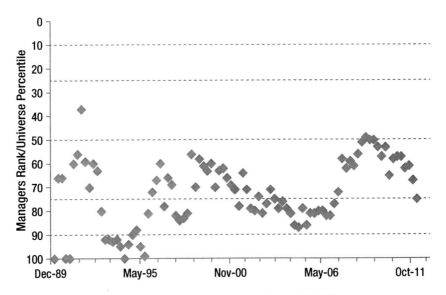

Figure 4-2. Performance of Enhanced Index Managers Versus S&P 500
*Data courtesy of eVestment Alliance

I've always believed that there is some logic to why enhanced indexation should make sense, given that you incur lower fees and the stock selection process is less emotional. Although this chart isn't perfect, the index has pretty consistently ranked below the 50th percentile, with only a couple of periods above that level. For the period studied, 2000 to present (I used a shorter time frame here given the relatively short history of the enhanced indexation industry), you appear to have a decent chance of finding a superior manager. The managers outperform about half the time, which is far better than we saw in Chapter 3 for traditional large cap core active equity managers.

Alternative Beta Managers

The last potential equity investment that pension plans are making occurs rarely among mutual funds and other investment options available to clients. Still, alternative beta managers have received quite a bit of press lately and are starting to see some traction in the retail marketplace.

To understand alternative beta managers, you first need to understand "beta," which is a fancy word that institutional investors use to describe "market exposure." If they "buy some beta," it means that they are moving from cash into broad stock market exposure, like index funds. Likewise, if a given investment strategy is described as "nothing but beta," it means that the investment manager isn't really delivering any skill in the portfolio and is earning returns that simply track the ups and downs of the stock market. Alternative beta strategies, then, are a very complicated, yet widespread, way of saying "market exposure that reflects the performance of something other than the index fund." These types of strategies come in a wide variety of forms and have even been used to try to replicate the returns of hedge funds and real estate (more on this in Chapters 8 and 10). For the individual investor, however, the most common of these is something called "fundamental indexing," which implies that something other than pure market capitalization is used as the basis for calculating the index weights.

In a traditional index, if the sum of all companies' market capitalizations is $5 trillion and a given company has a market capitalization of $100 billion, that company's stock will comprise 2% of the index. As a result, a money manager with $100,000,000 to invest in an index fund will buy $2,000,000 worth of that company's stock. This methodology reflects the simple fact that the market has spoken and priced this stock at $100 billion, for whatever reason, and that the full opportunity set of all stocks should include a 2% allocation to this company. In fundamental indexation, however, so-called real-world factors are used to compute the weights in the index. Instead of using the value of the company's stock market capitalization to determine weighting, fundamental indexation relies on a formula that includes things such as the revenues of all companies, their physical assets, their net income, total employees, etc., to re-weight the stocks in an index based on their real weights in the economy, not just the stock market's perceived value of their worth.

In practice, fundamental indexation strategies generally look like an expensive way to buy a mid-cap value strategy, with a few little twists thrown in. Fundamental indexation will underweight stocks undergoing bubbles and buy companies that the market is undervaluing. In general, this means that companies with slightly smaller market capitalizations might appear to be cheaper, all else being equal. In addition, growth companies that are being priced based on hope for their earnings in five years will be underweighted to allow for greater positions in solid but boring companies with larger sales but less growth: the very definition of a value strategy.

The bottom line is that although all these enhanced index managers may sound like "the better mousetrap" and the solution to avoiding all bubbles and speculation pricing forever, a much cheaper solution has been out there for a long time—value index funds. As is the case with so much else in this industry, always look twice at a new product that is promising the world. Either there is far more in the fine print that takes the promises down a notch or it is a repackaging of something that you can already get cheaper somewhere else.

Summary

As I have shown in this chapter and Chapter 3, although there is no easy or simple answer to the question of how to structure your portfolio, there are a number of rules of thumb that can help to diversify your investments and reduce unwanted and uncompensated risks. As they construct their equity portfolios, both pension plans and individual investors need to consider a wide variety of sometimes confusing topics, including active versus passive versus enhanced versus alternative beta, growth versus value, large versus small, and domestic market versus foreign markets once they determine their allocation to equities in the asset allocation step outlined in Chapter 2. In practice, however, balancing risk, return, and cost is actually very simple to do—just make sure that you are getting what you really want and what you paid for. Common mistakes such as investing small fractions of your portfolio in each of ten active growth funds and ten active value funds will most likely generate the return stream in aggregate of a very expensive index fund, not some kind of magical outperforming composite of 20 different investment managers. Another common mistake, taking a large style bias, such as over-weighting growth stocks 5 to 1 relative to value stocks in your portfolio may generate some very nice gains in a given year that growth stocks do well, but that same portfolio will significantly cost you when the value cycle returns (and it always has returned eventually).

Remember that asset allocation, as we discussed in Chapter 2, drives 90% of your expected return and total risk. In my experience, however, investment structure mistakes can drive 90% of an investor's unwanted risks. An over-weight to growth, or small, or emerging markets can be entirely unintended and merely a by-product of what was thought to be good manager selection, but this type of unintentional style bias is what will hurt you the most when you aren't looking out for it and growth or value rapidly reverts against the other like growth-biased investing did in 2001 when the NASDAQ boom came to an end.

Finally, it is common practice among pension plans to mix and match styles and types of investments when building an equity portfolio, and there is no reason you cannot do the same thing. Let's say you found an active large cap value fund that you love, but you cannot find a tolerable large cap growth fund. Then just invest in a growth index fund to offset that style risk from the value manager. If you want to index your large cap investments and choose active managers for your small cap dollars, just understand the risks that you are taking, and make sure that the risks you don't want to take are not finding their way into the portfolio on their own.

Above all else, remember this simple truth: there is no free lunch in equity investing. The sum of all the investors in stocks is the market return, or worse. Once you deduct the large active management fees charged to investors in mutual funds and other investment products, everyone does worse off in aggregate than if everyone had invested in the index. In Chapter 7 I will discuss the art and science behind how pension funds select asset managers, but bear in mind the moral of the story of the data I have presented here: active managers as a whole, especially in developed markets like the United States, have generally underperformed their stock market benchmarks the majority of the time. Sure, you can certainly pick a winner here and there that will serve you well for decades at a time, but those are few and far between. Be selective with your usage of active managers because they cost you far more than the index fund alternative and rarely live up to the high promise of outperformance in their advertisements.

Investment Structure for Fixed Income, Part I

The Basic Characteristics of Fixed Income

Parallel to the discussion of the investment structure for equities that I presented in Chapters 3 and 4 is a consideration of the investment structure for your fixed income investments (otherwise known by this asset class's simpler and more common name, "bonds") in this chapter and in Chapter 6. As you can see, we have moved to a new box that is parallel to our equity structure considerations in our recurring Road Map to Financial Success. As with equities, once you have determined during the asset allocation step how much you should invest in fixed income in general, you must then answer the question of how you should construct your fixed income portfolio. However, because the fixed income structure that you select is independent of your equity structure and really should be chosen at about the same time, these are simultaneous and not sequential steps.

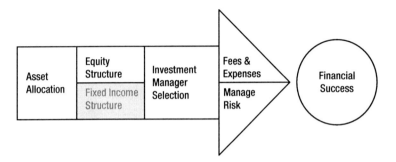

Fixed income investing is generally considered to be more complicated than equity investing because the mathematics and probabilities of yield (interest rate paid), duration (interest rate risk), and default risk (risk of losing money due to bankruptcy) are far more complex than the optimism of stock selection. However, determining the fixed income investment structure in your portfolio and for a large pension plan or endowment can really be boiled down to a few decisions:

1. How much "duration" do you want in the portfolio?

2. How much credit risk (default risk) do you want in the portfolio?

3. How much active or passive management do you want in the portfolio?

4. Do you wish to invest only in the United States, or are there advantages to investing outside of your home market?

I will review each of these decisions in turn, covering the more technical topics of duration and credit risk in this chapter and the more personal preference questions of desired manager risk level and global investments in Chapter 6.

Duration

There is a really long and complicated definition of what duration is, how it is calculated, and how it is used in practice. If you would like to really understand the concept, I can recommend some terrific textbooks such as *The Handbook of Fixed Income Securities*, by Frank Fabozzi, which is generally considered to be the bible of the fixed income industry. The simple explanation of duration, however, starts with the fact that most fixed income securities pay coupons (periodic interest payments) over the life of the bond and principal (the face amount of the bond) at maturity.

When you buy a bond, duration is the weighted average of how long it will take you to receive all of those interest and principal payments. Two bonds with the same final maturity date can have different durations if the coupons are meaningfully different. Imagine a bond that pays a semiannual 1% coupon and another that pays a 4% semiannual coupon. Even though both bonds pay you $1,000 at maturity, the bond with the higher coupon will have a somewhat shorter duration because a larger share of the total cash flows you will receive over the life of the bond are paid in earlier years.

I recognize that very few people reading this book are likely to be building their own portfolios of individual bonds; and those that are building their own probably understand fixed income concepts far more than I will explain here. Therefore, for the average person who invests in mutual funds, I will discuss duration in the context of how it should influence your choice of investment managers and how you should structure your overall fixed income portfolio.

Why Duration is Meaningful to You

Duration has a second purpose other than a calculation of time of cash flow receipt, one that really is meaningful to investors in mutual funds and other portfolios of fixed income that are constructed by professionals. In short, duration measures the sensitivity of a bond or a portfolio of bonds to movements in interest rates.

The total return to an investor from a bond comes from two different sources. First, the bond pays a set amount of interest (coupons) every year. Second, assuming the entity who issued the bond does not default or go into bankruptcy, you will receive the face value of the bond at maturity. In contrast to when you buy a stock and hope that its price will rise over the next 5 years, you know exactly what a bond will be worth at its maturity date—that aforementioned principal amount. Any difference between the purchase price and maturity face value is therefore part of your planned return.

Imagine that you bought a $1,000 face value bond for $900, with a maturity in exactly 4 years. This hypothetical bond pays a coupon of 3%. If you hold the bond for all 4 years until maturity, when you receive that $1,000 face value you will have earned a capital gain of $100 (the difference between the $1,000 you receive at maturity and the $900 you paid for the bond), or $25 per year for each of those 4 years. You will also have received $30 per year ($1,000 x 3%) in interest payments, giving you an annualized total return of $55. When you divide $55 by your purchase price of $900, you can see that your annual yield to maturity is 6.1% per year.[1]

---

[1] I am simplifying the math a little here. Again, please refer to Frank Fabozzi's *The Handbook of Fixed Income Securities* if you need to understand the precise calculations.

Table 5-1. Sample Yield to Maturity Calculation

	Cash Received
Year 1 Interest	$30
Year 2 Interest	$30
Year 3 Interest	$30
Year 4 Interest	$30
Year 4 Principal	$1,000
Purchase Price	$900
Total Accretion	$100
Accretion per Year	$25
Effective Annual Return	$30 + $25 = $55
Yield to Maturity	$55 / $900 = 6.1%

The $900 purchase price and $25 annual "accretion" in the price of the example bond is based on two factors. The first factor is the credit quality (an assessment of the likelihood that the bond issuer will default on the bond) of the issuer. Buyers of lower-rated bonds demand higher rates of return to compensate them for the higher probability of default. If our issuer is downgraded (i.e., at some point in time it is believed to have a higher chance of defaulting than was previously thought) by a ratings agency that is concerned that the issuer might go bankrupt, the price of the bond might fall immediately to $800, meaning that a buyer of this bond would now see a yield to maturity of 10.0% ($30 coupon plus $50 annual accretion equals $80 income/$800 face value.).

The second factor in the price of our bond is the market interest rate. If the world is humming smoothly along and government bonds are yielding 3%, our imaginary corporate bond might yield the investor 4% or 5%, since investors will require a moderate amount of additional return above the prevailing treasury yield in order to compensate them for the risk of default, however remote it may be. If, on the other hand, inflation is starting to rise and the Federal Reserve cranks government rates up to 6% to prevent the economy from overheating, now our bond will have to yield 7% or 8% to reflect the fact that the entire interest rate world has moved toward higher rates. These higher rates are also necessary because investors will desire some incremental return above treasuries (called the "yield spread") to compensate for the fact that their bond is carrying higher risk than treasury bonds are.

Because the coupon was set in stone when the bond was issued, the coupon can't change when the world moves to higher interest rates; yet our bond needs to have a higher yield to keep pace with the rest of the bond market. The only aspect of the bond that can change, therefore, is the price, which will fall when rates rise to increase the amount of the annual "accretion" for a new buyer. Through a quirk of mathematics, the amount that the price of a bond will rise or fall with a change in interest rates happens to be roughly equal to the duration of the bond![2] If a bond has a duration of 6 years, when rates rise by 1%, the price of the bond will fall by 6%. If rates fall by 0.5%, the price of the bond will rise by 3%.

Table 5-2. Bond Price Movements for Given Durations and Interest Rate Changes (Simplified)

	Rates Fall			Rates Rise		
	-0.50%	-1%	-2%	0.50%	1%	2%
Bond Duration						
1 Year	0.5%	1.0%	2.0%	-0.5%	-1.0%	-2.0%
2 Years	1.0%	2.0%	4.0%	-1.0%	-2.0%	-4.0%
4 Years	2.0%	4.0%	8.0%	-2.0%	-4.0%	-8.0%
6 Years	3.0%	6.0%	12.0%	-3.0%	-6.0%	-12.0%
8 Years	4.0%	8.0%	16.0%	-4.0%	-8.0%	-16.0%
10 Years	5.0%	10.0%	20.0%	-5.0%	-10.0%	-20.0%
12 Years	6.0%	12.0%	24.0%	-6.0%	-12.0%	-24.0%

This math also holds for portfolios of bonds, not just individual securities. If a given bond mutual fund has a published duration of 7 years for the entire portfolio, the price of that mutual fund will rise or fall by roughly 7% in response to a 1% rate movement.

What Duration is Right for You?

When considering which bond fund you should buy, therefore, the duration of the fund matters as much as anything else. A fund called a *short-term fund* will generally have a duration of a year or less. A *core* or *total return fund* will typically have a duration that falls in the 4- to 6-year range. A *long-term bond fund* might have a duration in excess of 10 years. If rates rise 2% over the course of a year in an improving economy, and that long duration bond fund is paying 5% in interest a year, you could lose 15% over that year[3], illustrating just how much risk duration really poses to the investor in a changing rate environment.

---

[2]Again, duration is not absolutely precisely the amount that the price will change in reaction to a change in interest rates, especially for very large movements in rates; but it is close enough that duration is widely used as a very good approximation of price movement.
[3]A 2% rate movement in a portfolio with a duration of 10 years will lead to roughly a 20% capital loss, partly offset by the 5% received in coupon interest over the year.

So, why invest in anything other than short-term bonds? Glad you asked. In most normal market environments, short-term investments have lousy returns compared to longer duration bonds. At the time of this writing, 1-year US government bonds are yielding 0.25%, 10-year bonds are yielding 2%, and 30-year bonds are yielding 3%. A given corporate issuer may see its 1-year debt trading at 0.50% above treasuries, but its 30-year bonds might have a spread above treasuries of 1.50%. An investor who thinks the economy is stable and isn't afraid of interest rate movements might view that 30-year corporate bond returning 4.5% (3% treasury yield + 1.5% credit spread premium) to be a far better investment than the 1-year corporate bond at 1.5% (1% treasury yield + 0.50% credit spread premium). Someone who is very concerned about rising rates or increased levels of default in the future, on the other hand, might consider the near certainty of the 1.5% return on short-term bonds to be far superior to the potential capital losses on longer-term bonds as rates rise, despite the higher yield for them. For a comparison of the yields on a 30-year Treasury bond and an AA corporate bond over time, see Figure 5-1.

The duration selection, therefore, is an incredibly important part of the construction of your fixed income portfolio. When pension plans make the duration decision, they typically balance the design of their fixed income portfolios using many of the same criteria that individuals can use.

For example, do you need the money soon? If a pension plan is holding cash to meet near-term benefit payments or to keep some minimal level of liquidity in the plan, short-term bonds are usually preferred. If you sold your house but planned to buy another one in the next 6 months, you would do the same thing and keep the duration very short term to avoid incurring large losses over that time frame.

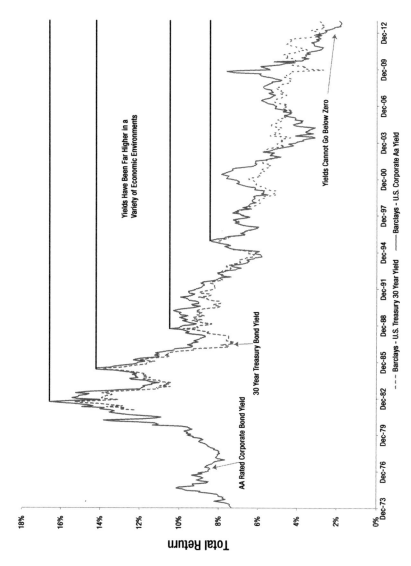

Figure 5-1. 30-Year Treasury and AA Corporate Yields Over Time

On the other hand, does the money fund a long-term need? Pension plans that keep a portion of their assets in fixed income to balance their risk exposure in other asset classes may not draw on their fixed income investments for years and years. The duration of the liability of the benefit payments that the pension someday will owe could be 10 or 20 years down the road. Keeping that long-term view in mind, many pension plans will take advantage of the generally higher returns for longer duration bonds and live with the associated volatility. In the same way, if you plan to retire in 1 year, long duration might put too much of your assets at risk; but if you plan to retire in 25 years, have only a 10% allocation to fixed income, and can live with short- or medium-term volatility, then the benefits of longer duration bonds might outweigh the risks for you.

Do the potential returns of long duration investing really outweigh the risks? The examples that I have given so far have been based on a "normal" interest rate environment, as shown in Figure 5-2. This chart illustrates a typical relationship between bond yields and time, where investors who have short-term objectives demand relatively low rates and investors willing to invest in very long-term securities wish to be more highly rewarded for their risk.

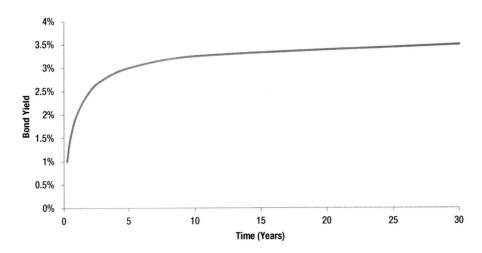

Figure 5-2. Normal Shaped Yield Curve

Whereas Figure 5-2 shows the most common environment, there are times that the yield curve could be flat or even downward sloping. For example, as shown in Figure 5-3, when short-term rates are very high and the economy is starting to weaken, longer-term rates could be lower than short-term rates in anticipation of rate reductions by the Federal Reserve to stimulate a future economic recovery. At these times, you could see yields of 5% for 1-year bonds and 4% for 30-year bonds and question the sanity of investing long term when long term means lower returns and higher risk. In these kinds of environments, pension plans will assess the relative merits of different durations and will normally shorten their durations to capture the higher return and lower risk nature of shorter duration investing, or they could anticipate significant large future rate increases and lengthen duration in order to profit from the upward movement in prices as rates fall. Which path they choose depends entirely on how much risk they are willing to take on a macroeconomic outlook like this that could be wrong.

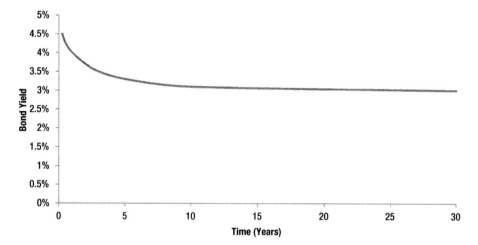

Figure 5-3. Inverted Yield Curve

What does the economic outlook look like today? I rarely advocate "market timing" to our clients, and large pension plans usually do not attempt to time economic cycles by moving their portfolio positions dramatically. However, there are times when the market environment must be taken into consideration. For most of the last 20 to 30 years, interest rates have been on a generally downward path, with a few notable exceptions, such as 1994. In the 1980s, 30-year bonds were yielding 8%, 10%, or even higher. In 2011 and 2012, 30-year bonds generally yielded around 2.75% or 3%, with a brief trip during the worst of the European economic crisis down to 2.5%. Although 30-year rates can still move lower and set new records below that 2.5% point, they generally cannot go below 0%. Practically speaking, 30-year rates, even in the worst crisis imaginable, probably cannot go below 1% or 2%. From their current levels, that isn't much of a fall.

On the other hand, although it is unlikely that bond rates will zoom upward on a moment's notice, given the commitment of the Federal Reserve to keeping rates moderate for the foreseeable future, they CAN go much higher someday. For example, 30-year bond rates could rise to 7% or 8% under the right circumstances. As a result, the risks are not balanced. One does not stand to gain much from further rate declines but could lose a lot from rate increases. In this environment, pension plans who wish to remain long-term investors and will hold their bonds to maturity may want to take advantage of the higher yields on longer-term bonds and might decide that a long-term buy-and-hold strategy is appropriate, even if it causes medium-term losses, since the total gain over the entire time period makes the investment worthwhile. On the other hand, a fund that has more flexibility in its portfolio may want to consider the likelihood that rates will rise and decide whether that possibility is worth the risk.

Given the greatly increased levels of perceived market risk since the credit crisis in 2008, as well as the apparent willingness of the Federal Reserve to take unprecedented steps to manipulate interest rates in a variety of markets and across all durations to manage risks throughout the economy, investors should be aware that the normal rules may not apply in the future and that the market interest rate may not react to economic ebbs and flows in the future as well as it has done in the past.

All of these factors that pension plans weigh in their decision-making process need to be considered by individuals and then some. As I discussed in Chapter 2 when I discussed a long term view on asset allocation regardless of short-term market movements, when pension plans take a calculated risk that goes wrong, they have time on their side. Pensions can wait years or even decades for assets to return to fair value. They also have the backstop of the sponsoring company or public entity to contribute additional cash to make up for a shortfall when needed.

When an individual has a large loss, on the other hand, the individual will need to reduce retirement spending plans, work for more years than planned to make up for the loss in extra savings, or simply hope that the loss turns around over the remaining time horizon. Frankly, none of these are great options, and so the risk of market movements going against you when making a duration decision in fixed income, the asset class that most people consider to be their "safe store of value" or their risk reducer, need to be considered very, very carefully.

Credit Risk

The bond market is built from three very different and specific types of investments—unlike the stock market, which is comprised of the aggregation of a bunch of individual company risks.

The Barclays U.S. Aggregate Bond Index is generally considered to be the broadest and most inclusive measure of the entire US investment-grade bond market. As of September 30, 2012, the Barclays Aggregate included more than $16.8 trillion in investment-grade fixed income securities[4]. Government bonds, including debt issued by the US Treasury and the direct debt of US government agencies, comprised 41% of the total index; corporate bonds constituted almost 27% of the index; mortgage-backed securities added 30% to the index; and other securities, like asset-backed securities and small amounts of some dollar-denominated foreign securities, made up the rest.

Unlike with stocks, these three main components of the index—government bonds, mortgage bonds, and corporate bonds—have unique risks associated with each of them, leading investment managers to "rotate" among these sectors in different economic environments in ways that stocks managers cannot. The simple explanation is that investment managers will buy corporate bonds (the debt of individual companies) and mortgage bonds (debt backed by the principal and interest payments of huge pools of homeowners) when the economy is improving or strong, since the low risk of default in these economic environments means that the incremental yield of corporate and mortgage bonds generates outperformance. In contrast, they will buy government bonds (generally considered to be a default risk-free investment) in times of crisis to protect their principal, since the chances of default or bankruptcy by the US or other governments is far lower than it is for corporations or homeowners.

As you can see in Figure 5-4, which compares the returns of investment managers who buy only corporate securities to the broader Barclays U.S. Aggregate Index, corporate securities portfolios vastly outperform the broader benchmark the majority of the time, where 100% of managers are outperforming the benchmark, with exceptions during times of corporate stress, such as the credit crisis of 2008 where the index ranked around the 1st percentile, indicating that 99% of corporate bond managers underperformed the index. Looking closely at the chart, there are extended periods—like 1992–1997, 2003–2006, and 2011–present—where the Aggregate Index ranked right at the 100th percentile, meaning that 100% of corporate bond managers had results better than the index. During these time periods, anyone exposed to corporate securities, regardless of skill or luck, would have outperformed the benchmark.

If you ignore investment manager returns for a minute, you can see a similar result if you compare the returns of the Barclays Credit (Corporate Bond) Index to the Barclays Aggregate Index. Figure 5-5 plots the rolling 3-year outperformance/underperformance of the Barclays Credit Index versus the broader Barclays Aggregate Index since 1980.

---

[4]Barclays Global Family of Indices monthly publication, September 30, 2012.

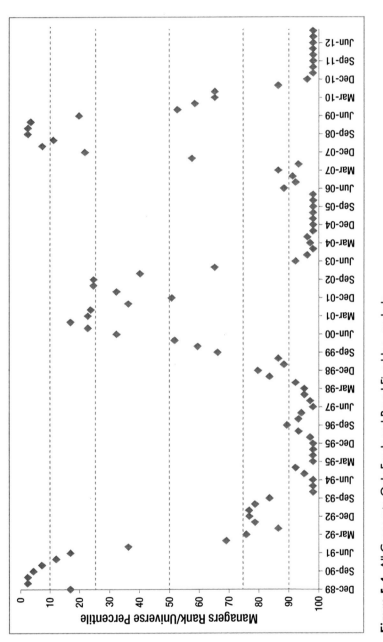

Figure 5-4. All Corporate-Only Funds and Broad Fixed Income Index
*Data courtesy of eVestment Alliance

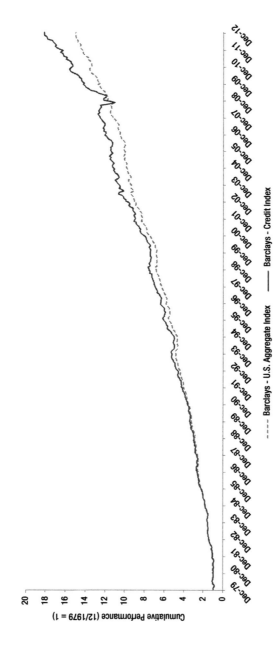

Figure 5-5. Cumulative Performance of Corporate and Broad Fixed Income Indices
*Data courtesy of Barclays Indexes

Over this time period, the Credit Index appears to outperform the Aggregate Index very consistently, except during crises and recessions. In fact, as Figure 5-5 indicates, the average annual outperformance of credit securities is 0.29% per year (0.57% median). If the first couple of years are discounted and recalculated from 1983 (remember, the very early 1980s were characterized by borderline runaway inflation and interest rates over 10%), the long-term average jumps to a 0.60% annual outperformance by corporate bonds over the broader index.

In Chapter 3, if you squinted hard enough, you might have been able to convince yourself that the growth or value equity style outperforms the other style in certain environments, but you would have been hard-pressed to find any real consistency. In addition, when a given equity style cycle ends, the reversal is usually violent and quick. When it comes to the bond market, however, I think it is pretty clear that corporate bonds generally have outperformed the entire fixed income market pretty consistently—with the exception of the "credit crisis" of 2008. This is why the vast majority of pension plans and investment managers tend to have long-term systematic biases away from the index toward riskier securities. After all, if you have a very long-term view and can survive periods of stress, there really is a long-term performance advantage to sticking with corporate bonds.

As you consider which types of mutual funds you wish to include in your fixed income allocation, I urge you to follow advice that is very similar to the position I took on duration earlier in this chapter. That is, if you have a long-term horizon, taking some credit risk can really pay off over the long run. If you have 20 or 30 years until retirement, this small annual advantage really begins to add up! Figure 5-6 adds the Barclays Government Bond Index to this analysis and shows that a lower-risk portfolio of only government bonds would have had a steadier path than corporate bonds over time but far less total return.

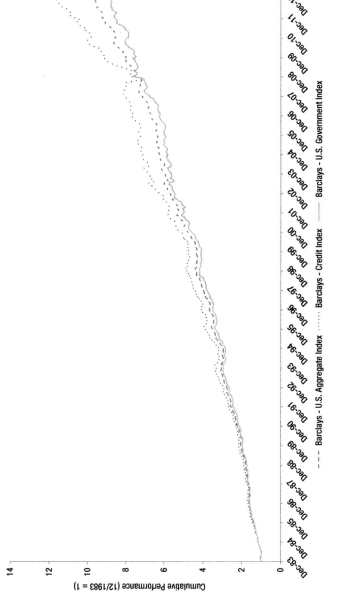

Figure 5-6. Cumulative Performance Government Bonds Versus Corporate Bonds and the Entire Investment Grade Fixed Income Market

*Data courtesy of Barclays Indexes

If you had invested a single dollar in the Barclays U.S. Government Index on December 31, 1983, it would have grown to $8.68 by June 30, 2012 (before fees and expenses). A dollar invested in the Barclays Aggregate (which contains government, mortgage, and corporate bonds) would have grown to $9.39, indicating the advantage of some broader diversification. However, showing the merits of taking even more risk, a dollar invested in the Barclays U.S. Credit Index would have grown to $11.09, or 6.7% growth over those 28 1/2 years.

As was the case with the duration discussion, again, all of this shows the benefits of taking reasonable risks over long periods of time. For those out there with a short time horizon, say, 5 years or less until retirement, this aggressive concentration in corporate bonds could be too much of a risk. Look back at the last two charts closely. If you had decided to heed my advice and invest in corporate bonds in 2006, your returns would have been horrible over the next few years as compared to someone who chose lower risk or more diversified assets.

This is precisely why pension plans manage their credit risk to fit their time horizon, just like they do with their duration risk. Short-term cash pools that are needed to pay benefits are invested in treasury bonds and extremely short duration, highly rated corporate bonds. On the other hand, long-term, strategic allocations to fixed income that may not be sold for many years seek the greater reward of corporate bonds. Although it is entirely possible that short-term risk may pay off quickly, never take on more risk than you can handle. If losses or market declines cannot be tolerated over the time horizon given, don't take on risks that can lead to intolerable losses, no matter how appealing the potential returns might be.

Summary

Unlike in the equity markets, the risks in fixed income investing are easily quantifiable and can be quite manageable if they are understood. The duration and credit risk of a portfolio can be designed to precisely fit the timeline and risk appetite of the investor (or a mutual fund with characteristics that match the investor's preferences can be selected), minimizing the potential impact of a catastrophic market movement. Whereas the underlying investment strategies of any given manager may be difficult for the average individual to understand, it is easy to obtain the duration and average credit rating of any fixed income mutual fund through your bank's or broker's web site, the mutual fund company or its web site, or a data aggregator like Morningstar.com. Once you understand your duration needs and your personal willingness to take on credit risk, finding a suitable fund for you should be a fairly easy task.

Investment Structure for Fixed Income, Part II

Manager Selection Considerations

In this chapter, I will continue the discussion of how to determine the appropriate fixed income structure for individual investors, but I would like to change the focus from the characteristics of the underlying bonds to those of the managers themselves. As I discussed in Chapter 3, when I covered the basics of the investment structure for equities, a strong case can be made that a global outlook for stock investing is the best way to reduce risk and maximize your opportunity set for returns. Does the same rule of thumb apply to bonds? In Chapter 4, I contrasted the results of active and passive managers across a variety of equity portfolio types and found that there is a mixed bag when it comes to whether there is any consistent value to active management among stock mutual funds. Are the results any clearer for bonds? Finally, whereas the discussion in Chapter 5 dealt mainly with traditional lower-risk, investment-grade fixed income investments, what about other types of bonds, like high yield and emerging markets? Is there merit to considering these in the portfolio? To keep things interesting, I will answer the second question first.

Active versus Passive Management

In Chapter 3, I made a pretty strong case for why most pension plans invest a large fraction (sometimes even 100%) of their equity allocation in index funds and why individual investors should generally do the same. I will not repeat that advice here! Very simply put, in contrast to my thoughts about indexing stock investments, I am not a fan of indexing fixed income, and I know of very few pension plans that use index funds for bonds. Why? The answer is simple. Unlike in equities, where the sum of all market participants equals the stock market index, the sum of all fixed income funds does not equal the bond market index.

How is this possible? Unlike in equities, the fixed income industry has plenty of participants with different interests or guidelines than the average investor has, which thereby skews how funds are actually invested. Insurance companies, for example, largely invest in government and highly rated corporate bonds, typically disdaining mortgage bonds and anything rated below AA. Sovereign wealth funds, the national investment companies of countries with positive national trade flows, tend to buy mainly government bonds in the United States and maybe a few highly rated corporate bonds. Meanwhile, central banks looking to manipulate exchange rates or manage international cash flows exclusively buy government bonds.

Lower rated corporate bonds and mortgage bonds are therefore more the domain of pension plans, investment managers, and retail investors. As a result, the sum of all the bond holdings of retail and pension plan investments looks nothing like the market as a whole. With insurance companies and sovereign wealth funds buying a disproportionate share of the government issuance, the investment funds that you and pension plans invest in will be heavily skewed toward the riskier corporate and mortgage bonds in most environments.

The question for you, the investor, then, is whether you are okay with that bias. Are you investing in fixed income for the perfect long-term safety of government bonds, or are you simply looking for a way to reduce and balance your stock market risk? If you are looking for the latter, then considering funds who take advantage of the long-term systematic outperformance (with the occasional major hiccup) of corporate and mortgage bonds over government bond returns is completely appropriate. Do you want a core or total return product that employs all sectors but usually underweights governments, or do you want to go full out and invest in a corporate-only portfolio?

The decision really boils down to what you view as the role of fixed income in your portfolio, your time horizon, and how well you can absorb the periodic corporate bond return collapses. As the charts in Chapter 5 have shown, anyone with a 10- or 20-year time horizon, or longer, would have done much better in a risky asset-biased portfolio over time, assuming they could have stomached the periods when corporate bonds and other risky assets fell off the proverbial cliff. Figure 6-1 compares the entire universe of institutional, active core, fixed income portfolios (the fixed income asset management products in which pension plans typically invest) against the Barclays Aggregate Index on a rolling 3-year basis. Here are the results, and they are rather shocking (at least to me).

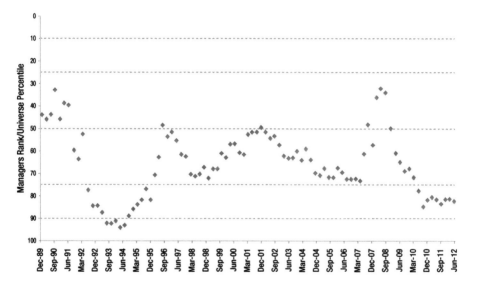

Figure 6-1. Performance of All Core Institutional Managers Versus Market Benchmark
*Data courtesy of eVestment Alliance

As has been the case in similar charts earlier in this book, the index's rank among the collection of available investment managers is indicated with the dots. If the index ranks at the 40% mark, for example, that would indicate that 40% of investment managers outperformed the index for the 3 years up to that point in time and 60% performed worse than the index.

In Figure 6-1, with the exceptions of the recession of 1991 and the credit crisis of 2008, more than half of all fixed income investment managers have always outperformed the bond market as a whole. Contrast that to the same charts we reviewed for equity products in Chapter 3, where actively managed funds enjoyed good periods and bad periods but did not consistently outperform the benchmark. That isn't the case here! Given the systematic bias by investment managers for riskier assets that outperform over the long run, as well as the ability of these managers to "rotate" among sectors during difficult market environments, I remain firmly convinced of the merits of investing all of a pension plan's fixed income dollars in actively managed products. Unfortunately, though, the retail bond market is one place where it is more difficult for individual investors to precisely copy that advice. Whereas Figure 6-1 plotted the returns of institutional portfolios, Figure 6-2 compares the entire opportunity set of mutual funds (636) that fall under the Lipper "Intermediate Investment Grade" fixed income definition.

Figure 6-2. Performance of All Core Mutual Funds Against Market Benchmark
*Data courtesy of eVestment Alliance

What happened to our great performance? Figure 6-2 would imply that individual investors should never invest in active fixed income portfolios because our odds of outperforming the benchmark seem to be so slight, directly contradicting the advice I would give to institutional pension plans based on Figure 6-1.

Remember that Figure 6-2 shows the results of mutual funds, whereas Figure 6-1 showed the results of institutional products that are available exclusively to very large investors like pension plans. There are a number of differences between mutual funds and institutional products that decrease the consistency of outperformance, but I do not think that they negate my predilection toward actively managed products.

Why? First, the mutual fund return data reflects the effect of fees, whereas the institutional return data typically does not. This difference by itself will move the index up a little in the rankings because index returns never reflect the impact of fees and expenses.

Second, institutional investment portfolios tend to be very tightly defined and controlled. Core fixed income portfolios are all benchmarked against the Barclays Aggregate, contain very little unwanted cash, and aim for roughly a market duration. Mutual funds, in contrast, need to keep a decent amount of cash available in the portfolio to supply liquidity for clients entering and leaving the funds. Mutual funds also are typically less well defined. If you read through the list of the 636 funds represented in Figure 6-2, there are lots and lots and lots of funds with "intermediate" in their names (implying shorter-than-market duration), an income focus (instead of a total-return focus, meaning that all they invest in is yield, not capital gains or sector rotation opportunities), sector-focused funds, and many other things that dilute the purity of this pool.

So, let's pull all of this together. In Figure 6-3, I have selected 10 total return-style fixed income funds from managers who tend to rule the roost. Even though I won't provide their individual names to avoid the appearance of endorsing any of these funds, rest assured that I'm not cherry-picking performance here. If you saw me on the street and asked me to rattle off the top of my head the "best" (most consistent, best resourced, most respected, etc.) fixed income managers without referencing a table of their performance, this is the list I would come up with.

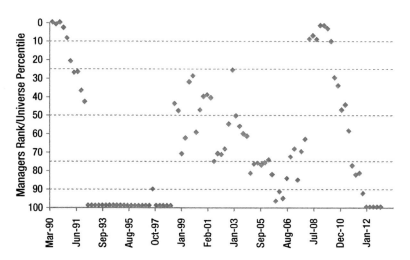

Figure 6-3. Performance of Selected Core Fixed Income Mutual Funds Versus Market Benchmark
*Data courtesy of eVestment Alliance

Looks a little better, right? For most of the 1990s, the index underperformed every single fund on my list. Performance got a little tougher during the NASDAQ collapse and then came back strong in the middle part of the last decade. Not unexpectedly, the credit crisis didn't do wonders for my list of managers, since they tend to overweight riskier corporate and mortgage bonds, but they have all come back great, with the index again ranking dead last over the past year. I will cover manager selection in the next chapter, but it sure looks like there are some pretty great managers out there that can outperform in most decent market environments.

Now, I know what you're thinking. Yeah, yeah, these look good, but they're not perfect. That performance spike or two is still really scary. Maybe we should give an index manager another look, and so I do in Figure 6-4.

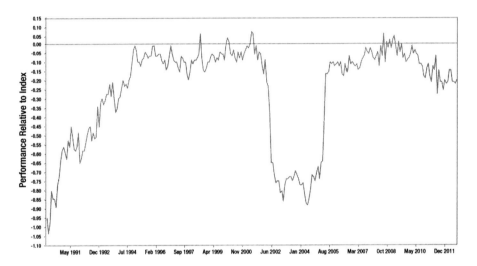

Figure 6-4. Performance of a Bond Index Mutual Fund Versus Index
*Data courtesy of eVestment Alliance

Figure 6-4 contains the full history of rolling 3-year returns versus the index for a major fixed income index fund. What is plotted is the rolling 3-year outperformance or underperformance versus the benchmark, regardless of market direction. If you compare this chart to the manager's returns for its S&P 500 index fund, which track the benchmark so closely they are virtually indistinguishable without resorting to a microscopic scale, you would think that this was an actively managed product. Given that the Barclays Aggregate Index has 7,999 securities in it,[1] and some are highly illiquid, the portfolio

---

[1] As of September 30, 2012

manager simply cannot buy a pro rata share of every security like you would for an index fund. Instead, a statistical sampling process is used as well as a small procorporate, antigovernment security bias to offset the impact of management fees. This slight deviation from an exact copy of the index results in a very slight increase of the yield in the portfolio.

Figure 6-4 shows that there may not be a perfect or even simple solution for individual investors. My list of dream managers in Figure 6-3 missed pretty badly a couple of times, but the index fund didn't fare a whole lot better. When recessions and crises hit, the fear of default rises. When default fears rise, yields and yield spreads rise, causing the prices of bonds to fall. Although having more credit exposure than the benchmark seems to lead to outperformance over long periods of time, as I showed in Chapter 5, there will always be short periods of time when credit quality fears impact these portfolios worse than others that have more exposure in less risky securities.

So, I know you really want to ask me who is on that list in Figure 6-3!! Have your city or state pension plan call me to solicit a bid, and I will let them know.

"Plus" Sectors

The "plus" sectors in fixed income are really some of my very favorite things to recommend to clients. High yield and emerging markets debt are the most common of the "pluses," with some small consideration given to a variety of other obscure investment types, like securitized bank loans. Although some of the rarer kinds of fixed income investments could be very relevant to a large pension plan, I will focus here on high yield and emerging markets debt because they constitute the vast majority of the "plus" sectors and are commonly available for investment in most core-plus funds as well as in individual portfolios dedicated to the asset type.

"Core" portfolios and the Barclays U.S. Aggregate Bond Index contain domestic investment-grade bonds, or bonds rated no worse than BBB–. "Core-plus" portfolios and "plus sector" investors therefore invest in things that simply are not in that 7,999-member list of securities that Barclays uses to build the U.S. Aggregate Bond Index,[2] mainly because emerging markets debt are not US securities and high yield bonds are, by definition, NOT investment grade. Instead, both emerging markets debt and high yield bonds are viewed by many, many investors as big, bad, scary demons that are not safe to invest in. Chinese, Russian, and South American debt? Scary! These countries default on their debts from time to time or may have weakly enforced rules of law.

---

[2] *Barclays Global Family of Indices* monthly publication, September 30, 2012.

High yield companies on the verge of default after falling from grace, or start-ups that have issued total debt equal to many times their annual revenues? These can be even scarier, which is one of the reasons why you might want to hire professionals to navigate these waters for you.

Here's the thing, though: everyone knows the risk of each of these types of securities, and everyone wants to get paid for the risk. I won't go into all the math and confusing charts, but the basic truth is that the incremental yield over treasuries offered by these perceived-to-be terribly scary bonds more than compensates the investor for the historical default rates and bankruptcy recoveries experienced by investors in these asset classes.

Howard Marks, the chairman of a widely respected high yield investment manager, has a mantra that he repeats in many of his letters to clients, articles, public speeches, and books: high yield investing is like amateur tennis. Whereas a pro like Roger Federer will win a match by hitting unreturnable shots, the amateur tennis player wins by simply getting the ball back over the net. If I, very much an amateur tennis player, make fewer unforced errors than you, I will win the game. The same is true in high yield investing. We don't need to make tremendous gains on individual securities like we would strive to do in an equity portfolio. All we need to do is make fewer errors (select fewer bonds that default) than the index, and we will outperform over time.[3] If you combine an asset class that overpays for default risk with managers who can mitigate the damage done by the worst bonds issued, hopefully this can lead to a long-term source of superior gains.

Figure 6-5 compares the cumulative returns of the Barclays Aggregate Index, the Barclays Credit Index, and the Citibank High Yield Cash Pay Index since the inception of the Citibank Index in December 1988.

---

[3]Howard Marks, *The Most Important Thing: Uncommon Sense for the Thoughtful Investor*, Columbia Business School Publishing, 2011.

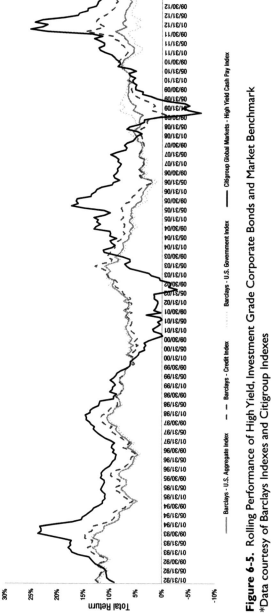

Figure 6-5. Rolling Performance of High Yield, Investment Grade Corporate Bonds and Market Benchmark
*Data courtesy of Barclays Indexes and Citigroup Indexes

The path is lumpy, but clear. High yield bonds have steadily outperformed both the broad investment-grade market and their investment-grade corporate brethren, except for those nasty bumps the chart seems to have hit in 2000–2002 and 2008. As I discussed in Chapter 5, investment-grade corporate bonds will outperform over long periods of time but experience negative shocks when the economy sours. Because high yield bonds are nothing more than higher-returning and more-volatile versions of corporate bonds, Figure 6-5 illustrates that both the long-term success rate is better and the impact of those shocks are greater. As I said in Chapter 5, these types of securities may be appropriate for an investor with a long-term time horizon who can ride out those short-term negative periods but should not be considered by someone who lacks the time or patience to allow the market to recover when it falls.

Figure 6-6 takes this discussion of corporate and high yield bonds a bit further with an "apples-to-oranges" comparison that still illustrates the point of the binary nature of high yield versus the broader market. In this chart, I have plotted the rolling 3-year returns of the core Barclays Aggregate Bond Index against the distribution of all high yield managers.

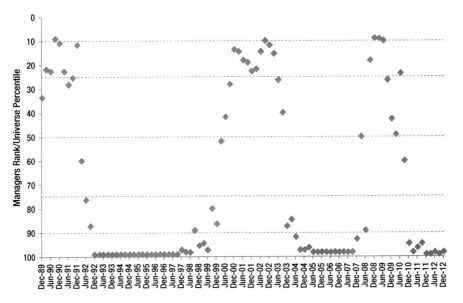

Figure 6-6. Performance of All High Yield Managers and Fixed Income Market Benchmark
*Data courtesy of eVestment Alliance

Not surprisingly, Figure 6-6 shows that high yield is either the hero or the goat, depending on the economic cycle. When times are good and default rates are coming down, the entire population of high yield investment managers outperforms investment grade fixed income, with the investment-grade index ranking at the 100th percentile, the absolute bottom. On the other hand, when the economy has hit a rough patch, like the recessions of 1991, 2000, and 2008, 100% of high yield managers underperform the broader market and the index ranks in the 1st percentile.

Taken together, these two charts leave me with the following conclusion: over long periods of time, high yield bonds will outperform the rest of the bond market but in a very choppy pattern. As a result, clients should pick one of the following two strategies for investing in high yield bonds, depending on their desired level of risk:

1. The Asset Allocation Approach: Invest for the long run, setting a steady and separate/dedicated allocation to high yield and living through the volatility in exchange for superior long-term results.

2. The Manager Approach: Invest the fixed income allocation in products with names like "Full Discretion," "Full Authority," or "Core Plus," where the investment manager is allowed to invest in high yield and other sectors as it sees fit, rotating the portfolio into and out of high yield as events warrant.

If you have a large amount of assets and want to select specific specialists in high yield, then the first strategy is appropriate, using periods of poor high yield performance to increase your investment with these managers in a bottom-picking, dollar-cost-averaging manner. If you would rather just trust professionals to do it for you, then an investment in more aggressive core-plus fixed income portfolios will get you the exposure you need. Either way, the long-term benefits of adding a moderate amount of high yield to your portfolio are clear, with superior long-term results for those that can stomach the risks.

Another common "plus" sector that pension plans include in their portfolios is emerging markets debt. This is the debt issued by lower-rated countries, like those in South America, Eastern Europe, and parts of Asia. Historically, emerging markets debt has been considered a more risky type of investment than investment-grade debt because many of the emerging markets countries have had crises that impact investors on a regular basis. These crises have included currency crises (like Mexico in the mid-1990s), economic collapses (the "Asian Tigers" in the late 1990s, many parts of Mediterranean Europe from 2008 to present), sovereign defaults (Russia in 1998), and re-nationalizations of assets (Venezuela about every 20 minutes). However, despite these periodic crises and considerable problems with governance and investor protections, the returns still look awfully good.

As shown in both Figure 6-7 (a chart of cumulative performance since the mid-1990s) and Figure 6-8 (a chart of rolling performance over a medium-term period), since the JP Morgan Emerging Markets Bond Index was created in December 1993, it has vastly outperformed all types of US investment-grade and high yield bonds, in spite of all those aforementioned crises, collapses, and other issues. In fact, the last 20 years have seen a steady prog-ress toward stability in the emerging markets. If one compares national debt to GDP or looks at trade balances, many emerging markets are now in a financially stronger position than the so-called First World. Some of these countries, like Russia, have even been redefined as investment grade, despite their very recent default history. (After all, 14 years really isn't that long ago in the memory of economists.) The continued migration of emerging markets economies into the developed world will continue with economic growth, but the debt issued by these countries has already had a tremendous track record. As a result, it is my opinion that this strong history argues for including emerging markets debt in the broader fixed income portfolios you select—but it probably does not merit a separate allocation to this asset class. As was the case with high yield bonds for investors who may not have the stomach for short-term volatility or large losses in a crisis, let your core-plus manager choose when and where to invest in emerging markets debt.

After all, I'm not absolutely convinced that this historical outperformance will continue forever, which is why I would rather trust the decision to include or exclude it from a core-plus portfolio to experts. If the trend shown in Figure 6-7 continues, you will profit from an allocation to emerging markets debt. However, the last 5 years shown in Figure 6-8 indicate that the rate of outperformance by emerging markets debt has significantly slowed. If that long-term positive trend stops once all markets are priced about the same, a broadly diversified investment manager will be able to redirect your invest-ment dollars elsewhere.

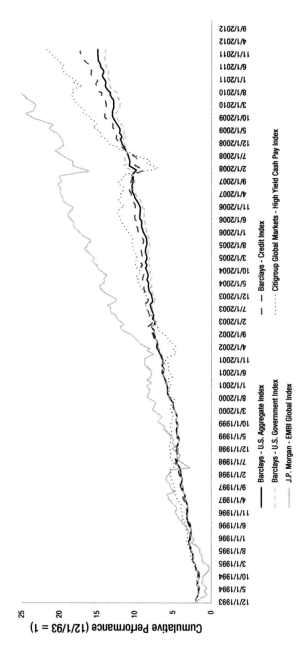

Figure 6-7. Cumulative Performance of High Yield Bonds, Investment-Grade Corporate Bonds, and Market Benchmark

*Data courtesy of Barclays Indexes, Citigroup Indexes, and JP Morgan Indexes

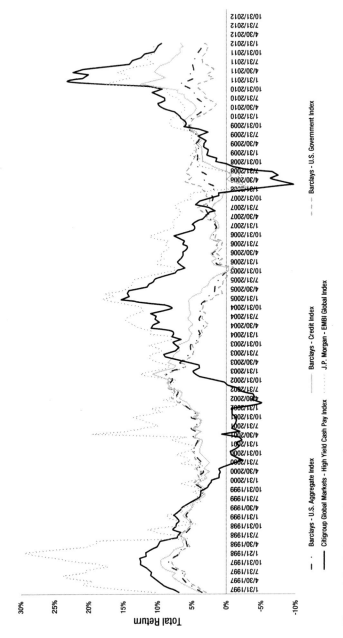

Figure 6-8. Rolling Performance of Emerging Markets Debt and Other Types of Fixed Income
*Data courtesy of Barclays Indexes, Citigroup Indexes, and JP Morgan Indexes

Should an Individual Invest in the US or Global Fixed Income Market?

When I meet with clients and we discuss the prospects for stock markets and economies, I am frequently asked to discuss how this or that economic factor or risk might affect their equity investments. As I outlined in Chapter 3, investing in US stocks really isn't a perfect proxy for investing in the United States anymore, given the foreign exposure of so many companies. A terrible economic meltdown that somehow affected the United States and only the United States (impossible, I know, but bear with me here) would not necessarily destroy the earnings or stock price of Apple or Coca-Cola or countless other companies that have significant non-US operations. Simply put, an investment in US stocks is not a pure investment in the US economy.

In contrast, when you buy US Government debt, you have 100% exposure to the United States. Consumer preferences in Germany or tax cuts in Australia have absolutely no impact on the probability that you will earn a return on those US bonds. US Government bonds depend 100% on the performance of the US government. Mortgage bonds depend 100% on US homeowners. Corporate bonds might pay part of their interest from foreign earnings, but the underlying rate regime that drives their total returns will flow directly from the government bond rate curve. In short, if you want to express an opinion on an individual country and its economy, fixed income—not stocks—is the place an investor can actually do it.

However, I do not normally recommend a separate allocation for non-US fixed income as a necessity for all investors, like I did for equities. In Chapter 4, I made a strong argument for why investors should think of stocks as global stocks and eliminate the "home country" bias that results from overallocation to the stocks of their native lands. That same logic, however, does not hold for fixed income.

The global investment-grade bond market is very different from the stock market. Whereas US, German, and Japanese automobile companies compete in a global marketplace for retail buyers, the US, German, and Japanese governments do not compete head to head, per se. US Treasury Bonds set the global baseline for all investments. Just as US corporate bonds or high yield bonds will be priced based on the "yield spread" (the incremental return demanded by investors to compensate for default risk) above Treasuries, so too will the bonds of other nations and their companies. Low-risk government bonds issued by countries like Germany and Britain will be priced to yield levels that are very similar to US government bonds, whereas risky countries like Greece or Italy will be priced to yield far more due to the possibility of default—not because Italy is a superior investment.

Although the sales, revenue, and profits of BMW could far outpace those of GM, thereby generating a much better appreciation in BMW's stock than GM's, German bonds will return basically the same to investors as US Government bonds over any reasonable time period. There are thousands of hedge funds, investment banks, and portfolio managers who trade in these securities and will buy the cheaper bonds and sell the more expensive bonds at any given time, keeping the prices and yields basically in line.

As a result, there are very small gains, if any, to be made from investing in bonds issued outside the United States or your home market. My advice to most of my clients for non-US investment-grade debt is very similar to my advice for high yield and emerging markets debt: allow your portfolio manager to invest in non-US bonds as he or she sees fit, but don't bother to seek out a separate portfolio for just non-US bonds. Except for cases of extremely large clients with massive economies of scale, or someone who wishes to increase or decrease the exposure to the dollar or other currencies on purpose to find some other source of returns, the benefits of any incremental yield may not outweigh the time and expense of finding and monitoring non-US fixed income funds.

Individual investors who wish to profit from the small differences between these markets should select mutual funds that are allowed to invest outside the United States in some moderate amount when the portfolio manager believes doing so is appropriate. A separate allocation to non-US bond funds is simply overkill given the limited opportunity that exists for gains. It may even hurt your performance when that static, non-US allocation is impacted by a crisis or other event that causes global capital to flow directly into US markets for security.

Summary

Bonds are, in many respects, a more direct investment in the real outcomes of a company's activities than are stocks. A company could double its sales but still see its stock price fall if a competitor triples its sales. For the bond investor, though, that doubling of sales will better insure that the company can pay back the money it has borrowed through the issuance of those bonds that the investor holds. Regardless of how the stock market wishes to view one company versus another, the bond market presents the clearest way to invest in a company's real balance sheet and long-term prospects. One can think of stocks as an investment in the hope of tomorrow, whereas bonds are an investment in the reality of today.

Before you determine the appropriate structure for your fixed income investments, you need to consider why you are investing in fixed income in the first place. If you are buying bonds to preserve principal and generate current income in retirement, all measures should be taken to minimize the prospects of short-term losses, including reducing duration and credit exposure. On the other hand, a long-term investor with many years until retirement can survive through periods of underperformance in exchange for the prospect of better returns when times are good. For this reason, long-term investors should explore the value that can be provided over the long term from the credit risk of corporate and high yield debt above and beyond long-risk treasury bonds.

Although the tendency by many investors is to simply view bonds as the low-risk balancing counterweight to the high-risk equity positions in their portfolio, I have shown in this chapter and in Chapter 5 that there is far more to fixed income than meets the eye. Duration decisions can result in great gains and losses as rates rise and fall with the economic cycle. Meanwhile, decisions about how much credit risk you can bear and which plus sectors you wish to include in your portfolio can result in returns that can rival stocks in many environments.

Investment Manager Selection

How to Find Tomorrow's Outperforming Managers Today

By this point in time, you should have a solid understanding of equity and fixed income structure under your belt. You also should have determined how much you should invest in each of the types of assets you are willing to consider and have worked out your plan for how to structure each asset class to minimize risk from unwanted biases and fees from active managers in asset classes where you have little hope of adding value. Now it is time to discuss the process of selecting money managers that will put your money to work in the markets; so you take another step on your path toward financial success, leaving the structure decisions behind and focusing your energy on selecting investment managers who will add value into your portfolio.

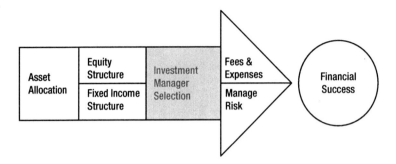

Selecting, reviewing, terminating, and replacing money managers is what the trustees of many pension plans or endowments spend 95% of their time doing. Your allocation of time and energy probably will not be that much different. However, even though this is the most time-intensive part of the entire investment process, it can also be the fun part—not to mention the part with the most obvious immediate impact. Investment enthusiasts love to spend their time poring over the quarterly or annual rankings of fund performance in the *Wall Street Journal* or *Money Magazine*. Some participants in 401(k) or 457 plans offered by corporations or public agencies drive investment committees crazy with requests for their favorite funds to be added to the plan options. And many investors love to join in the cocktail party chatter about how much better or worse than the market they are doing and how it is all thanks to some obscure mutual fund recommended to them by their dentist's brother-in-law's accountant (or something along those lines).

However, when it comes to determining whether you will retire with assets sufficient to your needs, manager selection is the part of the investment process that matters the least. Remember from Chapter 2 that asset allocation drives more than 90% of the variation in returns from investor to investor and from Chapter 3 that investment structure determines at least another 5% of your returns. Manager selection is really just the icing on the cake.

One of the best pieces of investment advice I can give to clients comes from an equity trader at an investment bank where I used to work. He used to tell me that when it comes to picking individual stocks, "If you outperform the market 50% of the time, your investments are average. If you beat the market 55% of the time, you are great. Win 60% of the time, and you are the best that's ever been. That's how thin the margin is between average and fantastic." I would argue that while we might hope to have a slightly more successful lineup of mutual funds in our portfolio, we should never expect that 100% of them will always beat the market because the individual security selection that makes such an important impact on mutual fund returns is so hard to do consistently. Frankly, if more than half of our mutual funds are outperforming for a given period of time and the fund selections are adding value to the portfolio in total, even after accounting for the underperforming funds and fees, we have done our job well.

These lowered expectations should guide your decisions for evaluating funds. In a properly diversified portfolio, you might have eight investments. Let's say you're invested in three US large and small cap stock funds, a core bond fund, a high yield fund, a non-US stock fund, an emerging markets fund, and a commercial real estate fund or real estate investment trust (REIT) fund (for more information on real estate and REITs, refer to Chapter 8). You might have a year where seven or eight of those funds are doing great, and you might have years where all eight underperform the market. However, over your 50-year investment horizon, you will most likely be able to look back and see that you basically earned the market return, or maybe a little better or worse, for the whole time on average.

Why is this?

Most major markets are generally believed to be "information efficient." The efficient markets theory, developed by Professor Gene Fama at the University of Chicago, presumes that all the information available about an asset is already incorporated into that asset's price, so no one can outperform the market due to "superior information" unless they have access to insider information (which is illegal).[1] Take a stock like General Electric, one of the oldest and largest companies in the world, as an example. Dozens of research analysts at Wall Street banks monitor every news item and earnings report with the scrutiny of a forensic detective. Hundreds or maybe even thousands of analysts at money management firms, mutual funds, and hedge funds do the same. Hundreds of thousands of individuals are invested in the stock.

What are the odds that out of all of those people, Joe Smith fund manager has superior information and knows more than all the others and is able to add value on the basis of it? Pretty small. The efficient markets theory says that any publicly available information is reflected in the price of the stock almost immediately because all investors have access to it and draw conclusions from it. The same is true for Exxon, Microsoft, AT&T, and all the rest of the stocks listed on the S&P 500. The odds that any one analyst has some piece of legal information that is truly unique are low. If you consider that the average mutual fund has 100 or 150 holdings in it, superior information on a single stock wouldn't make a lot of difference anyway. The fund manager would need to have unique and superior information on a dozen or more stocks, every day, to consistently add value based just on information. In the incredibly competitive environment that is the financial markets, that's a pretty hard assumption to make—and quite often it is just not realistic.

---

[1] The "strong form" of the efficient markets theory holds that even insider information is incorporated into the stock price.

In their book, *Active Portfolio Management*, Richard Grinold and Ronald Kahn[2] proposed the following model for categorizing the world of money managers. Let's assume for a second that you can break down investment managers in two ways: each is either Lucky or Unlucky and Skilled or Unskilled. We'll assume that, contrary to the efficient markets theory discussion previously, there actually is such a thing as skill when it comes to picking stocks. We'll also assume that skill can add some value to an investment, even in a relatively efficient market.

Each manager, therefore, can be placed into one of the four open spaces in Table 7-1, and four distinct personality types can result, as seen in Table 7-2.

Table 7-1. The Four Characteristics of Investment Managers

	Lucky	Unlucky
Skilled		
Unskilled		

Table 7-2. The Four Resulting Types of Investment Managers

	Lucky	Unlucky
Skilled	Blessed	Forlorn
Unskilled	Insufferable	Unemployed[3]

The adage, "It is better to be lucky than good," can apply to at least a quarter of the population in this analysis. I'll go through each of these categories in detail to help you understand how to pick the right manager of your investment funds.

The Blessed Money Manager

I'll start with the group of money managers that we all want to hire: the Blessed Money Managers. Trustees of, and consultants to, pension plans and endowments spend, as a group, millions of hours a year trying to find the managers that are most likely to deliver stellar future returns. Investment consulting firms hire armies of analysts that are tasked with sending out and

---

[2] *Active Portfolio Management—A Quantitative Approach for Producing Superior Returns and Controlling Risk*, Second Edition, Richard C. Grinold and Ronald N. Kahn, McGraw Hill, 2000.
[3] Grinold and Kahn referred to combination of the Unlucky and Unskilled as "Doomed," but I prefer to jump right to the end and think of them as the "Unemployed."

scoring questionnaires or requests for proposals from managers; meeting with managers; critiquing their people, resources, organizations, and investment philosophies; and then ranking the managers in an effort to develop lists of recommendations for clients for the future. Entire industries exist of database vendors that create software for slicing and dicing performance and holdings a million different ways to try to determine with any kind of statistical certainty if a series of great results was truly due to skill or luck. Trustees, consultants, and money management marketers then fly around the world to meet in the world's most expensive dating process to convince each other that they are meant to be together.

At the end of the process, every client hopes that these Blessed managers truly are as skilled as their slick promotional materials seem to imply and that their glorious past results persist forever.

The Forlorn Money Manager

At the end of the day, though, luck can change. As great as a manager might appear on paper, sometimes they just get it wrong—even if they have a team of MBAs from top schools building models based on data collected by 200 research analysts, each with 10+ years of experience, and are willing to invest whatever is required to have the best tools in the industry. Or, maybe their style falls out of favor with the industry for a few years, where the deep value stocks that they love to discover stay ignored (and depressed in price) by the rest of the market. Whatever the case may be, these types of firms fall into the Forlorn category. They know they are doing everything right. They have torn apart and rebuilt their processes a dozen times. They have held dozens of internal meetings and hired plenty of outside advisors to try and figure out what is going wrong, and yet the downward slide continues.

Forlorn Money Managers make consultants, including myself, lose sleep. There is brilliance there, and a consultant can tell clients over and over again to be patient, but there is always the question of whether or not patience and brilliance will pay off in the end. Managers in this camp are like the baseball player that falls into a 2-month slump after three great seasons. Is it just a slump? Will the past brilliance return? Maybe something changed. Maybe they actually don't have skill. Maybe they were simply lucky for years and were great at convincing people that their good luck was actually the embodiment of skill. Regardless of the reason, these managers are the main reason that picking future sources of outperformance is more of an art than a science.

Of course, I do have a few clients that will invest with these Forlorn firms from time to time, and their willingness to invest with someone at the bottom of the cycle has paid off in some cases. (Bear in mind that it is entirely possible that poor results can continue indefinitely, so don't take this example of bottom picking as a guaranteed source of great performance.) If you have faith in the manager's investment process but their performance is poor, maybe their process or philosophy is out of favor for the moment and is due for a return. If they like stocks with good R&D investment, for example, and the world has spent the last year bidding up the prices of companies that are cost cutters, perhaps this manager will come back strongly when the market starts to reward companies that are investing in the future.

The Insufferable Money Manager

Back to the baseball analogy. If those first three great seasons were actually just the result of luck and the player was never really any good in the first place, then the manager falls into Grinold and Kahn's next category: the Insufferable Money Manager. This group drives consultants crazy. You meet with them and listen to their story and see their results, but you just know something doesn't add up. They simply aren't that good. Their market-beating performance makes no sense. They lack the resources of the Blessed and Forlorn Money Managers. Their people aren't as experienced or impressive, they don't have as sophisticated a trading and database system, and they don't have the same depth of research resources.

What they do have, however, is an impressive track record and the most annoying team of marketing people on the planet. They trumpet their results from the rooftops, cold-call your clients, and harass you at conferences. Investment consultants can't figure out how they generate the results that they do, and clients resist them for years and years and years until a naïve consultant finally gives in, perhaps because they want the harassment to stop, and hires them anyway. But then, the Insufferable Money Manager's true lack of skill inevitably shows up when their good luck runs its course and they become part of the next category: the Unemployed Money Manager.

The Unemployed Money Manager

Unemployed Money Managers are not unemployed originally, of course, but they become that way over time. The firm's string of luck cannot carry on forever, and eventually its lack of skill becomes apparent. Clients may hang on to the fund for a few years, hoping that the past was prologue and believing that the good years are just around the corner—and in some cases, the manager's luck does return. However, most of the time their results get worse, asset levels fall, clients move on, and the manager begins to struggle to stay in business.

Applying Manager Performance to Your Investments

What does this mean for the average individual investor? Someone with a $10,000 portfolio certainly cannot command a meeting with a portfolio manager in the same way that a pension plan with $100,000,000 to invest in the strategy can. If it is hard enough for pension plans and endowments and investment consultants with unlimited access and tremendous resources to determine luck and skill, separating the Blessed from the Insufferable, how can the individual investor have any idea if they are picking the real winners?

Here are my rules of thumb:

1. Ignore overnight successes. I'd take a manager who has outperformed the market in 16 of the last 20 years but has stumbled the past 2 years over a sexy new manager with 3 highflying years any day. Statistically, there is a 1 in 8 chance that a new firm can beat the market during its first 3 years out of the box.[4] The odds that its string of successes continues—if those successes are indeed based just on luck—get longer every year.

2. Beware of Endpoint Bias. The problem with the rankings of top mutual funds in papers or magazines is that the criteria used to compile the list is always based on performance for the 1 year or 3 years or 5 years preceding the publication date. This tells you nothing about the fund's chances of long-term success. A manager with 4 lousy years and 1 utterly amazing year could generate a good 5-year number, despite a disappointing performance 80% of the time. Instead, investors need to look at the manager's 1-year returns from inception onward— or, better yet, its rolling 3-year returns from inception onward. How many of those periods have outperformed the index? Long-term consistency is a far better indicator of future success than just a recent snapshot of success. Because this point is so crucial to selection, I'll go into more detail when I discuss the pitfalls of Endpoint Bias later in this chapter.

---

[4] I'm assuming a 50/50 chance you randomly pick a portfolio that beats the market. Consider that 1/2 cubed is 1/8. If you throw in transactions costs and fees, the odds of a 3-year good string fall to maybe 1 in 9 or 1 in 10, which is certainly not an impossible feat given that hundreds of new firms or products launch each year. If 200 new funds launch this year, even odds of 1 in 10 mean that 20 of those could outperform the index in the first 3 years purely by luck.

3. Take a look at other portfolios within the same firm. How have they done? In most firms, research analysts are a shared resource. The analyst who covers the telecommunications sector gives the same information to the large cap growth portfolio manager as she does to the small cap value portfolio manager. If the portfolio that interests you is an outstanding star in a sea of mediocrity, something doesn't add up. If the research resources can't add value anywhere else, why is that particular fund doing so well? Maybe the portfolio manager is an utter genius, but the portfolio manager's results still rest on the shoulders of the research done by the analysts, which appears to have some issues in the other portfolios. Some firms make a point of advertising their success rates, such as 13 out of their 15 funds have beaten their Lipper peer group (these are performance rankings of all funds in a given fund category by Lipper, a division of Thomson Reuters) for the last 5 years. Although I have plenty of bad things to say about peer comparisons as a benchmark of success later in this chapter, a success rate like that, where the vast majority of the firm's products have similarly good results relative to peers—coupled with long tenures of key people with good, long-term track records—implies a far higher probability of continued success across the investment management company's product line.

4. Stick with firms that have the resources to cover the sector in question. Some asset classes, like non-US stocks or corporate bonds, require huge resource platforms. How can five people sitting in New York have a better chance of generating strong performance in a global portfolio than a competitor that has 300 analysts stationed in the regions they research? Make sure the firm's resources are up to the task at hand. In addition, look for teams and firms with low analyst turnover and long tenures of portfolio managers. The longer a team has worked together, the more they trust each other and the more they are prepared to weather the bad times together. Ignore the new guy with three analysts and a firm you have never heard of. When performance turns down, the new guys have no client loyalty, no employee loyalty, and little chance of surviving intact.

5. Ignore the firms whose employees are frequent guests on CNBC (unless the firm happens to have trillions of dollars in assets and that employee's words really do move markets). If you see a portfolio manager from a firm you have never heard of once a week on one of those "stock advice" shows where people call in and ask the "experts" what they think of this or that individual company, ask yourself these questions:

    1. Doesn't he have anything better to do? If his portfolio is based on intensive research, being on national television every morning may distract him. Perhaps the fund should spend less time developing a public persona and more time researching the stocks in my portfolio.

    2. Why is he giving his ideas away? Proprietary research is normally not free. The ideas might be stocks that the portfolio already owns and the manager is trying to build up some excitement for them by talking them up in public. Or, in the worst-case scenario, he really is giving away the results of his company's research to build his reputation.

Believe in the manager's investment philosophy. Many people are fans of Warren Buffett because he makes a point of saying that he invests in what he knows. As Mr. Buffett commonly says, seeing lines out the door of a given store is a better argument for the potential returns that company can generate than all the Excel spreadsheets of financial projections ever produced. Mr. Buffett, then, serves as the quintessential example of an investment manager who believes in the value of strong fundamental research.

Another type of investment manager you might consider could have a thematic style, for example, where the portfolio manager develops a handful of macroeconomic themes with the help of economists or analysts tasked with thinking 5 years down the road. Some common themes are the graying of America (medical services, retirement communities, cruise lines) and the greening of America (recycling, sustainable products, renewable energy, organic foods). The manager then tries to pinpoint the overall trend within each theme and buys a handful of either best-of-breed or next-generation companies, depending on whether that manager has a bias toward established large cap companies or small cap startups. A third philosophy could be buying growth stocks at a reasonable price by avoiding the real high fliers and instead looking for companies that offer comparable technology and sales growth—but without the markup in stock price that the industry's publicity leader might get.

As you can see in the examples given, none of these themes are revolutionary, but they do guide the manager's thinking. The point of any of these is that as long as you understand and believe in the manager's philosophy, you will be more likely to tolerate periods of underperformance when that philosophy goes out of style for a year or two. If you understand, believe in, and agree with how the portfolio manager picks stocks, you might be able to avoid the tendency to move on to a new fund just before things pick up again.

Endpoint Bias Case Study

The easiest way to underperform and lose money in the financial markets is to pick funds based on their most recent endpoint. Figure 7-1 shows how two real funds compare to the entire population of core bond funds as of March 31, 2009, on a 1-, 3-, 5-, and 10-year basis. The boxes denote the breakdown of all peers by quartiles. The top-most box contains the results for the top 25% of all funds, the second top-most box contains the 25th to 50th percentiles, and so on. The top and bottom 10% of the distribution are truncated from the graph to prevent absurd outliers from distorting the entire picture.

As of the date in question, which fund would you pick? The fund denoted by the small dot has 1-, 3-, 5-, and 10-year performance near—or even above—the top of the distribution, indicating that its results have been in the top 10% or better of all core bond funds over any time period. The small square represents a fund from another company that has been well within the bottom 10% of all core bond funds over all time periods displayed.

Making a decision about which manager to hire or fire based on Figure 7-1 illustrates what I refer to as Endpoint Bias. That is, a fund looks terrific or horrible based on its performance over some number of months or years up to a given point in time. Given procurement rules and minimum qualifications for bidders, Endpoint Bias is actually how many institutional investors are required by law to find and hire investment managers. The plan requires that all candidates perform above the benchmark through some given date. Then, human nature being what it is, the individuals searching for an investment manager typically select one of the managers that looks the best over the recent past under the assumption that the trend will continue.

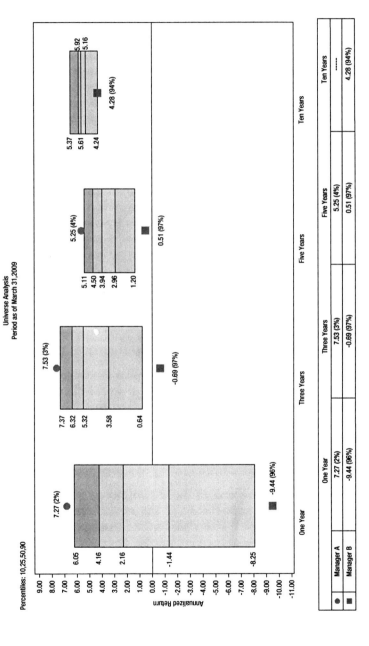

Figure 7-1. Peer Group Ranking Example

*Data courtesy of eVestment Alliance

As an individual investor, however, you can pick whomever you want to without fear of being sued for violating some procurement law. And, in this case, picking and choosing whoever you want would serve you well. What do I mean by that? Take a look at Figure 7-2, which plots the two managers' results in a different way, showing their results above or below the benchmark on a rolling 3-year basis. The chart for each manager begins at the inception of the investment fund and extends through the worst of the 2008 credit crisis. When the line representing each manager pulls above the gray horizontal line, this indicates that the manager was outperforming the Barclays Aggregate Bond Index. Meanwhile, when the line representing each manager falls below the zero line, this indicates that the manager was underperforming.

The scenario in Figure 7-2 paints a significantly different picture from that shown in Figure 7-1. As it turns out, our underperforming manager from Figure 7-1 has had a pretty great track record from its inception right up to the beginning of the credit crisis in 2008. Over its 16-year rolling history prior to the credit crisis, this manager never underperformed the benchmark. Clearly, something went wrong with the portfolio when the credit crisis hit, but a 16-for-16-year track record of outperformance up to that point should count for something, shouldn't it? Maybe this manager has more skill than that prior universe chart implied in Figure 7-1. In contrast, take a look at our great manager from Figure 7-1. From their (more recent) inception of 1999 through late 2008 (also beware of my admonition earlier against funds with shorter track records), this manager has been decidedly mediocre. Their performance was briefly decent relative to the benchmark in 2002, but for most of their history this manager basically delivered index-like returns to their clients.

Which analysis do you trust for selecting where to invest your money? The most recent end point data or the entire body of work? Many people invest with the manager that looks great today, based on that data ending point, instead of the one who looks great over the course of its entire history. As you probably could have guessed by now, I would recommend choosing the entire body of work as the basis for your assessment rather than succumbing to the Endpoint Bias that results from looking at a brief snapshot in time.

If an investor were to choose one of these two money managers to invest with in early 2009, I certainly hope that he or she would have ignored the most recent data and invested with the terrible-looking manager from Figure 7-1. After all, 2008 was the worst year for fixed income since the Great Depression, and any manager with credit risk in its portfolio (see Chapters 5 and 6 for more detail) would have had terrible returns over that year. Investing in credit securities at the expense of an allocation to government bonds was an investment philosophy that had worked for years and years, but it was radically out of favor in early 2009. However, as Figure 7-3 demonstrates, it turns out that credit securities actually presented a fantastic opportunity.

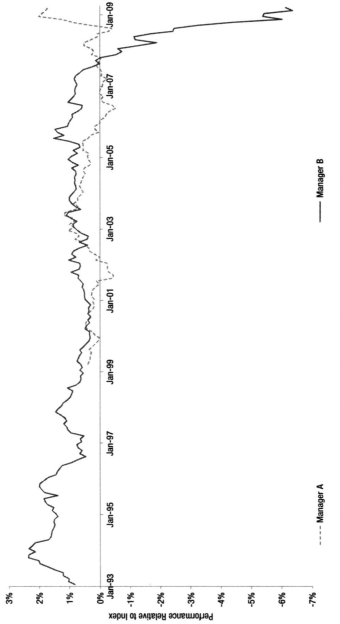

Figure 7-2. Rolling 3-Year Performance of Sample Managers Relative to Index Through 2008

*Data courtesy of eVestment Alliance

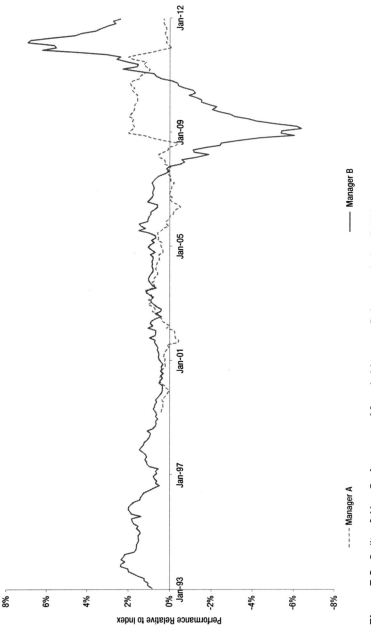

Figure 7-3. Rolling 3-Year Performance of Sample Managers Relative to Index, Full History

*Data courtesy of eVestment Alliance

As you can see in Figure 7-3, the underperforming manager from Figure 7-1 came roaring back from the bottom in 2008 to deliver phenomenal performance in 2010 and beyond. In contrast, the manager who looked good in early 2009 for the first time in its history returned to mediocrity in 2011. Although every advertisement for mutual funds on TV and in print always says that past performance is not a guarantee of future results, it certainly can be a rough indication of what possibilities the future might hold. In the example in Figure 7-3, a fund that had looked great for almost two decades hit a rough patch and then returned to greatness, whereas one that had never done much of anything briefly outperformed its peers and returned to obscurity.

How do you avoid the tendency to let yourself be governed by Endpoint Bias? After all, most individual investors do not have access to databases and charts. But guess what? Although they are fantastic for really getting into the weeds for analyzing returns, you don't need all those fancy tools for a quick approximation of this kind of review. All you need are three highlighters: green, yellow, and red. When you are interested in a fund, go to the fund's web site, the prospectus, or some general industry web site like Morningstar.com and find the fund's year-by-year performance versus the benchmark. Then, look at the results year by year, highlighting outperformance by the manager in green, underperformance in red, and a rough tie in yellow. Table 7-3 contains two hypothetical examples.

Table 7-3. Annual Performance of Two Hypothetical Funds

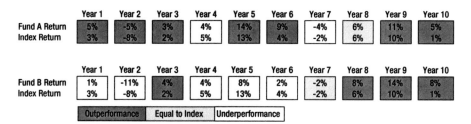

	Year 1	Year 2	Year 3	Year 4	Year 5	Year 6	Year 7	Year 8	Year 9	Year 10
Fund A Return	5%	-5%	3%	4%	14%	9%	-4%	6%	11%	5%
Index Return	3%	-8%	2%	5%	13%	4%	-2%	6%	10%	1%

	Year 1	Year 2	Year 3	Year 4	Year 5	Year 6	Year 7	Year 8	Year 9	Year 10
Fund B Return	1%	-11%	4%	4%	8%	2%	-2%	8%	14%	8%
Index Return	3%	-8%	2%	5%	13%	4%	-2%	6%	10%	1%

Outperformance	Equal to Index	Underperformance

As you can see, Fund B has much better endpoint results than Fund A does and has generated very solid results in the last three years of this series. According to this data, which would be easily accessible on the Internet, Fund B's outperformance during the last 3 years was better than the benchmark— and it was better by a greater magnitude than Fund A's outperformance. If you were making your decision based on the 3-year number as of Year 10, Fund B would be your selection. However, if I were choosing a fund to invest my retirement in, I would choose Fund A. Fund A outperformed by less than Fund B recently, granted, but it outperformed 70% of the time versus only 40% for Fund B. Maybe something has changed and Fund B is suddenly the best in the business, but I would rather rely on the long-term successful track record of Fund A for managing my assets.

Remember, you can't go back in time and buy last year's results. All you can do is identify funds with the higher long-term batting average and hope that the consistency of success persists.

Peer Comparisons

As I mentioned previously, it is very common to hear a television advertisement for a mutual fund company say something like, "80% of our funds beat the Lipper Peer Group Average for the last 5 years." When they say that, my mental response is always, "So what? The average fund isn't the only alternative to yours." Although I will explain at length the reasons for my disdain of peer comparisons later on in this chapter, I can make this advice really simple: ignore peer comparisons, especially when they do not include the index results.

A peer group comparison (see Figure 7-1 and Figure 7-4 for examples) is a database ranking of the returns of every available fund of a given type or in a specified asset class over certain periods in time, with the fund in question highlighted. Look back at Figure 7-1. The shaded boxes reflect the returns of every core bond fund in the industry lumped together into a demonstration of the size of the distribution, whereas the dots show how the two funds in the discussion and the index compared to that population. When someone says that a fund beat the peer group average, it means that the fund is in the top 50% of all the funds in its type. In this example, it means that the dot representing the fund's return would be higher than the median.

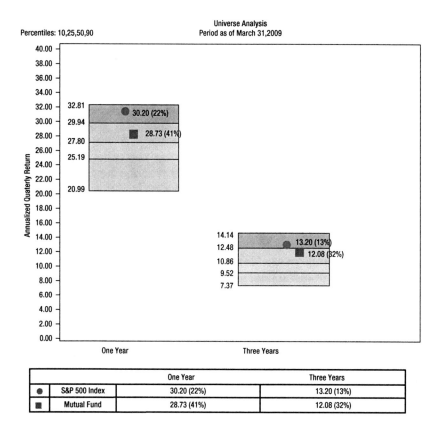

Figure 7-4. Sample Fund and Index With All Large Cap Core Mutual Funds
*Data courtesy of eVestment Alliance

Peer group comparisons, although interesting, have three major problems associated with them and should not be used as the sole basis for investment decision making. First, peer groups disseminated in the popular press or on the web are almost always generated as of a single point in time, resulting in the aforementioned Endpoint Bias. Second, the peer group isn't a homogenous universe of funds that have a similar construction, risk profile, or turnover level. Concentrated, high-risk, large capitalization core equity managers with 20 stocks are in the same peer group as large cap core enhanced index managers with 300 stocks. If a fund beats its peers because the portfolio manager took more risk and the market went up, what happens when the market goes down? The fact that the managers outperformed their peer group tells me absolutely nothing about *how* the manager outperformed their peers—or, more importantly, how much risk they took to generate those results. Third, and this is the most important point in my mind, what about the return for the index? An index fund or ETF is the real alternative to selecting a given actively managed fund. If no one can beat the index, why do I want to pay active management fees in the first place, no matter how good my selected fund looks compared to the other underperforming options?

Figure 7-4 is an example of a fund (the round dot) that outperformed its peer group median for two time periods, ranking in the top 41% of all funds for the prior year and the top 31% for the last 3 years. This is a perfect example of one of those funds that "outperformed the Lipper peer group median." The index, however, ranked in the top 21% for the last year and the top 13% for the last 3 years and ranked roughly 20 percentage points better than the supposedly superior fund did. Although it is nice that the fund did better than its peers, you could have been invested in an index fund that performed even better and paid a lot less money in expenses and fees.

This is why no pension plan takes peer comparisons for individual investment managers seriously as the sole basis for fund selection. The alternative to a given fund isn't the peer group; it's the index that investors can get virtually for free by investing in an index fund with a very low manager fee. When managers start saying in their commercials that their fund has outperformed both the Lipper Peer Group average and the index every year for the last 10 years, then I will start to consider making more use of peer comparisons. I need to know that the fund has consistently been a better choice than BOTH most other funds and the index fund over long periods of time to make it worthy of consideration for investment.

The Secret to Selecting Managers for your Money

Because peer comparisons and endpoint results are not good criteria for selecting managers, how should individual investors select them? I will give the same advice here as I did for how to build a successful, long-term asset allocation plan that works for you: consistency, consistency, consistency, consistency—consistent track record, consistent people, consistent philosophy, and consistent organization.

Consistency of Track Record

As outlined previously in this chapter, investors need to be aware of Endpoint Bias and focus on consistency. A manager that outperformed the benchmark in 10 of the last 12 years, with all else being equal, is a far better choice than a manager who has looked good only for the last 3 years. While history does not guarantee the future, the odds are far greater that an investment manager who has had relatively good results for a long time will have a better chance of future success than will one who has done fantastically well for just the last two years.

Consistency of People

Most mutual fund web sites will list the tenure of the portfolio manager and other key staff. This is incredibly important information because the track record of any investment product is 100% dependent on the people who built it. If a fund has a great 20-year history but everyone who built that history retired 2 years ago and the team is new, that fund really has a 2-year track record. Anything before that can be credited to someone else and should be ignored in your analysis.

Consistency of Philosophy

This one is the hardest to determine but also the least likely to change. If an organization has built its reputation around well-researched, diversified, risk-controlled stock portfolios and then shifts to a new line of products that offers highly concentrated portfolios with high turnover, look somewhere else to invest your money. When a manager's investment philosophy changes, their track record should be discarded. Anything prior to the new philosophy was generated in a different manner and has no bearing on the possible returns you might experience.

Consistency of Organization

There are generally two kinds of investment management companies in the world: dedicated firms and afterthoughts. Dedicated firms may be partnerships, publicly traded companies, family-owned companies, or part of a parent company. Regardless, they are alike in that they devote 100% of their time, energy, and resources to generating investment returns for their clients. Afterthoughts, on the other hand, is my nickname for investment management firms that comprise 1% of the income statement of a commercial bank, insurance company, or industrial conglomerate. In most cases, these firms do not control their own destiny and are frequently under pressure to deliver sales or revenue targets to their parent companies that have little to do with the market environment or the needs of their clients.

The organizations with which you should invest should demonstrate a long-standing and stable commitment to investment management and the resources needed to provide solid returns to their clients. All too often, the afterthought organizations are forced to reduce staff when the market gets tough to deliver financial results—which is exactly the time when more resources are needed to seek out opportunities in a difficult market.

Summary

An April 2012 white paper by Wilshire Consulting[5] detailed just how difficult it can be to find managers that outperform the benchmark year after year. Among large capitalization core equities managers, for example, only 15% of those managers who ranked in the top quartile for the three-year period between 2006 and 2008 remained in the top quartile for the subsequent three-year period between 2009 and 2011. If there was evidence that the best managers always rise to the top, we would expect to see half or more of those that had done well in the first survey remain among this top group in the second time period. A completely random distribution would result in 25% remaining in the top quartile from three-year period to three-year period. Instead, that 15% result demonstrates how incredibly difficult it can be to deliver top performance year after year because 85% of those that were able to rise to the top for one 3-year period were unable to stay in the group for the next period. This survey is conducted on an annual basis across a variety of asset classes, and while the results may vary slightly from year to year, they don't change very much. As such, it is highly unlikely that managers operating within any asset class (with the possible exception of asset classes like emerging markets stocks and high yield bonds, where the spread of information is considered to be very inefficient) to remain in the top group year after year after year.

Investors cannot expect to get perfect results every year. The process or investment philosophy that any particular money manager uses to select the companies in which it invests can very well come in and out of favor in different market environments. Periods of great performance can be followed by periods of poor performance, and the worst-performing managers in the industry can suddenly jump back to life when their style comes into favor and their results leap up the rankings table.

Consistent outperformance of the market is a difficult endeavor, and finding mutual fund managers that outperform the market every single year is not realistic. An investor looking to guarantee a long-term investment for a comfortable retirement should focus on selecting investment portfolios that have delivered above-benchmark performance for a long period of time in aggregate. When you do this, you will be well ahead of the game and should consider yourself a sound investor who has done your homework.

---

[5]"2011 Active Management Review," April 4, 2012, Wilshire Associates Incorporated.

Alternative Asset Classes

Going Beyond Stocks and Bonds

Alternative investments are generally the biggest differentiator between the asset allocation mixes of institutional investors, like pension plans or endowments, and individual investors. Whereas a major university endowment might have 50% or more of its portfolio invested with private equity managers or hedge funds, the average person normally does not have access to these kinds of investments in a typical 401(k) plan.

If you choose to invest in alternative asset classes, you are making an asset allocation decision. However, because your ability to invest in alternative asset classes is highly reliant on who you chose as an investment manager, you are also making an investment manager selection decision. As a result, I have highlighted both the Asset Allocation and Investment Manager Selection boxes in the recurring Road Map to Financial Success to help you visualize how to think about these investments.

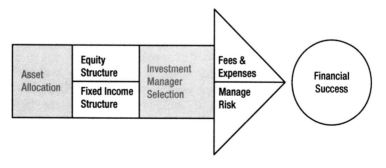

In this chapter, I cover what alternative investments are, if and how they should be included in your asset allocation plan, and how an individual investor can participate in these kinds of investments.

What Are "Alternatives"?

What are these "alternatives" anyway? Alternative investments is a broad label for pretty much any asset that is not a plain old stock or bond. Some people might have a broader or narrower definition of a few types of assets, and they may exclude real estate investment trusts (REITs) or commodities from the list of alternatives. For the sake of organization, however, I will include all of these types of alternative investments in this chapter to keep them all in one place.

Broadly speaking, alternatives can be lumped into four major categories:

1. Private equity, including leveraged buyouts, distressed debt, and venture capital

2. Real assets, including real estate, infrastructure, and, for the purposes of this book, REIT stocks

3. Hedge funds

4. Commodities

Many of these types of assets, including private equity, most real estate and infrastructure funds, and hedge funds, are available to investors by invitation only. These investments are typically structured as limited partnerships, as opposed to, say, publicly available mutual funds. As a result, they carry significant legal restrictions and typically require that an investor have a sufficiently high income or net worth before qualifying as an "accredited investor." Even those who do qualify as accredited investors still need to be allowed into the limited partnership by the general partner. Without fantastic personal connections, that is a high wall to breach by most people. In addition, most of these investments are created with a preplanned fund size in mind and are either explicitly capped in the partnership documents (private equity and real estate) or implicitly intended to be so by the portfolio manager (hedge funds). The general partners or portfolio managers for private equity partnerships, real estate funds, and hedge funds then control who is allowed to "subscribe" or "commit capital" to their funds.

As a result of these limitations of fund size and the requirement to be invited to invest, the most successful and desirable funds are simply unavailable to the vast majority of clients, regardless of who they are. A private equity firm like Kleiner Perkins, the original source of funding for many of Silicon Valley's most successful companies, has not added a major new partner since its first fund.

If the firm wanted to, it could open its doors to new clients and see immediate inflows of five times (maybe 100 times) as much money as it currently invests. Because the firm would have trouble finding places to invest that much money and could be unable to repeat their historical success rate, however, they limit the fund to a manageable size and select only the investors that they want to have as partners—those investors that have been there since the beginning. Many other top tier venture capital funds can tell a similar story—their success in the past and their desire to limit their funds to a manageable size makes it very difficult to gain access to this asset class. In many cases, new potential investors, if any were admitted, would need to prove to the general partner what benefit they bring to the table (advice, prestige, relationships) as a limited partner to displace some other long-term client. If your last name is Gates, Ellison, or Zuckerberg, you might have a chance of joining the party and investing in the next fund. For the rest of us, though, we would likely need to find some other way to gain exposure to these asset classes, such as investing with lower tier funds or trying to replicate the returns of the asset classes in other ways, as I will discuss later.

Over the last few years, a number of firms have begun to offer mutual funds that invest in some of these alternative investments. While these funds enable individual investors to indirectly invest in alternative assets, I have yet to see any information that indicates that these products perform much better than the asset class as a whole. In many cases, when you invest in these funds, you are essentially buying something like an index fund that captures the return of the asset class. Keep in mind, then, that your investment will not necessarily benefit from a tremendous amount of outperformance due to manager skill. For those considering investing in these types of funds to gain broader asset class exposure, I urge you to pay close attention to the analyses that follow, where I try to determine whether there is really anything to gain from achieving only the asset class median return in alternative assets.

Private Equity

While "equity" and "stock" investments are made up of portfolios of publicly traded securities that can be bought on a stock exchange through a broker, "private equity" is a catch-all term for investments in companies that are not publicly held. These types of investments come in three general flavors.

Leveraged Buyouts (LBOs)

LBOs, also known as just "buyouts" because "leverage" is thought to be a four-letter word by some, constitute more than 80% of the private equity industry. In this type of investment, a private equity fund (or a group of funds that pool their capital and work together) purchases a publicly traded company that is either underpriced or underperforming and in need of restructuring. Part of the money to pay for the purchase comes from the invested capital from clients in the fund(s), and part (usually most) comes from new debt issued to pay for the deal. As the company's balance sheet and income statement improve over time, cash flow from operations is used to pay off the debt bit by bit, making the remaining equity more valuable.

Let's say a company with a $3 billion market capitalization is having trouble. Its employees are unmotivated, its CEO is failing, its products need refreshing, and inventory is building up. On the plus side, it has a recognizable name brand in the consumer market and a huge number of great patents. Now let's say Buyout Fund XYZ looks at the company and sees its potential, so it announces an offer to buy all the stock in the company at a premium price of $4 billion to reduce resistance against selling by current stockholders. To raise the $4 billion, Buyout Fund XYZ takes $1.5 billion from the capital invested in the fund by clients and issues $2.5 billion in new debt. It then brings in a new management team, replaces the board, reinvests in product growth, and hopes for a turnaround.

Over the next few years, improving operations generate enough cash flow to pay down $1 billion of the debt, and the advice and industry network provided by the buyout firm helps the company come back to life. After a few years, Buyout Fund XYZ sells the company or reissues public stock in the amount of $7.5 billion, reflecting the tremendous improvement in the company's operations and potential. The investment of $1.5 billion in cash from the fund is now worth five times that initial amount. On the flip side, suppose the company does not make a dramatic turnaround. In this case, Buyout Fund XYZ shuts the company down; sells off its inventory, fixed assets, and patent portfolio for $2 billion; and defaults on the debt. For $1.5 billion invested, the fund gets back $2 billion. Some of that $2 billion might need to go to bondholders, but the buyout firms often structure the deals so that profits and management fees will flow to them throughout the restructuring and the debt has little recourse in the event of failure, resulting in a hefty profit even when the buyout doesn't work as planned.

Not a bad business model. It reminds me of the old "heads I win, tails you lose" game I played with my brother when he was 2. Although not quite every deal works out with a profit like I just outlined, win or lose, the success rate of private equity firms is awfully high. Protections for bond holders in the event of default have improved in recent years, and the fire sale of assets when a deal goes bad doesn't always cover costs. Overall, however, this isn't a bad business to be in if you like to buy houses that have an elevator for your cars.

Venture Capital (VC)

Venture capital is the type of investment that most people associate with the concept of private equity. Venture capital funds often serve a critical function in the life cycle of a company because they provide money to early or middle-stage companies in exchange for a share of the equity in the firm. This money often helps a new company move from the "idea phase" of its development cycle to the prototyping or launch phase. In addition, venture capital funds also typically provide other services to the companies in which they invest. Many funds, for example, connect the companies with seasoned executives to help them transition into maturity. Others may supply contacts with companies in affiliated industries with which they can work to grow their businesses and network. Some even offer to help the founders cash in on the value of their company by managing either the company's initial public offering or its outright sale to a strategic buyer.

Typically, venture capital funds focus on the technology, medical device, or telecommunications sectors; and the classic examples of companies that were assisted in their early growth populate the lists of the most successful start-ups of the last few decades. As a result, it should come as no surprise that Microsoft, Apple, Google, Facebook, Cisco Systems, Yahoo!, and Oracle—as well as high-profile failures like Pets.com, GeoCities, WebVan, and Kozmo—all received a substantial portion of their early funding from venture capitalists. However, venture capitalists aren't always spot-on with their investments; beyond those I just listed, there were a large number of late 1990s NASDAQ bubble companies that were backed by venture capital and yet ceased to exist by the time 2003 rolled around.

Despite the abundance of household-name companies that have been backed by venture capital, these types of funds generally make up 10% or less of the private equity market and, as mentioned above, are extremely difficult for new clients to invest in. After all, the team managing the venture capital fund doesn't want to invest in an endless number of companies because it will be unable to help each of them with their management strategies and business plans if its portfolio is spread too thinly. A typical number of investments by a venture capital fund might be 25 start-up companies, with an expected success rate far below that of the buyout firms. Of those 25 investments, venture capital funds typically hope that one or two might turn into wild successes, three to five will generate a moderate return, and fewer than the remaining 20 will muddle along unsuccessfully for years—or fail outright.

The investment a venture capital fund makes in any one company will be rather small, maybe $10 million to $50 million, because a new start-up isn't trying to build a massive factory or supply chain and usually doesn't need the billions of dollars that a candidate for investment by a buyout firm might require. Rather, it wants to either prove that a concept or product works in practice before selling it or launch a new service that requires money only for the first round of employees and computers. As a result, whereas a buyout fund might have a portfolio of multibillion equity positions in each of several companies, yielding a total fund size of $10 billion or more, a venture capital fund may invest an average of $20 million in 25 companies, requiring the fund to raise no more than $500 million—which it can easily do just by tapping its happy investors from prior funds.

Mezzanine and Distressed Investments

Mezzanine and distressed investments are often overlooked in the realm of private equity strategies. So, what does the process of investing in these two investment vehicles really look like? Let's start with mezzanine investments.

Mezzanine investors provide a middle step between venture capital funds and an initial public offering or sale of a company. Once a start-up, with the help of venture capital money, has proven that its product works and has lined up customers, it might need a large infusion of cash to ramp up production. However, given the still-young nature of the company, it might not be able to find a bank willing to give it a large loan, in which case a mezzanine fund will step in and provide a far larger amount of money than the venture capital fund did. The mezzanine fund will supply this money either as a high-interest loan or in exchange for equity in the company, and it will expect a return on the investment higher than the interest rate the bank would have charged on a similar loan to a more established company. The fund's expected return, however, will be far lower than that expected by a venture capital fund because the odds of failure are so much lower now than when the company was just getting started. As a result, the terms investors can demand from companies in need of capital may not be as generous as those that a venture capital fund can obtain.

Meanwhile, a distressed investment fund provides a similar kind of service to companies that a mezzanine fund does, but it works with a very different kind of company. A firm that has come on hard times—whether through mismanagement, competitive pressures, or a variety of other circumstances—but isn't a great candidate for a buyout fund may need a large infusion of cash to turn its operations around and get back on the right track. Maybe the company is largely held by a few stockholders and can resist the takeover efforts a buyout firm would mount, or perhaps the management team is key to all operations and vision and cannot be easily replaced. Whatever the case may be, like with the mezzanine fund, the distressed investor will provide cash in exchange for an equity stake or interest payments that again fall between what a bank would charge and what a venture capital fund hopes to earn.

The fraction of the private equity market that falls under the definition of these two kinds of funds tends to ebb and flow with the economic cycle and the boom and bust nature of some industries. However, distressed and mezzanine investors generally do not comprise more than 10% to 20% of the entire private equity opportunity set.

Why Do Pension Funds Invest in Private Equity?

When private equity investments work, they generate fantastic returns. Imagine being one of the first investors in Apple or Microsoft or Google. Estimates vary, but most economists and academic studies tend to show that private equity investing over a long period of time, like a complete economic cycle, should be expected to generate returns that are 3% to 5% better than the public stock market—and that is just on average. The best private equity investors return far better than that.

I have seen numerous studies from a variety of sources that show the "dispersion" between top and bottom investors in a variety of asset classes. One such chart is shown in Figure 8-1. In this chart, the performance of each investment manager in the entire population of similar managers in an asset class is plotted to show how large or small the distribution is for active managers' outperformance or underperformance relative to the index for that asset class. For core fixed income portfolios, for example, Figure 8-1 shows that the difference between bond managers in the 25th percentile and those in the 75th percentile (the width of the middle two of the four segments in the chart) might be 1% over a market cycle, a very tight spread of outcomes that indicates there are not large differences among them. For large cap core equity investors, that performance gap between good (25th percentile) and poor (75th percentile) has been around 8%, a wider spread that indicates that success at picking active managers can have a significant impact on returns, yet that performance difference will still likely be dwarfed by the broader returns of the public equity markets, which can often be up or down 20% in a year. For private equity investors, however, the gap between 25th and 75th percentiles has been far wider—around 15%—whereas the difference between the very best and the very worst private equity managers (the entire width of all four segments) is 45% per year, indicating that the impact of good or bad manager selection can often overwhelm the impacts of the market returns and can be the single largest driver of an investor's total return.

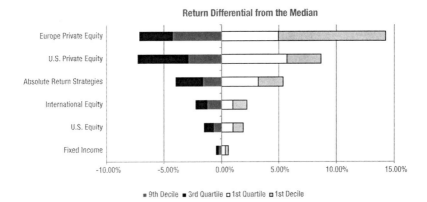

Figure 8-1. Dispersion Among Active Managers
*Data courtesy of Wilshire Private Markets (data through June 30, 2010)

Every client I have ever worked with that invests in private equity wants to be a "top quartile" investor and reap the superior returns shown by the best-performing funds in that far-right bar in Figure 8-1. Many clients even have that goal specifically delineated in their governing policy documents. Of course, only in Lake Wobegone can everyone be above average, and so three-quarters of all dollars invested in private equity will, by definition, miss that top quartile. Given the long-term, illiquid, and opaque nature of private equity investments, however, it can often be unclear how many investments really do miss this mark.

Private equity managers (and some clients) repeat the mantra of that top-quartile goal and will discuss at length the investments they have made that have generated great successes. Meanwhile, those investments that detract from overall performance will be dismissed as "early stage," having "potential," or "will generate improved returns as valuations warrant." No one ever wants to acknowledge that three out of four private equity funds will miss that top quartile and that almost half of all private equity investments will do about the same as, or worse than, public equities. If a fund invests in a company that generates a return of ten times the invested capital but loses money on every other investment, the fund as a whole will lose money. Still, the manager will trumpet the fact that they were an early investor in that successful company for the next decade. Such is the allure of the asset class, and the hope that every fund that invests in private equities can be among those top performers that new assets continue to flow into private equity year after year.

Simple math indicates that even those institutional and individual investors with real insight into which firms will outperform the rest of the pack will have trouble maintaining that "top quartile" status. According to private equity manager Preqin,[1] private equity funds have raised an average of a little less than $300 billion a year over the last few years. The "Top Quartile Funds," assuming you could identify them with precision, therefore have raised less than $75 billion a year. In the United States there are 134 state pension plans (some states have more than one) with more than $2.5 trillion in assets. If the average plan has a 10% allocation to private equity and spreads that investment over four years, those state plans are investing $62 billion per year, which amounts to virtually the entire top quartile of investments. Now add in the hundreds of billions of dollars poured into private equity funds by university endowments, very high net worth individuals, city and county pension plans, corporate pension plans, and foreign pools of money including sovereign wealth funds, and it is clear that the total of all the investments by sophisticated investors in private equity clearly overwhelms the opportunities presented by top quartile funds.

For investors who are not certain that they can obtain access to funds that are guaranteed to be in that mythical top quartile of great performers, or for those who lack the ability to qualify as an accredited investor for investment in any fund, the question remains whether the inability to invest in private equity as a whole will have a negative impact on performance versus those investors, like large pension plans and endowments, that are able to make such investments. In Figure 8-2, I show the performance of the entire buyout market against some stock indices that might be considered to be a proxy for this type of asset to determine if there is another way of gaining a similar return stream for those without access to the best private equity funds—or even to private equity funds in general.

---

[1] See various "Private Equity Quarterly Reports" sent to clients by Preqin over the last few years.

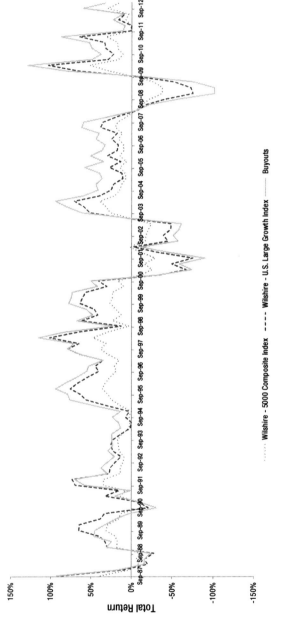

Figure 8-2. Rolling One-Year Performance of Buyout Funds and Stock Indices

*Data courtesy of Wilshire Associates and Venture Economics

When I produced Figure 8-2, I was shocked. The solid line in this chart combines on a capital-weighted basis the quarter-by-quarter results of a vast universe of buyout funds, culminating in more than $435 billion in assets by the final data point. On a rolling one-year basis, I've compared that performance history to the rolling one-year performance of the Wilshire 5000 stock index and the Wilshire Large Growth stock index. Because buyouts are a fairly new asset class and have a limited history, because they were created in the 1980s, the first few years of this chart do not tell us much. However, since the late 1990s, it is clear that the average investor in buyout funds is not getting what they pay for. The after-fee results track the two stock market indices closely enough that I consider this to be pretty clear evidence that the entire buyout industry as a whole may not produce any value above a passive stock index return. As Figure 8-1 showed, whereas there is a clear performance advantage to investing in top quartile funds, investors who are not able to access the top-performing funds may earn nothing more than the public equity returns.

Given that buyout funds charge huge fees for the results they produce, if you are getting average returns on your investments in these funds, you are far better off just skipping the asset class entirely and investing your money in public equities. Yes, everyone expects that private equity should have a return premium over public equities, and the top funds certainly have added value for those clients who have access to them, as was shown in Figure 8-1. However, as Figure 8-2 illustrates, the market for buyout funds as a whole looks just like the market for ordinary stocks. Furthermore, given both the huge spread between the performance of the 25th and 75th percentiles that was shown in Figure 8-1 and the fact that the average return looks like the stock market, anyone who is getting below-average results would be significantly better off investing in an index fund of publicly traded stocks.

This is not meant to be an indictment of private equity in general, or buyouts in particular, for the large institutional investors who pursue these opportunities. After all, they very well may have a chance of finding and investing in those top funds that have results far better than those shown in Figure 8-2, and the long-term results earned by many large pension plans and college endowments certainly indicate that there is value to be had in the best investments. However, for individual investors who cannot access those top buyout funds, and, at best, might be able to find their way into a second- or third-tier fund, the evidence that anything but the best investments in this asset class have merit is far less than compelling.

Figure 8-3 shows a similarly constructed four quarter, rolling return series for venture capital funds, which were comprised of a high of $145 billion in total assets a few years ago. I was as surprised by this chart as I was by the result in Figure 8-2, and I will draw the same conclusion here as I did for buyout funds: There is no discernible difference between the returns for the average venture capital fund and a public equity index (in this case, a small capitalization growth stock benchmark). Yes, the public benchmark is more volatile than the venture capital industry returns, but the good performing peak times for stocks are better and the long-term trends are very similar.

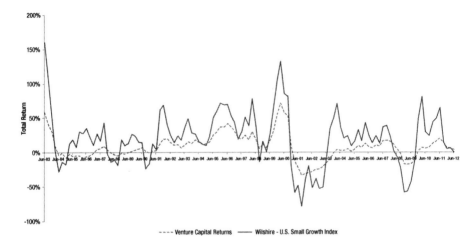

Figure 8-3. Rolling One-Year Performance of Venture Capital Funds and Stock Index
*Data courtesy of Wilshire Associates and Venture Economics

In Figure 8-4, I show the same return series for venture capital as compared to stock indexes for just the technology and telecommunications sectors. These sector-specific indices started in the early 1990s, so the chart is a bit truncated when compared to Figure 8-3.

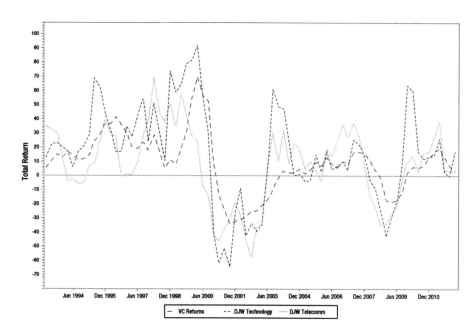

Figure 8-4. Rolling One-Year Performance of Venture Capital Funds Versus
Telecommunications and Technology Sectors
*Data courtesy of Wilshire Associates and Venture Economics

These sector exposures, which are widely available in index funds, ETFs, or
actively managed sector mutual funds, track the venture capital industry-wide
return data as well as, or maybe even a little better than, the small cap growth
index. As was the case with buyout funds, if you cannot find your way into
one of the most sought-after venture capital funds, it appears that there is no
reason to go with the second best, as it is doubtful that you will get anything
better than just a public stock market return.

Most economists and consulting firms estimate that the private equity industry on average should return somewhere in the neighborhood of 3% to 5%
above public equities, but the previous charts show some pretty convincing
evidence that the average fund has not delivered results anywhere near that
level for more than a decade. Although there are certainly some very high-
profile college endowments and public pension plans that make large investments into private equity and then tout their superior results in the press,
there are plenty who have also stuck a toe in the water and been disappointed
with the results.

In short, whereas the average investor cannot get broad access to the same
set of opportunities that the largest public pension plans can and may find
himself or herself unable to invest in a variety of private equity funds, this
might not be a bad thing because the returns of the private equity industry

as a whole do not appear to deliver the consistent added value above public stocks that should be expected. Instead, individual investors can save money and find far lower fee alternatives to these highly illiquid asset classes without negatively impacting their results.

To be clear, this does not mean that no one should invest in buyouts, venture capital, or any other form of private equity. There certainly are plenty of examples of investors who have achieved tremendous success in these asset classes. Rather, the evidence indicates that whereas the best funds have generated fantastic returns for their clients, the entire industry as a whole has not performed much better than the public stock market. Pension plans, college endowments, and high net worth individuals who can obtain access to the best funds may find continued success in this asset class. For those of us who lack such access, however, the returns on the whole do not seem to be any better than stock investments.

Real Estate

Of the alternative assets discussed in this chapter, real estate is undoubtedly the easiest to explain and understand because we see it every day. Investible real estate, at least from the perspective of institutional investors, generally includes commercial office buildings, industrial factories and warehouses, "multifamily" apartment buildings, student housing, assisted-living facilities, retail locations (like malls), and self-storage warehouses. Although raw land can occasionally find its way into a real estate fund, individual residential properties (houses) generally do not.

As a result, an investment into a real estate fund in your portfolio likely will have very little overlap with the real estate you already own, such as your primary residence or a vacation property. While both of these residential properties would fall under the broader definition of "real estate," their growth in value and any potential income you may generate from them is driven by somewhat different economic factors than the types of commercial real estate just outlined.

The types of real estate in which pension plans invest can be further broken down into three categories based on expected return and risk: core, value-added, and opportunistic.

1. Core real estate investments are fully leased, steady-as-she-goes properties that are managed for cash flow and minimal capital gains.

2. Value-added real estate includes properties that are underleased, require some moderate decorative work, or need a change in the marketing or management plan to get back on track.

3. Opportunistic real estate contains raw land under development, existing properties in need of a major remodel, or properties that will be demolished and rebuilt.

Moving across the spectrum from core to value-added to opportunistic, the potential for returns increases with the opportunities that the property presents—but so does the risk. As a result, pension plans tend to view each of these types of real estate as having a very different rationale for inclusion in the asset allocation. In fact, they often will treat each of these categories as its own distinct asset class, identifying a fraction of total assets that should be invested in each of the three types of real estate, just as they would assign a target allocation of, say, 35% of total assets to stocks or bonds.

From an asset allocation perspective, core and lower-risk, value-added properties are typically viewed as replacements for some fixed income investments and can often generate higher yields than fixed income with moderately more risk. Although these types of properties experience some mild ups and downs as the business cycle runs its course, office buildings, retail space, and the like tend to have fairly steady returns over time because the property manager's main job is to keep tenants happy, keep the building full of tenants, and pass on the rental income to the investors.

Higher-risk, value-added investments and all opportunistic investments, on the other hand, are more like equity investments, especially private equity. Some investments will succeed fantastically well, and some will fail. On average, the ongoing need for the creation of more real estate over time to match the growing economy and population should be a driver of returns. However, any given property could be mismanaged, overleveraged, or poorly developed. Condominium development in the mid-2000s in South Florida and Las Vegas are two great examples of opportunistic investments that yielded tremendous returns for several years before facing a significant and extended downturn when demand for such properties diminished.

To gain exposure to all three types of real estate investments, public pension plans and other institutional investors typically will invest in both limited partnership real estate funds, which pose all the same limitations for individual investors that private equity limited partnerships do, and real estate investment trust (REIT) stocks. REITs are publicly traded companies that invest solely in real estate properties, typically through the use of a buy-and-hold strategy. Because they are publicly traded, a wide variety of individual REIT stocks, REIT index ETFs, and REIT mutual funds, both indexed and actively managed, are available to individual investors. Many companies that are not legally defined as REITs[2] yet still have significant real estate industry exposure, like property developers, hotel managers, and construction companies, are also available for investment. As a result, although individual investors may not be able to invest in some manager's latest limited partnership that is only open to a handful of special clients, they can certainly gain exposure to the industry as a whole and benefit from the asset allocation benefits of investment in an asset class that is driven by different macroeconomic factors than regular stocks and bonds.

Because REITs are publicly traded securities and are subject to many of the short-term whims of the stock market, the returns of any given REIT fund will be more volatile than those of privately held real estate investments. Therefore, it is appropriate to compare their performance relative to the underlying properties over a very long-term horizon to smooth out short-term market fluctuations.

In Figure 8-5, I have compared the returns of the Wilshire Real Estate Securities Index to the NCREIF National Property Index (which tracks the value of the underlying properties contained in all the real estate benchmarks) and the NCREIF ODCE Index (which tracks the aggregate returns of more than a dozen of the largest real estate investment partnerships). Given that REIT stocks are valued every second by the stock market while the underlying properties in real estate indices or funds are appraised about once a year, the two NCREIF indices look much "smoother" than the REIT index in Figure 8-5. However, over the time horizon of a long-term investor, they all demonstrate the same general trends, ebbing and flowing in value with the overall economy and real estate market. This leads me to conclude that an individual investor who is not part of a multibillion limited partnership real estate fund can actually gain exposure that is relatively similar to that of the private real estate market over long periods of time using REITs.

---

[2]To become a REIT, there are some legal tests that a company must pass, including distributing 90% or more of its income in the form of dividends. Some real estate companies may not pass this rule and therefore will not technically be considered REITs. However, most real estate mutual funds will invest in anything that is "close enough," including companies in the real estate industry that may not legally be considered REITs but are real estate businesses in every other sense.

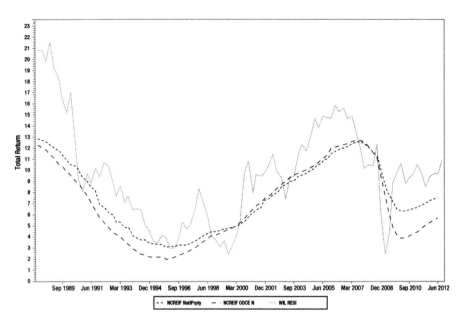

Figure 8-5. Comparison of Long-Term Returns for REITs and Private Real Estate Limited Partnerships

Why Invest in REITs?

At the present time, many asset managers, economists, bankers, and investment consulting firms expect stocks to return between 7% and 9% and bonds to return around 3% to 4% on average over the next several years. As a result, a 70% stocks, 30% bonds portfolio should therefore earn in the range of around 6% per year. Meanwhile, the consensus view is that core real estate funds and REITs should return 5% to 6% in the same market environment. This means that if you were to change your asset allocation from 70% stocks, 30% bonds to 65% stocks, 25% bonds, and 10% REITs, your expected return would still be around 6%—but you would now be diversifying your risk across three asset classes instead of two.

In Chapter 2, I introduced three hypothetical investors who committed to three different asset allocations over time. In Table 8-1, I take a look again at the returns that Bob, one of the investors from that section, would have earned under his prior plan (80% US stocks, 20% bonds) versus what he would have earned with a more diversified portfolio (75% US stocks, 15% bonds, 10% REITs).

Table 8-1 shows that Bob's portfolio would have experienced worse per-formance with REITs than without them in 2007 and 2008, given that these were down years for real estate. However, every other year that saw a total return of less than 7% would have experienced improved results with REITs in the portfolio, not to mention a moderately better total return over the entire period. As such, Table 8-1 is a clear demonstration of the value of diversification.

Table 8-1. Impact of REITs on Asset Allocation

	DJ Wilshire 5000 Index	Barclays Aggregate Bond Index	Wilshire Real Estate Securities Index	Bob	Bob with REITs
1991	34.20	16.01	20.03	30.56	30.05
1992	8.97	7.41	7.4	8.66	8.58
1993	11.29	9.76	15.23	10.98	11.45
1994	-0.07	-2.92	1.64	-0.64	-0.33
1995	36.46	18.47	13.65	32.86	31.48
1996	21.22	3.62	36.89	17.70	20.15
1997	31.30	9.68	19.76	26.98	26.90
1998	23.43	8.68	-17.43	20.48	17.13
1999	23.56	-0.83	-3.17	18.68	17.23
2000	-10.89	11.63	30.7	-6.39	-3.35
2001	-10.96	8.44	10.45	-7.08	-5.91
2002	-20.86	10.27	2.66	-14.63	-13.84
2003	31.63	4.11	37.08	26.13	28.05
2004	12.48	4.34	34.83	10.85	13.49
2005	6.38	2.43	13.82	5.59	6.53
2006	15.77	4.33	35.67	13.48	16.04
2007	5.62	6.96	-17.66	5.89	3.49
2008	-37.23	5.24	-39.83	-28.74	-31.12
2009	28.30	5.93	29.2	23.83	25.03
2010	17.16	6.54	29.12	15.04	16.76
2011	0.98	7.84	8.56	2.35	2.77
2012	0.00	0.00	0.00	0.00	0.00
Average Annual Return	8.65%	6.61%	10.24%	8.55%	8.88%

Hedge Funds

Hedge funds have gotten a tremendous amount of press in the past decade but remain one of most poorly defined categories of investments. Just as "modes of transportation" is a very broad term that can include both a Boeing 747 and a kid's tricycle, so too can hedge funds include funds that invest in stocks, bonds, emerging markets, and currencies. In addition, hedge fund portfolio managers can use any number of tools that are simply not available to the regular mutual fund manager.

Because hedge funds invest in assets that are available to other types of investment vehicles (mainly stocks and bonds), by most definitions and industry consensus, they are not considered to be a unique asset class. However, in my opinion, given that hedge fund managers can invest in ways that are not available to other investment managers, they should be given separate and distinct consideration from other asset classes in an asset allocation plan. Furthermore, the returns from hedge funds can be sufficiently different from the stocks and bonds in which they invest that they warrant a separate discussion and allocation within the asset allocation process, even if they are investing in underlying assets that you might already hold through more conventional portfolios.

Before diving into the merits of hedge fund investing, there are five terms that are important to understanding how hedge fund managers invest differently than other asset classes: shorting, leverage, multi-asset classes, strategy consistency, and portfolio concentrations.

Shorting

The most basic difference between hedge funds and mutual funds is the ability of hedge fund managers to "short" securities. To short a security, the hedge fund manager will borrow the security from the portfolio of an index fund or some other large investor via an investment bank, paying a specified rate of interest for the loan. The hedge fund manager will then sell the security on the market, hoping that the price will fall over time and he or she can buy it back at a cheaper price to replace the borrowed shares while earning a capital gain. If the price rises, the hedge fund will suffer a loss when it buys back the shares it borrowed and sold at that higher price, but will make money if the stock falls before it buys it back and returns it to the party from which it was borrowed. A "short" can either be a position expressing a view that a single company is overpriced and will fall in value, or it can be done as part of a paired trade, a strategy I will discuss following in the section that details the main types of hedge funds.

Leverage

If you give a mutual fund $1,000, the portfolio manager will buy $1,000 worth of stocks, maybe minus some small amount of cash the manager holds on hand. If you give a hedge fund $1,000, the fund could set up positions worth $2,000, $3,000, or even more. These positions could be highly directional, meaning that you are 200% or 300% exposed to the equity market. On the other hand, they could be offset, with 100% bought long and 100% sold short market exposure, resulting in no directional bias and returns based solely on the manager's skill in picking securities to buy and sell.

Multi-Asset Class

When you invest in a stock mutual fund, the manager mostly buys stocks. When you invest in a bond mutual fund, the manager mostly buys bonds. In a hedge fund, some managers might have positions in stocks, bonds, currencies, and commodities, short and long, all at the same time.

Strategy Consistency

Although most hedge fund managers adhere to a stated investment philosophy, many managers are opportunistic and change direction and strategies as events warrant. Whereas this can be positive for your portfolio because the manager can respond to market events, it can also be negative because you never have a perfectly clear idea of exactly what some managers are doing, resulting in unwanted biases and risks at your total portfolio level.

Portfolio Concentration

Whereas a public stock manager might hold 75 to 200 positions and a bond manager might hold hundreds or even thousands of securities at once, some hedge funds might have only a few high-conviction positions at any given time. Because hedge fund managers are generally compensated predominantly for portfolio performance, instead of in accordance with an annual percentage of an asset's base fee, they are generally not afraid to take on disproportionate levels of risk when they feel it is appropriate to do so.

Hedge funds can use the five tools outlined previously (and others) to take many forms; a few of the most common types of hedge funds are listed following. This list is not intended to be exhaustive, as there are at least 14 distinct types of hedge funds, and more are being created all the time. Rather, the following is an indicative list of the types of strategies in which you might invest if you choose to add hedge funds to your portfolio.

Macroeconomic

For many people, investors like George Soros, who strides the world for opportunities and once forced the Bank of England to devalue the British Pound, are the first thing that come to mind when they think of hedge funds. Although the hedge fund world has moved away from a reliance on macroeconomic funds over the last 20 years toward more stock- and bond-focused strategies, the quintessential hedge fund strategy is still to invest anywhere and in any asset, using leverage and large positions to move markets and generate a profit.

Long/Short

Let's say that a manager has no interest in positioning a portfolio for a rising or falling stock market over the next year but has a strong conviction that GM will experience better returns than Ford. In this case, the hedge fund will buy 100 shares of GM and sell short 100 shares of Ford. If the market goes up 20% over the next year, both stocks will likely have returns in that same ballpark, generating no market return for the manager. However, if GM goes up 22% in that bull market and Ford only rises 18%, the manager will make roughly a 4% profit on the difference between the two stocks' prices completely independent of the movement of the overall stock market. A portfolio of long and short positions across a variety of industries or countries, therefore, generates returns based on the manager's skill at picking companies to buy and sell while remaining agnostic on the market as a whole.

Merger Arbitrage

Let's say that Company A announces that it is acquiring Company B for $50 a share, which was trading for $40 a share at the time of the announcement. Between the time that the merger is announced and the time that the transaction is concluded, shareowners of both companies will need to approve the transaction, government regulators will weigh in regarding whether the combined company violates antitrust laws, and other suitors could offer higher bids for the company that is being acquired. As a result, the stock of Company B may only trade at $45 or $47 a share until all these concerns are resolved, despite the offer price of $50 a share, because investors are not convinced that this transaction will actually be finalized. A merger arbitrage manager will weigh the pros and cons of the merger and assess the likelihood that the merger will be concluded. Then, if that assessment is positive, the manager will take a position that allows them to earn that remaining $3 or $5 premium below the transaction price if the merger succeeds. On the other hand, if they think the merger is doomed to fail, they will take a position that will profit from the corresponding movement in stock prices after the merger is called off—when the prices of the buying company and target company return to their preannouncement levels.

Index Arbitrage/Statistical Arbitrage

This type of fund exists in many varieties, but the commonality among all of them is that they take advantage of small and temporary mispricings in the market. One example would be a stock that trades in New York and Paris. At any given instant, the share price in New York and Paris, after accounting for currency, could be different by a very small amount. If a manager could buy the stock in one location, sell it in the other, and buy or sell Euros for US Dollars as needed, they could lock in a small profit. Maybe the trade generated a fraction of a penny a share, but it only took milliseconds to execute with very little risk. If the manager could do that 1,000 times a day across a wide variety of securities and markets, the results could add up to a significant return.

Convertible Arbitrage

Convertible bonds are fixed income securities that can be exchanged for shares of stock in the underlying company at certain prices under certain conditions. A hedge fund might buy or sell the stocks or bonds of these companies to take advantage of the mathematics behind the price relationship between these two connected securities.

Fixed Income

If AAA-rated corporate bonds rarely default but are priced to yield 0.75% more than similar maturity treasury bonds, why not buy the corporate bonds and sell short the treasuries to lock in that 0.75% return, less any cost of financing? Although a net return of 0.25% or 0.50% may not sound like much, if you can leverage that up high enough, it starts to generate a significant return. Long Term Capital Management, prior to its collapse in 1998, was leveraging this trade hundreds of times and generating fantastic results for its clients right up to the point that it collapsed.

Capital Structure Arbitrage

Many companies that issue debt do it in a variety of tiers. Some bonds may have a higher or lower preference in the event of bankruptcy or a higher or lower priority for interest payments. As a result, these bonds, although they are issued by the same company, will trade at different yields to reflect their relative likelihood of being impacted by a default. A hedge fund can invest in one tier and short another, capitalizing on the spread between them if the manager believes that the default premium for the lower-rated tier is overpriced.

Short-Biased Equities

Some people are just pessimists. Short-biased managers are the muckrakers of the hedge fund world, trying to uncover every bit of sordid news about a company, its management, and the skeletons in its closet that they can find. Then, when they discover a company that they think is doomed for a comeuppance, they take a short position and spread the word, telling the press, online message boards, their peers, regulators, and anyone else they can think of.

If the truth comes out and is as bad as they hoped, the price of the company's stock will fall dramatically, delivering great returns for those who were short that stock.

Generally Anything Else that Doesn't Want to Be Constrained and Can Charge a High Fee

Yes, this is a catch-all category and includes leveraged emerging markets managers, opportunistic investors, and quasi-private equity investors that will buy private investments in public companies. In some cases, it can even include hedge funds that buy a large stake in a company, pressure management to make some change in strategy, personnel, capital structure, etc., and then hope to profit from the improvement in the share price. If someone can think up a new strategy, charge a big fee for it, and find investors who are willing to invest in it, it is probably a hedge fund.

As you can see, there are a wide variety of hedge funds that share few commonalities—except maybe consistently higher fees, leverage, and risk concentration than those normally found in more traditional investments, like single asset class mutual funds. Hedge funds, as this list makes clear, really can encompass any manager who doesn't invest in just plain old stocks and bonds.

Do Hedge Funds Generate Returns That Are Commensurate with Their Fees and Risk?

For years, hedge funds have promised to the pension fund and endowment community that they will generate "stock-like returns with bond-like risk." I heard those words in sales pitches and presentations to my clients by managers more times than I care to count. Hedge funds have promised for years to be an "all-weather" strategy to the pension fund and endowment community, claiming to be agnostic to the direction of the markets and capable of generating returns in all environments. In reality, though, the truth was not quite so rosy. In 2008, when stocks fell 40% or more, measures of the broad hedge fund universe were down about 20%—which was better than the market as a whole but terrible for an investment that promised returns without directional market exposure. Although the value of the average hedge fund has since recovered, the damage done to the industry in the eye of many of my clients is immeasurable. Many of them are asking the same question that you should as you consider including them in your portfolio: Are they simply a high-fee way of getting limited market exposure, or do they really offer a unique source of returns, investment manager skill, and value?

In Figure 8-6, the solid line represents the rolling one-year return for the Credit Suisse Dow Jones Hedge Fund Index. The dashed line is a 50/50 blend of the MSCI World (stock) Index and the Barclays Aggregate (bond) Index. Although the two lines were fairly divergent prior to about 2000, they have basically experienced the same results ever since. What this means is that over the last 10 years, hedge funds on the whole have devolved from an asset class with a unique and diversifying return and risk stream into simply a high-cost way of constructing a 50/50 stock and bond portfolio, where everyone with a Bloomberg terminal can call themselves a hedge fund and make a fortune. For the math wizards reading this book, the correlation between these two series has averaged 0.79[3] since mid-2003, which is an indication that there is far less diversification between hedge funds in general and simple stock and bond exposure than the industry would lead you to believe.

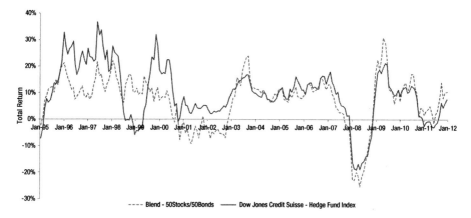

Figure 8-6. Performance of Hedge Fund Industry Versus 50% Stocks/50% Bonds Passive Portfolio
*Data courtesy of Dow Jones Credit Suisse Indices, MSCI, and Barclays Indices

As was the case with private equity earlier in this chapter, I firmly believe that some hedge funds are capable of generating unique sources of return through unique investment strategies and tools as well as through the expertise of the large number of great investors who have left institutional asset managers or investment banks over the years to start their own companies. The analysis previously, therefore, does not discount the case for all hedge funds from investment. As was the case with private equity and real estate, it is entirely possible that large institutional investors may be able to find a few hedge funds that will have superior returns relative to the population as a whole and invest in them, generating returns far better than the chart preceding shows.

---

[3]Correlations based on monthly observations.

For an individual investor, though, broad exposure to the entire industry of hedge funds through some of the nascent hedge fund mutual fund and ETF structures may not add much real value to your portfolio, especially when the extremely high fees of hedge funds are considered.

Commodities

It can be difficult to watch 30 minutes of cable news without seeing at least a few advertisements for investments in gold. Although gold, and many other commodities, is often discussed as a store of value in times of crisis or a protection against inflation, investors need to carefully consider the nature of, and problems with, commodities investments before investing their money in them. Some pension plans invest in commodities to hedge against inflation, although a clear link between commodities prices and inflation is dubious, as shown in the chart following. Others will include commodities trading strategies within hedge fund portfolios because there can be gains to be made by skilled investors trading in commodities, just as there was in stocks and bonds.

Figure 8-7 compares the rolling three-year returns of the GSCI Commodities Index against the US Consumer Price Index (CPI). If you can see a clear pattern, please let me know. The commodities index has been far more volatile than CPI and does not appear to track it in the slightest.

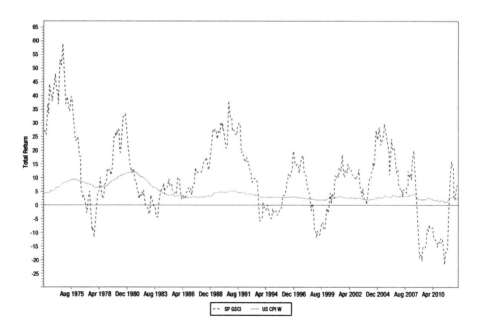

Figure 8-7. Rolling Three-Year Performance of Commodities Index and Inflation
*Data courtesy of Standard and Poors and the Bureau of Labor Statistics

In the pension industry, the common view is that commodities generally are not an appropriate asset for long-term investors to buy and hold like one would with an index fund of stocks or bonds. A government bond pays interest over the time that you hold it. A share of stock may fluctuate in price as much as commodities, but over time the company may pay cash dividends and grow in total value due to operating success. A bar of gold, a barge full of copper, or a barrel of oil, meanwhile, pays no interest or dividends and generates no economic activity on its own. The value of that investment from one day to the next fluctuates not as a result of the cash yield or reward to the investor but rather as a sole result of what someone else is willing to pay for it. Some commodities, like wheat, cocoa, soybeans, pork bellies, and even oil, can actually decline in value over time due to the fact that food products rot and oil can turn into tar, supporting the case that a buy-and-hold strategy may not be appropriate over the long term.

There is a stronger argument in favor of investing in commodities as part of a hedge fund portfolio, though. As you can see in Figure 8-7, the prices of commodities have been volatile over time, and there is nothing that traders like more than volatility because it presents opportunities for profits. Whether a hedge fund is trading short-term stock movements, currency fluctuations, bond yields, or commodities prices really doesn't matter to the hedge fund. Trading is trading, and short-term profits are all good. After all, the more volatile the price of an asset is, the more opportunity there could be to find a profit in trading it.

In my opinion, individual investors are best served by staying away from commodities as long-term investments. If you are really concerned about inflation, there are investments like Treasury Inflation Protected Securities (TIPS), which are Treasury bonds whose principal and coupons are linked directly to inflation and therefore make a much better inflation hedge. Trading in commodities should be reserved for individuals or funds that wish to speculate solely on short-term movements.

Fees

Although alternative investments are very different from one another in practice and in results, they do have one thing in common that investors should be aware of: fees.

I will go into great detail on fees in Chapter 9, but here is a quick summary. Hedge funds, private equity funds, and private real estate funds all charge fees that are far higher than other types of investments. (Commodities investments can be made through high-cost hedge funds or through moderate-cost index funds.) All of these active managers typically charge a base fee of 1% to 3% plus a share, typically 10% to 30%, of the profits. For a hedge fund, for example, that charges the industry standard 2% base fee and 20%

performance fee, a 7% pre-fee return on the portfolio yields clients a net return after fees of 3.6%.[4] In contrast, a 7% pre-fee return on a stock port-folio will generate net returns of 6% to 6.5% for actively managed portfolios and about 6.95% for index funds. If you invest with a "fund of hedge funds," an investment manager that finds hedge funds for you and builds you a portfolio of hedge fund investments, bears all the cost of managing the portfolio, and conducts all due diligence on the underlying hedge funds in which your money is invested, you will often be charged 0.5% to 2.5% more in fees, plus another 10% of the performance. That 3.6% net return on just the hedge fund invest-ments could be very close to zero for you when all the fees from the fund of funds are taken into account.

I periodically meet with hedge funds in places as diverse as Switzerland, the United Kingdom, Hong Kong, and Singapore, and the results of these econom-ics are obvious. While pension plans struggle to improve their returns and decrease the burden they impose on the taxpayers, it is difficult in hedge fund meccas like Geneva, Switzerland and Greenwich, Connecticut to walk 25 feet without tripping over a Ferrari or passing a store selling $20,000 watches. The amount of wealth that is created by using money from others to generate 7% returns and then pocketing the vast majority of it as fees is overwhelming. It also illustrates quite clearly why there is so little profit left for clients that their net returns basically track the public markets, as shown in Figure 8-6. The 100-foot yachts parked in the harbors of Stamford, Connecticut, are no different and are often purchased with wealth generated by incredible fees on private equity funds, which return on average to investors the same amount that the stock market does, as shown in Figure 8-2 and Figure 8-3, or worse.

Again, although there are a handful of excellent managers who can generate superior returns for clients, my experience with the vast majority of these types of funds is that the fees charged are not proportionate to the real value created for clients. Over the last few years, even as returns have gotten worse, fees in alternative investments have remained constant or have even gone up, especially among hedge fund managers. Clients have seen their disappointing results and tried to move into funds that they think will do better than their current portfolio is doing, putting tremendous upward pressure on the top funds. This, in turn, tends to shift the pricing of the entire industry upward, despite the dubious evidence that the hedge fund industry in total adds any net value in the first place. Some efforts have been made to shift the balance between base fees and performance fees more toward performance fees to reward only superior performance. However, in an industry where demand far outstrips supply, the ability of discerning investors to change the pricing marketplace is scarce.

---

[4]$7\% - 2\% - (20\% \times 7\%) = 3.6\%$

Summary

Does the average investor need any of these?

The inclusion of alternative investments tends to be the single biggest differentiator between the total portfolios of large pension plans and endowments and those of individual investors. In the right markets, they have added tremendous value, but in the wrong markets they have magnified pension plan losses. Does the individual really need exposure to these asset classes to compete, or is he or she better off replicating what can be replicated and ignoring the rest?

The evidence in this chapter seems to illustrate very clearly to me that the excess returns generated by some alternative investments might be a thing of the past. Although there are still some fantastic private equity funds and hedge funds out there, the average fund is no longer as enticing as it once was. In both industries, fund sizes have grown and grown to the point where the portfolio managers are often working more to protect their base management fees than to maximize their incentive (performance) fees. In this new reality, 2% of a few billion dollars produces a lot more income for the portfolio manager than 2% of the far smaller fund sizes from a decade ago.

The continuous flow of new talent into the hedge fund industry from proprietary trading desks at investment banks or concentrated investment managers complicates this issue because many investors are willing to pay the newest hedge fund managers any price to join the industry. Quite often, however, the driver of the returns these traders generated when they were at an investment bank was not their own brilliance. Rather, it was their ability to access information flows and resources that the bank provided to them as employees—advantages that they are no longer privy to now that they are on their own.

Real estate, despite the debacle of the 2008–2011 period, seems to be the only place where individual investors can still improve their overall outcomes through the diversification that another asset class can add to their portfolios. Whereas large pension plans often generate their exposure to this asset class through investments in limited partnerships that are unavailable to the average person, the preceding evidence shows that publicly available REIT securities are a reasonable proxy for the private real estate investment industry over very long periods of time. Given that REITs (and the broader real estate-related companies sector) are available in ETFs, index funds, and actively managed mutual funds, there are plenty of ways in which the individual investor can add exposure to real estate in both a higher- and lower-risk manner.

No matter which course you choose, to invest in alternatives or to remain focused just on plain vanilla public securities, bear in mind that although alternatives have helped to improve the returns of large investors like endowments and public pension plans for years, the vast majority of the returns that large pensions have generated have come from stocks and bonds. Private equities, real estate, commodities, and hedge funds usually constitute less than 25% of all of an institutional fund's assets. In many cases, pension plans have used logic similar to what I have outlined in this chapter to decide against investing in most or all of the alternative investments, yet their results have not suffered irreparable harm. Given the lack of access to these types of investments by individual investors, their high fees, their lack of liquidity and transparency, and their sheer complexity, you may be very well served by simply devoting your energy to increasing your savings rate, reviewing your asset allocation more frequently, or increasing the amount of time you devote to researching public securities funds.

Fees and Expenses

Reducing the Inevitable Drain on Assets

Now that your asset allocation and investment structures have been set up to generate the best return/risk trade-off, and you have selected a lineup of investment managers and funds to help you generate the best outperformance possible, now it is time, as the Road Map to Financial Success graphic implies, to make sure that you are getting what you pay for. Fees and expenses are the only certainty in your investment portfolio—they will drive your returns and assets down. Although there are some expenses that are worth paying, especially if they can generate a higher rate of return, it is important that investors understand just how impactful even small differences in fees can be over the time span of a career and retirement.

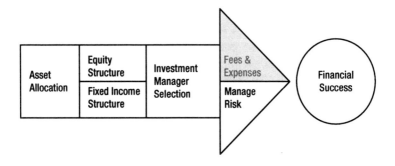

Seeking to minimize these costs wherever possible is the most surefire way to send positive results right to your bottom line. Ben Franklin's famous saying "a penny saved is a penny earned" was never more true than when it comes to the costs of managing your retirement portfolio. Every penny you do not pay out to a broker, bank, or mutual fund is one more penny, plus interest, you will be able to call on some day. I have often been told that the greatest benefit that my profession (investment consulting) brings to large pension systems, endowments, and foundations is our hardnosed attitude toward fees and unnecessary risks, some of which were covered in my discussion of investment structures and alternative investments. In this chapter, my focus will be on the potential cost-related risks and alarm bells that you will want to look out for to make sure the majority of your investment dollars are used to make you, and not your financial planner, richer.

I'll start with a personal example to show how intelligent people can make unknowing mistakes when it comes to fees and expenses.

When I was growing up, my parents invested $10,000 in a college savings account for my younger brother and me. At the time, brokerage commissions were generally fixed and were very expensive in comparison to the low-fee and no-fee brokers that pervade the market today. There was no CNN, CNBC, or Fox Business yet; Michael Bloomberg was still an employee at Salomon Brothers; and the *Wall Street Journal* was predominantly read by people who rode subways to work in lower Manhattan. In short, the amount of information readily available to the average investor was very limited.

My parents checked around with some friends, and the name of a financial planner was suggested. After a meeting or two with him, the planner suggested that they invest all of the money in our college savings account in one single large cap growth fund. It was a relatively new fund, but it came from a well-known mutual fund company and had lots of "potential" in the financial planner's eyes. It sounded like a reasonable suggestion from an expert, and so my parents opened accounts for my brother and me and made the initial investment. Thereafter, when my brother or I made some extra money over the summer or at after-school jobs, we would diligently send checks over to the financial planner to add to the account.

In the end, the fund did rather well by the time we both graduated from high school, although the never-ending bull market probably had more to do with the success of the fund than the manager's particular skill. Given that I was closer to the beginning of my freshman year in the late 1980s than my brother was, the Black Monday crash of 1987 cost me a bit more of my balance than it did him, but that wasn't really the fault of the financial planner. Everyone lost money in that decline.

All in all, the fund did relatively well and it seemed like the financial planner did a reasonable job for us; and I can't recall any complaints we had at the time. In fact, I'm sure we passed his name to others who needed someone to advise them. It wasn't until years later, once I had several years of experience in the financial services industry under my belt, that I thought back to this investment and realized just how many mistakes were made.

As you could probably guess from discussions in previous chapters, I am of the opinion that the financial planner's decision to put 100% of my family's money into an aggressive, large cap, US growth stock fund was NOT a smart idea—especially because my brother and I had less than 10 years to go before we needed to access the funds in the account to pay for college. First, given the relatively short time frame until the money would be needed for college, the asset allocation should have had some balance between risky and less-risky investments, or additional contributions should have flowed into a lower-risk investment to dilute the weight to that single fund. Second, the sole selection of a large cap growth fund imposed two unwanted style biases (large capitalization stocks and growth stocks) on this portfolio.[1] Third, choosing a single manager for the entire investment amount left us open to a large amount of idiosyncratic risk, or risk from just one investment manager's decisions. Investing smaller amounts in each of a few funds would have reduced the potential impact of poor performance from any of them.

Now, I know what you're thinking. As the title implies, this chapter is supposed to be about fees and expenses, not about all the mistakes my family's financial planner made when he gave us advice regarding asset allocation, investment structure, and manager selection. Well, up to this point, I have left the details about what the planner's advice cost out of the story; and, frankly, setting all the poor advice just mentioned aside, this is the part that has really bugged me over the years.

First, the management fee for the mutual fund was more than 1.5%. I'm sure the planner showed my parents data that said that this fee was better than those they would have to pay for the average fund at the time, but 1.5% was still ridiculously high. Saying this fee is below average is like saying that I can run faster than half the world population, as long as you include babies and the elderly in that other half. Not exactly a strong statement regarding

---

[1] A combination of growth and value funds would have been much better and more risk controlled. Imagine if this story had taken place in the late 1990s instead of the late 1980s, and my college savings suffered through the extended collapse in technology stocks instead of the relatively short 1987 crash. As bad as the overall market losses were during the dot-com collapse, growth stocks dramatically underperformed the broader market. With only a few years to go until college, there simply would not have been time to repair that damage and regrow my assets.

the planner's supposedly superior fee structure. Second, the fund paid the planner an annual "12B-1" fee of 0.25% to help pay for marketing and distribution. Part of that 0.25% probably flowed back to the planner every year we remained invested. Third, and this is the worst part of all, the fund charged a "front-load" fee of 5.25% for every contribution my family made to the fund. This fee went directly to the financial planner as compensation for recommending the fund to us. For that initial $10,000, he earned an immediate $525. Each time my brother or I saved up $500 from summer jobs and sent it to him, he made another $26.25 for doing nothing subsequent to that initial recommendation.

So what is the end of the story? The $10,000 invested on Day 1 was only worth an initial $9,300.[2] Every year, an additional 1.75% was subtracted from the value of that portfolio as a management and sales fee, regardless of performance, plus 5.25% from any new contribution.

I don't disagree that the broker was owed something for that initial meeting and recommendation. However, an additional 5.25% every time we made another investment over the life of the fund simply doesn't sit well with me today, now that I have the benefit of hindsight. In addition, whereas one could argue that maybe that first $525 was an appropriate amount of compensation for the time and effort he spent determining the right investment strategy and recommendation for us (although I would guess that the vast majority of his clients received similar recommendations to invest in that same fund that took little incremental work), imagine if we had invested $50,000 instead of $10,000 and he had made the same recommendation to put 100% of our money into that mutual fund. Would $2,600 have been a fair amount of compensation for the exact same amount of effort? Now we are starting to talk about really meaningful amounts of money coming out of your pocket. If he has two new clients who are both rolling over 401(k) accounts into IRAs, and he gives similar advice to each client, should the person who saved $500,000 over a lifetime pay him five times as much as the person who saved $100,000—for precisely the same advice?

Put even more simply, was it appropriate that he recommended to us a fund that paid him 5.25% up front plus 0.25% every year on top of more fees from future contributions? Was that really the single best option he could have found, or was it the single best option for his personal income statement? This, in a nutshell, is a real-world example of everything that can go wrong with an advisor, and everything that you need to avoid.

---

[2]$10,000 minus 1.75% in annual management and sales fees plus another 5.25% subtracted due to the front load.

Planners vs. Brokers

Although it may seem like a broad generality, in my experience the global financial services industry breaks down into one of four models. In the next few pages I will explain these models and what to ask and watch for when choosing money managers and expert advice. Although there are certainly well-intentioned people in the financial services industry who have their clients' interests first in their hearts, investors and customers need to be aware of these industry models when searching for truly trusted advisors and partners.

Per-Transaction Model

The first and most common business model in the financial services industry includes those professionals who work on a per-transaction basis. This is the model that your typical stockbroker falls into. If he convinces you to buy 1,000 shares of XYZ, he makes a commission. If he isn't sufficiently persuasive or fails to call his entire client list on a regular basis, he simply doesn't get paid as much. Under this model, salesmanship equals profits. Most of Wall Street works this way, with investment banks earning fees only when they can convince companies to merge or divest; a start-up to issue an initial public offering (IPO); or a money manager or private client (you) to buy or sell a stock about which they have a strong opinion (or in which they have a large in-house position that they need to reduce by selling it to their clients). At the end of the day, the more that professionals working on a per-transaction basis can get their clients to churn their accounts or engage in transactions, which may or may not be beneficial in the long run, the more they get paid.

Whereas this business model might help Wall Street firms improve their bottom lines and decide who are their best performers and deserve to be the most richly rewarded, this is the single worst model for you as a client. If a broker is able to convince you to trade 10 times as often as you need to, with dubious benefits to you as a client, that broker is paid 10 times as much as he would be if he simply gave you longer-term, buy-and-hold advice. In my personal example previously, the financial planner clearly had a strong incentive to sell us the highest fee and highest load fund he thought we would agree to buy because that would generate the most income for him through that initial transaction fee (the 5.25% front load).

Retainer-Based Model

An alternative to the per-transaction model is the retainer-based model, where the financial advisor or investment consultant simply provides advice for a fair fee that is based on the time she or he spends with you. Regardless of whether you have $100,000 or $1,000,000 to invest, the fee is generally the same because the amount of work is virtually the same. Your accountant or lawyer doesn't charge ten times as much for the same project for a very rich client as he does for a middle-class client, unless the complexity and time commitment requires it. Why should your financial advisor? If the goal is to find an appropriate asset allocation and manager lineup, it really doesn't matter if you have $10,000 or $10,000,000 to invest. All you are doing is adding a couple of zeros after some of the line items.

Most of the consultants who advise public pension plans work based on this model. When you are talking about tens or hundreds of billions of dollars, a per-transaction fee is simply impractical and does not encourage the consultant to share in the long-term success of the fund. In addition, a predetermined annual fee helps to ensure that the consultant or advisor has the client's best interests at heart because the consultant's only goal is to keep the client happy, and he or she receives no compensation for any of the advice and recommendations provided. Like so much of the advice in this book, if this philosophy works for a huge pension plan, why shouldn't it work for you?

In Chapter 2, I suggested that meeting with a representative from the IRA services area at your local bank or maybe a client service person at a store front for a discount brokerage firm might be a great way to get more information about the asset allocation that is right for you. Assuming that this service is provided "free" to you as a client, you are dealing with a firm that employs a retainer-based business model because you are already paying for that advice somewhere in your account (like quarterly account fees or a lower interest rate on your cash balances than you might be able to get somewhere else). As this client service professional is not paid on a per-transaction basis but rather is paid a salary by the bank to keep you happy as a client of the firm, the advice is more likely to have your best interests in mind. On the other hand, if he starts telling you that all the bank's in-house mutual funds are the best in their asset classes and are the only things you should ever consider buying, you should start questioning whether he really is getting a transaction-based fee after all through some kind of fee rebate or sales incentive.

Percentage of Assets Model

The third model I will detail is the model commonly employed by asset management organizations. Most money managers, ranging from mutual funds to private equity funds to hedge funds, are paid a fee equal to some percentage of assets per year. If assets grow passively due to market movement or actively due to superior performance or the addition of new client accounts, the firm earns more income because the assets under management have increased. Similarly, if markets decline or clients leave the firm, income and profits decline.

From the client perspective, if your account grows in value, regardless of whether that growth is the result of a strong market return or actual manager investment skill, you pay more. If it declines, you pay less. Fundamentally, this seems more equitable than the transaction-based model because the manager is generally rewarded for successful outcomes for clients.

Another very fair aspect of this model is that the very large clients that I work with, and even some individual investors, tend to benefit from "breakpoints" in their fees. If the client gives a manager $10 million to manage in some strategy, their fee might be 0.30% per year. If they give them $50 million, the fee might fall to 0.25%. Although a larger amount of assets might eventually cause the manager to add additional trading or research staff, the incremental cost of servicing a $50 million account versus a $10 million account is practically zero, and the fees reflect those economies of scale.

Although an individual investor may not be able to negotiate their own fee schedule with an investment manager as a pension plan would, most mutual fund firms offer multiple share classes of the same funds, where larger portfolio sizes will have lower fees. So, whereas you might not be able to pay the bottom dollar, low fees that large pension plans pay, some smart shopping or research might enable you to find the fund you want for less than you initially thought.

In fairness to the managers, there is one problem with this model: market movements can cause unwanted effects. Imagine a scenario like the 1990s, where stock prices rose more than 100% over a few years. A manager who underperforms the market but manages to not lose any clients will see their income double, despite demonstrating no skill in their client accounts and simply tracking (or even trailing) the market return. Similarly, in a bear market, a manager who protects significant amounts of value (i.e., loses less money than the market as a whole) and does a great job for their clients will see their income fall due to the lower asset base.

Payment for Results Model

The fourth model is based on payment for results and is most commonly levied as a performance-based fee, which is also known in some asset classes as carried interest. For a typical stock or bond portfolio, a pension plan that employs performance-based fees will pay a lower management fee than for a similar base-fee-only arrangement but then will pay an additional fee to the manager when returns exceed the market index or some other benchmark. In other words, a money manager could be paid, say, 0.50% a year by clients who prefer pure management fees, or, for those who want a performance-based fee, a 0.30% management fee plus 20% of the amount the portfolio exceeds the S&P 500 over a given time period.[3] The benefits of this fee structure are obvious: when the money manager does poorly, the client pays a far lower fee than the normal base fee and does not reward the money manager for mediocrity. When times are good and the money manager outperforms the benchmark for that portfolio, the client theoretically should be sufficiently happy with the superior returns to cut a far larger check. In practice, though, if a number of performance-based fee managers outperform at the same time, a client might see their calculation of total fees paid jump significantly, sometimes drawing unwanted attention to that bottom-line number.

There are also fee structures that use a combination of the preceding. As I discussed briefly in Chapter 8, private equity, real estate, and hedge fund managers, for example, tend to charge management fees of 1% to 3%, and even sometimes more, plus a performance-based fee of 20% to 30%, often above a benchmark of 0%. For a hedge fund that charges a 2% base fee and a 20% performance fee—which is the most commonly used fee structure for hedge funds (usually referred to as "2 and 20")—a mediocre performance of 6% in a year can result in a fee of 3.2%![4] That's right. The manager generates a 6% return in a year with your money and you only get a 2.8% return. No wonder there are so many private jets parked in Westchester, New York.

What Fee Structure Is Right for the Personal Investor?

I know that was probably a lot more detail than you ever wanted or needed to know about fee structures, but it is extremely important to understand the motivations of your service providers in the financial services industry. When you make savings and investment decisions, a great deal of your future can be at stake, and there are some people in the financial services industry (as there are in many other industries) looking to take as much of your money as they can legally (and sometimes illegally) get away with. You need to thoroughly understand the motivations behind the advice and services that they provide to you and, where possible, negotiate terms that protect you against those that will try to use your assets to enrich themselves. At the end of the day,

---

[3] In practice, these types of structures usually have stated maximum fees, which discourage excessive risk taking by the money manager, as well as some kind of long-term smoothing mechanism to ensure that years of bad performance are held against the money manager during periods of good performance to avoid overpaying for middling results in aggregate. I'm simplifying the concept here slightly to avoid making this example too complicated.

[4] A 2% base fee plus a performance fee of 20% equals 2% plus 1.2% (20% times 6%) for a grand total of 3.2% in fees. With a gross (before-fee) return of 6%, that leaves 2.8% for the client.

you and your service providers should have an alignment of interests: only when and if you do well are they rewarded or retained for their services.

Of the previously mentioned compensation models, the quickest one that you need to rule out involves any funds that charge front-load fees and the advisors that sell them. It is difficult for me to imagine a scenario in which the interests of an advisor who is paid on a per-transaction basis are truly aligned with those of his clients. In my preceding personal example, the advisor was paid a sales commission up front and had little ongoing reward for maintaining a successful relationship with my family beyond some fraction of that small marketing and distribution fee. For per-transaction fee providers, simply put, the incentive is to sell you as much product as they can and advise you to sell underperforming funds the instant they think the funds look weak to free up your money for more funds that pay them a front load. Each time the advisor successfully advises you to follow his or her recommendations, you lose another 5.25% of your money. You also lose, as I did in my youth, each time you make a periodic contribution into your savings and buy more of that fund, paying another 5.25% for the advisor's original advice.

In Table 9-1, I imagine three different arrangements with financial planners. In all examples, I start with $25,000 to invest and then add $2,000 to the investor's savings at the end of each year. To keep things simple, I will assume that the investments earn 8% every year. The first column is an example of the investor who falls for all the tricks, including a front load of 5.25%, high management fees of 1.50%, and 12B-1 fees of 0.25% (which is the full slate of fees and expenses that hit my account years ago). The second column represents an investor who pays an advisor a hard dollar amount of $500 for advice every 5 years and then invests in a different share class of the same fund with a management fee of only 1.00%. The third column is for an investor who uses the free resources at her or his bank to develop the asset allocation plan and invests much of that portfolio in the lowest-cost index funds and ETFs, resulting in an average fee of 0.30%.

Table 9-1. Comparison of the Impact of Fees

	Investor 1	Investor 2	Investor 3
Initial Contribution	$25,000	$25,000	$25,000
Front Load	($1,438)		
Investment Gains	$1,885	$2,000	$2,000
Management Fees	($445)	($770)	($81)
Year 1 Ending Value	$25,002	$26,230	$26,919
Year 2 Ending Value	$28,530	$30,184	$31,139
Year 2 Contribution	$1,885	$2,000	$2,000
Investment Gains	$2,433	$2,575	$2,651
Management Fees	($575)	($348)	($107)
Year 3 Ending Value	$32,273	$34,411	$35,683
Year 4 Ending Value	$36,245	$38,930	$40,575
Year 4 Contribution	$1,885	$2,000	$2,000
Investment Gains	$3,050	$3,274	$3,406
Management Fees	($721)	($442)	($138)
Year 5 Ending Value	$40,460	$43,763	$45,843
Year 9 Ending Value	$60,057	$66,064	$71,282
Year 9 Contribution	$1,885	$2,000	$2,000
Investment Gains	$4,955	$5,445	$5,863
Management Fees	($1,171)	($735)	($237)
Year 10 Ending Value	$65,726	$72,775	$78,907

As you can see, even small differences in fees really start to add up. The low-cost investor (3) has almost $13,000 more than the high-cost investor (1) after just 10 years, and more than $6,000 more than our reduced-cost investor (2). After 20 years of saving money (not shown in this table), the difference between Investors 1 and 3 grows to more than $50,000. That's $50,000 extra that Investor 1 put into the advisor's pocket instead of his or her own. It shouldn't be a surprise that if three people put the same amount of money into an account every year and earn the same results, the person who pays the lowest fees will have the most in assets in the end. The amazing part is how much those differences in fees really can make.

Simply put, you should never, ever invest in a fund that deducts either a front-load fee (which is deducted up front from each contribution you make) or a back-load fee (which is deducted from your account when you sell the fund) from your hard-earned money. The one possible exception to this rule is if the only advisor that you trust in your area, for whatever reason, only works for commissions from funds with loads. In this case, you should give that advisor the absolute minimum amount of money that is required for an account size (assuming that the dollar amount of the front or back load is acceptable to you as a fair amount to pay for the advisor's time and advice) and then invest the rest of your money in other share classes of the same funds that do not charge a load.

The vast majority of fund families that offer funds with loads have other versions of their funds without loads and often with lower management fees. These funds are run in precisely the same manner as the load funds and are managed by the same people using the same resources. As such, they should have nearly identical returns to load funds. If you absolutely, positively disregard my advice and invest in a fund with a load, make sure that any savings above the required minimum and, especially, any future contributions, all flow to the load-free version of the fund.

Are All Fees Bad?

One of the largest purveyors of indexed mutual funds (low-cost mutual funds that are designed to track a market index as closely as possible) has been running ads in newspapers and magazines for years, bemoaning the impact of fees on performance and touting the benefits of investing your money in their inexpensive index funds. If every mutual fund offered the same performance regardless of investment philosophy, their point would be 100% on the money. If two funds earn 9% per year for 10 straight years and one fund charges 1.00% while the other one charges 0.20%, the expensive fund will turn a $10,000 investment into $21,589 after 10 years. The cheaper fund, meanwhile, will give you a portfolio value of $23,243 after 10 years—an improvement of almost $1,700 just from paying a lower fee on the same portfolio. All else being equal, a lower-fee fund will always generate a better return than a higher-fee fund because it will deduct less from your account every year.

Obviously, though, not all funds are equal. No one buys into a fund that charges a management fee of 1.00% and expects to get a return that mirrors that of the S&P 500. If you want the market return, then invest in an index fund. If, on the other hand, you believe that a given manager can consistently out-perform the market, then a higher-fee, actively managed portfolio may be right for you.

Let's reconsider the example from the prior paragraph and assume that the actively managed fund (before fees) outperforms the stock market by 0.50% every year. Unfortunately, the fund's outperformance (0.50%) amounts to less than the incremental fee versus the index fund (0.80%), and the value of your investment at the end of 10 years is $22,610. That's better than the high-fee fund mentioned, but it is still $600 less than would have been earned in the index fund. If the manager can add 2% of value to the fund every single year, though, you can start to see the real benefits of active management. That 2% outperformance less the 1% fee yields an after-fees annual return of 10%, whereas the index fund is only returning 8.8% (9% market return less 0.20%) after its fee. Now the actively managed portfolio is worth $25,937 after 10 years, which is $2,700 better than the index fund.

In answer to the question posed, then, no. Not all fees are necessarily bad. If an investment manager can actually deliver performance that is 2% better than the benchmark every single year, that is something that is worth paying for.

In theory, if I have 100% certainty that the manager will always deliver 2% above the benchmark, I should be willing to pay any fee up to 2.19% for a net annual return of 8.81%. After all, my alternative to this fund is the index fund, which will return 8.80% per year after fees.

As I showed in Chapter 7, however, finding managers that can deliver precisely 2% of outperformance year after year, in good markets and in bad, is a tall order. The data I shared in that chapter might probably (and rightfully) lead you to conclude that this type of outperformance is impossible. Although it very well could be the case that you could find SOME mutual fund in some asset class that has had at least 2% outperformance every year for some 10-year period, it is difficult to imagine that this fund's perfect track record will continue for another 10 years.

Finding a balance between a reasonable expectation of outperformance and the fees that you are willing to pay for that outperformance becomes the key driver of the decision regarding whether you will choose an actively managed fund or go with a low-cost index option. Although I cannot give you a hard and fast rule for how to find that balancing point, you need to consider how successful you think the manager will be in the future, how reasonable that performance is in light of other alternatives, how much the fund charges in fees, how that fee compares to the fees of the fund's peers, and how willing you are to stay with that fund when it inevitably underperforms. Even the best funds might underperform for 3 or 4 out of every 10 years. Are you willing to continue to stay with those funds bearing the higher cost versus an indexed alternative, as long as the manager's style is out of favor? If you don't think that you will have the courage of your convictions to ride out the full market cycle, you may find yourself buying at the top of a manager's outperformance record and then paying high fees right down to the bottom, when you finally throw in the towel, sell, and invest in another highflyer that is perfectly timed for its own underperformance.

I will give you one caveat to all this "lower fees are better advice": even very large investors have their vision clouded by fee comparisons sometimes, and I advise you not to let fees and expenses become the be-all and end-all of your mutual fund selection process. Paying 0.10% higher in fees for a fund that returns 1.0% more than its peers can be a good deal, as long as you have confidence that the 1.0% outperformance will persist. Whereas the lower cost of two identical funds is usually the better choice, try to choose between actively managed funds, if that is what you want, based on how much you believe in the manager's approach, the likelihood that the strategy will do well in the future, and how the fund fits your overall investment strategy. A cheaper fund may serve you less well over the long run if the performance advantage of a higher-priced fund exceeds the incremental cost.

Diversification and Fees

Up to this point in this chapter, I have discussed whether higher fees for a single fund versus an indexed alternative are worth it. Meanwhile, the rest of the advice in this book clearly says that you should never put all your eggs in one basket and should be as diversified as possible. If you are investing in several different asset classes and plan to include a few mutual funds in each asset class in your portfolio, it is very possible that you could quickly find yourself with investments in six or more mutual funds at the same time.

As thin as the odds are that any fund could outperform every single year, the chances that every fund you select will always outperform are exponentially more remote. (Frankly, based on my experience, I would say that it is impossible for every fund an investor selects to outperform its benchmark every single year.) As a result, with a sufficiently broad selection of funds, it is likely that outperformance by some funds in some years will be at least partially offset by underperformance by others, resulting in a total portfolio that could underperform the market as a whole. Remember, whereas the sum of all fixed income managers may not necessarily equal the entire bond market (see Chapters 5 and 6), the sum of the portfolios of 20 large cap stock managers will be virtually the same as the companies constituting any major index. As a result, in aggregate those 20 portfolios will generate a market return for you, less the average active management fee the funds charge, leaving you far better off simply buying as cheap an index fund as you can find.

As I discussed previously in this book, it is therefore imperative to selectively decide where you want to take, and pay for, active risk. An investor might select indexed large cap funds, active small cap funds, indexed non-US funds, aggressive emerging markets funds, and active fixed income funds based on the advice I've given—not a bad combination of funds. In this example, investors are paying high fees where they think that their managers can add value and paying low-cost index fees where they think they will just earn the market return. By using a select number of active managers and indexing the rest, investors increase their chances of outperforming the market versus investors that select four high-fee, actively managed mutual funds in every asset class and hope for the best.

Breakpoints

Many mutual fund companies offer different classes of shares based not just on whether or not the funds carry a load but also on the amount the client is willing to invest in a given fund. As you develop your asset allocation plan, you should give prime consideration to whether greater diversification results in higher expenses.

When a pension plan is considering investing in an institutional portfolio, a fee structure for a given fixed income portfolio might look like the following:

- 0.40% on the first $25 million
- 0.30% on the next $25 million
- 0.25% on the next $50 million
- 0.20% on any amount above $100 million

Let's say the client has $300 million to invest in fixed income and several good manager candidates to choose from. If the client gives the entire investible amount to a single manager, they will incur a large amount of idiosyncratic risk[5] associated with that investment but will pay a fee of only 0.23%, or $700,000 per year. If the client selects two managers that offer the same fee schedule, they diversify the risk of any given manager, but each manager's fee increases to 0.27%, or a total of $800,000 per year. If the client splits their investment three ways, they must pay an average manager fee of 0.30%, or a total of $900,000.

The client's lack of conviction in a single manager and selection of three different fixed income managers results in an annual increase of $200,000 in fees and lower exposure to underperformance by any individual manager. However, it also results in lower exposure to outperformance by any individual manager and a better chance that at least one poor performer in any given year will negatively offset the good performance of the others. By hiring three managers instead of one, the client is paying more money for less performance in any given year—but reduces the risk that their entire portfolio will completely melt down.

Although not many people make $300,000,000 investment decisions, this thought exercise still applies to the individual investor. Even for smaller asset sizes, fee breakpoints still exist. For individual investors, mutual funds are often offered in a variety of share classes with different minimum investment amounts and management fees. For example, a large, well-known index fund manager charges 0.17% for accounts over $3,000 and 0.05% for accounts over $10,000 in one index fund. A household-name fixed income firm charges 0.75% for assets over $2,500 and 0.50% for accounts of more than $100,000 in one of its flagship products. When you decide how many investment managers you need in a risk-controlled portfolio, that 0.12% or 0.25% increase in fees by selecting more, smaller portfolios might really start to add up and

---

[5] A really fancy way of saying "manager-specific" risk. In other words, the risk that the manager does a terrible job all alone and underperforms the market and the manager's peers due to specific stock picks, industrial sector weights, excessive trading, or anything else that creates a uniquely poor return for just this manager.

impact your returns. Or, you might decide that those are minimal costs to bear to reduce the impact that a single manager might have during a period of catastrophic underperformance.

As was the case for our pension plan example, you need to balance your desire for diversification against the cost of diversification. It may be scary to put all of your money in a single bond fund. If you don't, though, and instead choose to split your investment between two managers, you could miss the opportunity to take advantage of the breakpoint between two share classes, which will increase your fees by a significant amount every year. Is that a cost you are willing to bear to have less fear that one of your funds will underperform? On the other hand, if you are so concerned that one of your funds will blow up that you need to pay more to diversify that risk by investing in peer funds, should you invest in it in the first place? Maybe the fact that the risk is so scary to you that you feel you must diversify it away should guide you in your decision to find other funds that let you sleep easier at night.

Likewise, you can invest $10,000 in the S&P 500 index fund and pay a fee of 0.05% per year, or you can put half of that $10,000 in the index fund and the other half in two growth and value actively managed funds. Not only will you pay significantly higher fees for those two active funds, but the cost of the index fund portion of your portfolio will increase by 0.12%. Are you sufficiently convinced that those two active managers are worth that incremental cost? At the end of the day, both pension plans and individual investors need to perform the same balancing act between the number of funds they feel they need to have in their portfolio to properly diversify their risks, the incremental cost of adding more funds to their portfolio, and the probability that having too many funds leaves them with a high-cost mess that cannot outperform in aggregate.

Exchange Traded Funds (ETFs)

Pension plans can have huge cash flows both into and out of the funds in which they are invested. For a very large plan, monthly contributions from the government entity that sponsors the plan or monthly benefit payments to beneficiaries can amount to inflows and outflows of hundreds of millions or even billions of dollars a year. No plan wants to wait until the last minute to sell securities to raise $2 billion or more, and so pension plans will often keep large amounts of cash that was recently received or awaiting disbursement in cash form instead of investing it in stocks, bonds, or other investments.

Unfortunately, though, if a plan holds, say, 2% in cash instead of remaining fully invested in its target asset allocation strategy, that cash can act as a drag on returns. If stocks are up 10% and bonds are up 5% over some period of time, but cash returns only 0.10%, the pension plan will underperform its benchmark and targets, all else being equal, due to that "cash drag." As a result, plans will often buy derivatives contracts, like stock and bond futures, which are highly liquid and closely track the index returns, to "equitize" (convert into an equivalent market exposure) their cash and eliminate the negative impact that holding cash can have on performance.

In some cases, instead of making actual investments in stocks, pension plans skip over "physical securities" altogether and instead invest in futures. After all, if the futures contract is designed to track the return of the stock market almost perfectly, then why bother trading actual stocks, which are much less liquid? What's more, investing in futures in place of stocks allows a pension plan to reduce the cash drag in its portfolios at the same time that it makes it easy to convert to cash when the time comes to distribute disbursements. True, there are some costs and complexities involved in buying futures, but for some clients the costs are roughly equivalent to what it costs to manage the physical stock portfolio.

This brings us to the personal investor and how this pension plan strategy translates to the individual level. Unfortunately, investing in futures is probably beyond the reach of most individuals. Individual stock and Treasury bond futures contracts are priced in the hundreds of thousands or millions of dollars. A single S&P 500 futures contract could exceed the value of your entire life's savings. This is precisely why these types of investments are perfect for large pension plans: if they need to turn $100 million of cash into a short-term market exposure, they can do it by buying less than 85 derivatives contracts at the time of this writing. Fortunately, however, there is a roughly equivalent instrument to futures for individual investors: ETFs.

ETFs, short for exchange traded funds, are very similar to typical mutual funds but trade on stock exchanges and carry different legal requirements. Due to how they are structured, ETFs often have lower fees than even index funds— although buying some ETFs can incur commission costs, depending on which ETF you buy and who you use for a broker. ETFs are available from a wide and increasing variety of providers and can offer the investor a broad selection of market and other exposures, ranging from large cap indexed stocks to crazy structures, like 200% levered portfolios that profit when treasury bonds fall in price (and rates rise). Due to the market liquidity of these instruments, though, they are far more appropriate for individual investors than they are for large pension plans. If a pension plan needed to buy $500 million worth of large cap stock exposure and was given the choice of trading 450 futures contracts or 10 million shares of an ETF at $50 a share, clearly the futures contract is the more efficient instrument for a huge investor.

Because ETFs normally trade on stock exchanges, you may need to pay brokerage commissions to transact, depending on your broker and the ETF producer. However, the lower management fees of ETFs may offset those commissions if you have a long-term strategy. The ETFs from one major provider of index funds, for example, might cost you 0.05% less per year than their indexed mutual funds do. If you are investing $10,000 in one of their ETFs and have to pay $10 per transaction, that transaction fee is 0.10% of your investment amount. If you plan to hold that investment for a long time, after 2 years you will have saved more money on management fees than you lost from commissions. However, if you plan to change your asset allocation every three months (see Chapter 2 for advice against doing that!), then you are probably better off with a mutual fund because the higher management fees will cost you less incrementally than all those $10 transactions costs—which, if you trade a lot, can add up awfully fast. Remember that selling one ETF and buying another through a broker that charges a commission for ETF trades incurs a total of $20 from two discrete transactions—which, in this example, amounts to four years' worth of savings from using ETFs instead of mutual funds.

In some cases, your bank or broker might offer their own in-house ETFs and will let you transact for free, like some discount brokerage firms do. It is up to you to compare the expense ratios of those proprietary ETFs against ETFs offered by other companies, keeping in mind your asset allocation and investment style, to see if you are better off paying more in transactions costs or in management fees to minimize the overall cost to you.

Summary

The most important thing to bear in mind when looking at what it will cost you to implement your investment strategy is that fees and expenses can impact your investment bottom line often as much as manager performance does. Frequent trading or a reliance on multiple money managers for the same strategy can lead to far higher costs than those incurred with a long-term buy-and-hold strategy or a portfolio of fewer money managers.

More important, though, than the fees involved in mutual funds and ETFs is the understanding that the investment industry is a business. It is designed to make money for those who work in it. This is not a charity. As long as you understand that premise and work diligently to find service providers that actually work on your behalf, as opposed to just their own, you will be ahead of the legions of investors who simply trust the fast talking, convincing guy in the nice suit with the slick hair. Before you work with anyone as an advisor or investor on your behalf, make sure that you understand exactly what they will be charging you both today and in the future, how they make their money off of your assets, and whether their interests are aligned with your goals of long-term steady growth or simply their own financial goals.

Risk Management

Avoiding the Unexpected

Throughout this book, I have described many of the basic errors investors make that cause harm to their portfolios and diminish their returns over time. In Chapter 2, for example, I discussed the problems that undisciplined savings, changes to your expected cash needs in retirement, and asset allocation strategies that ignore the long term can present. Chapters 3 and 4, meanwhile, listed the many uncompensated risks that can impact your portfolio when you allow your judgment to be clouded by size, style, and home country biases. Chapter 7 showed how inconsistent even the best managers can be when it comes to outperforming their benchmarks, and Chapter 9 illustrated the point that fees and expenses can drain your savings and long-term growth over time. In other words, I've spent a good portion of this book discussing the various risks that can negatively impact investors' portfolios and, by extension, their returns in the long run.

In this chapter, I will tackle the subject of risk management head on and review some of the major risks that arise in portfolios that do not generate compensating returns. I will also give a few real-world examples of mistakes that investors make to illustrate how to better guard yourself against following suit. Although I have waited to directly address risk management until now, keep in mind as you read this chapter that this all-important topic needs to be something that every investor considers both periodically, when major financial decisions are made, and continuously, as investments are monitored.

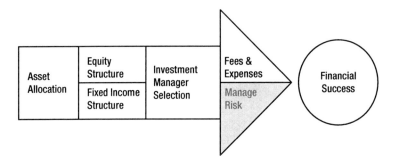

The Road Map to Financial Success graphic may indicate that managing risk is a single step on the path to retirement security, but, as was the case with the fees and expenses that it costs you to implement your plan that were discussed in Chapter 9, risk management really should be an overarching discipline. As you develop your asset allocation strategy, your asset structures, and your manager selections, you should consider the risk of each step as you go. Then, periodically you should look at the big picture of your investments and see if anything sticks out. Does something keep you up at night? Does it seem like 50% of your returns or problems are coming from one single investment? If so, you need to consider whether the cause of all that trouble is sufficiently valuable that it really ought to be included in your portfolio. In practice, it seldom is worth the trouble.

People in the medical profession adhere to a code of conduct that begins, "First, do no harm." That is also a terrific rule of thumb for handling your own investments. If you can avoid making basic mistakes that will cost you money over time, you will be far better off in the end than you will be if you fiddle with things, even with the best of intentions, to the point that you are a detriment to your own results.

For Most Investors, Diversification is a Must

Andrew Carnegie once said, "The way to become rich is to put all your eggs in one basket and then watch that basket." If your dream path to retirement is to open a store, start a restaurant, or launch a product that you hope will generate the wealth you require, I wish you all the luck in the world. Risking everything for a dream can be a noble pursuit and can have tremendous financial and personal rewards, as long as the dreamer understands the potential costs and consequences of failure. For everyone who lacks the ability to control their own destiny, though, diversification of their investments is a must. Sure, Mr. Carnegie grew fantastically rich by watching his basket of one investment, but that investment, over which he had complete control, was U.S. Steel. (Not to mention that he also had a virtual monopoly over the steel output of an entire country at the very beginning of the Industrial Revolution.) For an individual investor who follows Carnegie's one basket advice and puts 100% of his investments into an S&P 500 index fund, however, it really doesn't matter how much you "watch that basket." You can't will the S&P 500 to go up or down on your command. As a result, for those investors who are amassing wealth through steady contributions into a retirement account and disciplined asset allocation, fundamentals that were discussed in Chapter 2, diversification across a wide variety of strategies and asset classes is the best way to reduce the risk of any one investment costing you your future.

Figure 10-1 shows what is referred to as the efficient frontier in asset allocation. The curved and upward sloping line indicates the expected return and risk for a variety of combinations of assets and shows the most optimal return tradeoff for any given level of risk.[1] At the far end of the line are combinations of mostly cash and fixed income investments, where expected returns and expected risk are both fairly low. The portfolios that make up the upper right part of the line would be comprised mainly of stocks, private equities, and other risky assets. Note that the line is not straight and has an upward bulge in the middle. This indicates that diversification, or having a portfolio that combines both risky assets and safer assets, changes the relationship between risk and return and leads to the potential for better outcomes than more concentrated portfolios do.

---

[1]When selecting an asset allocation strategy, the most common measure of risk at the total portfolio level is the standard deviation of returns. If your expected return is, for example, 7% with a standard deviation of 12%, your returns in two out of every three years should be between -5% and +19% (7% plus or minus 12%). In one out of every three years, your returns should be worse than -5% or better than 19%—which is a very inexact projection. As a result, asset allocation mixes need to be selected with the very long term in mind, allowing exceptionally good or bad years to offset each other over time. While it is virtually impossible to project the expected return for a portfolio in advance for any given year, experts can predict what some diversified portfolios should return on average over a decade or more with a reasonable level of accuracy.

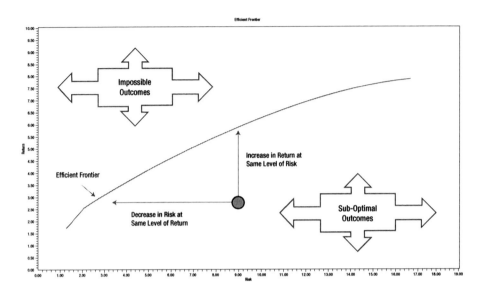

Figure 10-1. Hypothetical Efficient Frontier for Stocks, Bonds, and Cash

Since the line represents the most optimal portfolio at any given level of risk and return, a portfolio that plots above the efficient frontier line is simply impossible. While we all would love to live in a world where 15% returns are possible with a minimum of risk, that data point would be above and to the left of the line and therefore, as I just said, impossible. An asset allocation combination that resulted in a point below the line is entirely possible, with a lower payoff in expected return per unit of risk taken, and would reveal that the investor could increase return at the same level of risk all the way up to the efficient frontier, or decrease risk at a constant level of return, again moving to an optimal asset allocation combination that is on the efficient frontier.

In Figure 10-2, using the 2012 return, risk, and correlation asset class assumptions from a major investment consulting company, I plot the expected return and risk for a variety of portfolios, ranging from 50% global stocks and 50% bonds to 100% global stocks and 0% bonds in 10% increments. As you can see, whereas the 100% stock asset allocation mix has the highest expected return, it also has the highest risk, as measured by the standard deviation of that return. For an aggressive investor with a long time horizon and a healthy appetite for risk, decreasing an allocation to stocks by 10% or 20% retains a fairly high expected return at 7% per year or better but leads to a dramatic decrease in expected risk. The change from a 100% stock and 0% bond portfolio to an 80% stock and 20% bond portfolio decreases expected return by 0.80%, from 7.80% to 7.00%, but it also decreases expected risk from 17.05% to 13.85%. That's more than three percentage points of risk reduction for less than one percentage point of expected return.

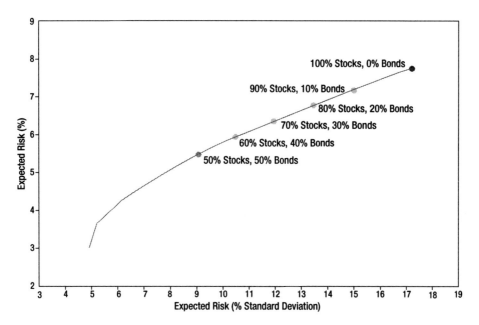

Figure 10-2. Expected Returns and Risk for Portfolios with Stocks and Bonds

In Figure 10-3, I have added small allocations to real estate investment trusts (REITs) and high yield bonds to spread the risk from two eggs in the hypothetical basket to four eggs. The advantages of greater diversification are obvious; both new plotted portfolios, as well as the entire range of outcomes, have a higher expected return and a lower expected risk than the comparable stock/bond-only portfolios.

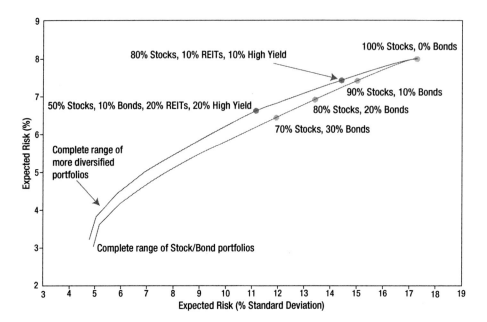

Figure 10-3. Expected Returns and Risk of Diversified Portfolios

The portfolio that is 80% invested in stocks, 10% invested in REITs, and 10% invested in high yield, for example, holds 90% of its assets in stock-like investments, counting REITs as an equity investment. That portfolio's expected return is about 0.10% higher than the 90% stock and 10% bond portfolio, and its expected standard deviation is 0.65% lower—which is exactly the kind of improvement you should be seeking. One of my clients likes to say, "When someone offers you a free lunch, eat it!" As an investor, the free lunch that you should be looking for is the opportunity to simultaneously decrease your risk while increasing your returns. This is the best possible outcome of an asset allocation decision-making process, and it is also the very definition of risk management.

The bottom line is that being diversified across many asset classes instead of just one or two is the single best way to reduce your portfolio's total risk, as diversification will minimize the risk exposure you face from any one investment.

Beware of False Diversification

Despite the many benefits of diversification, all investors do need to beware of the risks of adding diversification just for the sake of diversification. What do I mean by this? Let me give you an example. In 2006 and 2007, in the aftermath of the recession and market collapse that occurred during the 2001–2003 period, many investors diligently tried to spread their risk across a wide variety of investments in order to limit the damage that any particular investment could do to their overall portfolio. By 2008, many large pension plans and other large investors held investments in US stocks, non-US stocks, emerging markets stocks, private equities, opportunistic real estate, value-added real estate, non-US real estate, hedge funds, commodities, and high yield bonds, as well as fixed income, cash, core real estate, and/or REITs. Some investors were allocated to 10 or more different asset classes and consequently felt as though they were sufficiently diversified to weather any storm.

Then, the credit crisis of 2008 happened, and all risky assets saw their values drop in lockstep. No matter whether an investor was invested in US stocks, emerging markets stocks, or private equities, every asset class except Treasury bonds decreased in value, including many cash money market funds. Whereas a seemingly diversified portfolio would have protected the investor from an isolated crisis in one or two asset classes, the lesson of 2008 was that the global financial markets are far more interconnected than they were widely believed to be. The interest rates required for any bank loans or non-Treasury debt skyrocketed, putting pressure on fixed income values and real estate investments that needed financing. The stock market value of banks around the world fell dramatically due to the declines in the values of the assets that they owned or claimed as collateral, leading to a further increase in rates and a decrease in lending. This caused the global economy to slow into a recession, making all other public and private equities fall in value as a result. As consumers started losing their jobs and saw their borrowing capacity decline, their interest in buying real estate fell to zero, leading to a downward spiral in the values of real estate investments and a further decline for the financial institutions who loaned money to real estate purchasers. And so the spiral continued.

Investors who thought that their allocations across 10 or 12 different asset classes would protect them from a broad decline found that the value of their treasury bonds increased (as they usually do in a crisis) while that of virtually every other asset class fell. Their great diversification was a myth.

The New Way to Manage Asset Class Risk

Out of the experience of the 2008 credit crisis came a new way of looking at asset allocation and risk management that is directly applicable to all investors, both large and small. Instead of determining a proper allocation to US stocks, non-US stocks, and emerging markets stocks as if each was truly a distinct asset class, many investors have shifted to a new paradigm wherein they allocate assets according to the purpose to each type of asset and then lump a variety of asset classes together accordingly. For example, public equities, private equities, high yield bonds, and higher-risk real estate generally generate good returns when the economy is expanding and poor returns when it is contracting. As a result, these assets could be thought of as the "growth" portion of a portfolio. Meanwhile, investment-grade fixed income investments, especially treasuries, tend to hold up better when the economy slows because interest rates fall and (as was discussed in Chapter 5) the prices of bonds correspondingly rise. Accordingly, these assets could be thought of as the "income" or "safety" portion of a portfolio. Finally, commodities, income-producing (core) real estate, and inflation-protected bonds like TIPS should perform better when growth is stagnant or positive but inflation is rising. As such, these assets could be thought of as the "inflation protection" portion of a portfolio.

Under this new paradigm, investors assess the risks that they see in the marketplace or the amount of risk they are willing to tolerate in their portfolio. Let's say that you are eight years away from retirement, are starting to think about de-risking your portfolio, and are concerned about the prospect of rising inflation. Based on your own personal understanding of the likelihood of various market events coming to pass or your asset size and cash flow needs in retirement, you might decide that you want to allocate 20% of your portfolio to inflation protection, 30% to income production, and 50% to growth. Other allocation categories could include "safety," wherein you make investments solely in short-term treasuries; "home runs," wherein you make investments in micro-cap technology companies to replicate venture capital returns; or whatever other categories you wish to define that help you to better understand and manage how your money is invested. Either with or without the help of a financial advisor, you can then determine how to fill each of those allocation "buckets," "themes," "categories," or however else you wish to think of these functional definitions of your investments.

Maybe you agree with me (see Chapter 8) that commodities are an unconvincing opportunity for a long-term buy-and-hold investor, so you invest half of the inflation-protected portion of your assets in TIPS and the other half in REITs. For the income-producing category, maybe you believe that it is most appropriate to keep 25% of that allocation in high-quality, shorter-duration fixed income and 5% in high-income REITs. Next, let's say you apportion 40% of your growth allocation in global public stocks, 5% in high yield, and 5% in growth-oriented REITs. At the end of the day, all three buckets have an allocation to REITs because REITs have some of the characteristics of each of your buckets, resulting in a total allocation of 20% of your assets to the REIT asset class; but those three allocations all have different and understandable purposes.

The end result of this category-based asset allocation planning process, ideally, should generate a similar outcome to what I discussed in Chapter 2. However, for those of you who prefer a more qualitative way of understanding how you are allocating their money and minimizing your exposure to risk, this approach toward risk management may allow you to sleep easier at night, knowing that your asset allocation plan is specifically designed to counter those risks that most concern you. As macroeconomic events warrant or your life plan changes (marriage, divorce, children, new job, inheritance, etc.), you can shift your assets among these various categories in a way that makes sense to you, bearing in mind my guidance from Chapter 2 to invest for, and keep in mind, the very long-term horizon.

Other Risks to Avoid

There are a wide variety of other risks that investors face in the marketplace, and no investor is immune to all of them. In this section, I will outline a handful of major risks that I have seen my clients face over the years and discuss the best ways to minimize their impacts or damage.

Churning Managers

In Chapter 7, I illustrated how difficult it is for any investment manager to consistently outperform the majority of his peers and a broad market index year after year after year. Even the most talented and well-resourced investment managers will have periods in which their investment philosophy simply does not work. A manager that is fantastic at finding the true underlying value of companies will generate great results during periods in which value stocks outperform growth stocks and the market is focused on deep fundamental research; but that manager will underperform when speculation and momentum drive the prices of securities with no connection to reality. Over long periods of time, I would expect that if the investment manager truly is skilled at stock selection, she or he will create value for clients, allowing for years here and there where the investment approach employed simply does not work.

It is during those poor performance times when investors stand to lose the most money. Let's say a mutual fund has performed terribly in recent years, lagging most of its peers and the index by several percentage points. If you don't sell the mutual fund and move your money somewhere else, you will lose even more if the fund continues to fall. If you do sell that fund and invest in another fund, however, you stand to lose if the original fund recovers and your new fund cannot continue the recent success that attracted you to it and falls in value.

What is an investor to do?

Most large institutional investors write investment policy statements that govern their decision making processes for asset allocation, manager selection, and so on. These policies provide a way for the organization to maintain continuity in its investment philosophy as investment committee members or employees come and go. They also provide legal protection for investment decisions that were entirely well-intentioned but produce lower-than-expected results. As long as a good policy is in place, a prudent decision that complies with the policy but ends up losing money can protect the investment committee from liability because they acted in accordance with their governing rules and lost money from a market movement or an unlucky outcome, not an imprudent decision.

In many of these policies, the pension plans that I work with have also written clear guidelines for when to fire and replace underperforming investment managers. The time frames vary from client to client somewhat, but generally large institutional investors will designate an underperforming investment manager as being "on watch" after one to three years of underperformance. Then, the client will closely monitor the manager's performance for another six to twelve months. If, at the end of that entire time period, nothing has improved, the client will undertake an effort to replace the investment manager. Keep in mind that there is nothing magical about a one- to three-year period. I have one client that uses a five-year rule and another that uses a rule of two consecutive underperforming years. The point is that each client has disciplined guidelines that they follow that overrule any emotion they might bring to the table when confronted by an underperforming manager. In every case, the formal process for making changes reduces the amount of rapid turnover, or churn, in the portfolio that can lead to compounding underperformance over time.

It is far too easy to watch a mutual fund in your portfolio generate a terrible one-year performance number, panic, and replace the investment manager a few months before that manager becomes the best performer of the subsequent year. If the fund is down, you cannot undo the damage that has been done and recoup your losses. All you can do is make your best guess about how performance will fare in the next period. The point of these watch-list periods is precisely to slow down the process of deciding to replace a manager. It takes a year or two or three of poor performance to place a manager on watch, then another year to monitor the manager for a recovery. If no improvements are made while the manager is on watch, then—and only then—is the manager replaced. As I discussed in Chapter 7, it can be very difficult to discern which managers are truly terrible and which are simply unlucky in any given quarter or year. Taking a reasonable amount of time to consider if a manager should be replaced allows for random variance in returns to filter out and a clearer picture to emerge that reveals whether the manager is truly skilled or not.

I recommend that you pick a time frame for your own pain threshold, starting with maybe a two-year review period, before placing your investment managers on your own watch list. Then take another year to see if they begin to recover. If you find after a cycle or two that you are constantly adding and deleting managers from your watch list due to the lumpiness of returns over any two-year period, try lengthening your time frame to three years or more. Although some investment managers really do make a permanent change from good to bad (due to changes in staff or a loss of a competitive advantage versus their peers) and honestly need replacement, I think you will find that most of the underperformance of formerly great managers is a transient result of market volatility, not a change in skill level—in which case, your patience may be rewarded with subsequent improvement.

The Exceptions to the Watch List Rule

The watch list process and time frames discussed previously should guide you through the process of evaluating whether to keep or replace investment managers that have normal periods of outperformance and underperformance. Keep in mind, though, that the application of long time frames for review does not apply in every case.

If performance is bad and the portfolio manager quits, half the firm is laid off, or three-quarters of the investment manager's product lines are shut down, you should not wait before deciding to move on. The company, the investment process, and the resources available to the portfolio management team have changed and no longer resemble what attracted you to this investment in the first place. Although it is entirely possible that the fund could bounce back, there are plenty of other great managers out there that are working in more stable organizations. The watch-list process is not intended to make you wait to see whether poor performance that results from, or causes, major organizational changes is a random occurrence. Similarly, if members of the team or organization are found to have broken securities regulations or other laws, get out immediately. Pension plans and endowments have no tolerance for these sorts of legal improprieties, and neither should you. Whereas many pension plans and endowments might take a week, a month, or even a calendar quarter to set up a meeting, discuss, vote, and then terminate a manager, you can react more quickly and sell a fund in a day—and you could be better served by being first out the door than the last.

Here is a real-world, worst-case scenario that illustrates when it may be appropriate to fire a manager quickly, without allowing for a long watchlist review period. A few years ago, a large investment manager reported to clients that it was replacing several key individuals because they had found a significant error in their computer-driven investment process and had hidden it from management for several months. Following the internal revelation of the programming problems, the company management then took another six months to terminate these individuals and inform clients about the errors. Within a matter of several weeks, the firm's assets dropped by more than 90% as virtually every client ended their relationship with this manager based on the perception of misplaced trust from the long delays before revealing what had happened. As much as I had admired this particular manager's cutting-edge research and portfolio construction process in the past, I agreed with my clients that trust comes first, so I helped them all through the termination and replacement process far more quickly than would have been allowed under the usual watchlist process.

As an investor in daily-valued mutual funds, you have a significant advantage over many large institutional investors because you can be out of a fund by the end of a given day. When necessary and appropriate, I strongly urge you to use that to your benefit.

Getting Scared

A 2012 study by Goldman Sachs showed that if you were fully invested in the stock market from 1992 to 2011, your annual return would have been 7.81%. If you were out of the market for the ten best days (which amounts to only one day every two years over that 20-year period), your returns would have been 4.14%. Without the best 40 days, you would have returned -2.31%; and without the best 70 days, you would have lost -7.20%.[2] Various other studies over the years from firms like Putnam Investments[3], Franklin Templeton Investments[4], and GE Asset Management[5] have used different time periods, different methodologies, and different numbers of missed days, but they have all reached generally the same conclusion: if you are not invested in a small handful of specific days over long periods of time, your returns can be radically impacted. In fairness, there have been a number of studies that have pointed out the exact opposite point: if an investor misses the 10 or 20 worst days of market performance in a given time period, their returns can be tremendously improved, too[6]. However, since these and other studies have shown that 50% or more of the best days occur within a few days or weeks of the worst days, often as a rebound that occurs shortly after a major fall in the markets, I posit that the existence of terrific days has less impact on the actual behavior of investors than does the existence of terrible days.

---

[2]The Penalty for Missing the Market, Goldman Sachs, January 30, 2012.
[3]Don't Miss the Market's Best Days, Putnam Investments, January 2012.
[4]5 Things you need to know to ride out a volatile stock market, Franklin Templeton Investments, 2012.
[5]Stock Market Ups and Downs, GE Asset Management, 2012.
[6]Missing the Ten Best, Paul J. Gire, CFP, Journal of Financial Planning, 1999, and "The Tale of 10 Days," Invesco Aim, August 2009.

Few people would ever watch the market jump up 5% in a day and sell off all their assets in fear that it might soon go down, thereby dodging the potentially terrible day to follow (because half of all worst days follow shortly after a great day). However, it is human nature for investors to experience a day where the market is down 10% or more and want to sell off all their assets to protect themselves against future losses. When crashes inevitably happen, and they will always happen again in the future, the investor who has converted his investments to cash could miss that "best day" recovery shortly thereafter, assuming one comes along. As a result, the investor who sells every time the market significantly falls (but not when it rises) might capture half of the market's good days (those that happen before the bad days) and all of the bad days that occur on their own.

My advice is to avoid being afraid and to stop reacting to short-term market movements out of fear. As I showed in Chapter 2, a diversified investor who rode out the 2001–2003 bear market earned back their entire portfolio value by 2005. Similarly, the 2008 crash and credit crisis were terrible, but many stock indices were close to their pre-crash highs by the middle of 2012—and a diversified investor would have fully recovered by about that same point in time. What should you do instead? Treat down days or weeks as buying opportunities. If you have 10 or 20 years or more until retirement and you are investing $500 a month regardless of the price of assets, why not invest $1,000 in a month when everything is half-off? If your time frame is sufficiently long to ride out even an extended downward market, like 2001–2003, steadily investing more than usual prepares your portfolio for an enhanced gain when markets recover.

Overconfidence

There are more than 25,000 mutual funds, 10,000 institutional-sized portfolios, and 8,000 hedge funds in operation in the world today, as well as hundreds of millions of individual investors. What are the odds that any one of those investors legally knows more about General Electric, Apple, or Citigroup than any other? Furthermore, what are the odds that any single investor has a systematic edge month after month and year after year over any other individual investor? I'm going to take a guess that the odds are rather low. In fact, I'm going to speculate that the odds that tens of millions of individual investors all have the ability to outperform the market and the industry professionals year in and year out are nil.

The stock market today is a place where rapid-trading hedge funds pay the stock exchanges huge fees to park their computer equipment a few feet away from the exchange's computer servers to make tiny profits on every transaction that crosses the market by minimizing the time that it takes for the electrons to move at the speed of light through the wires into their computers, through their trading algorithms and software, and back to the exchange's servers. If the hedge funds' and investment banks' computers were merely across the street, let alone miles away, they would be at a significant competitive disadvantage because those computers that are more closely positioned to the exchange's servers get to trade first. How can an individual investor who is trading at home, hundreds of miles away from the exchange, and using the relatively slow power of human thought to decide when to buy and sell hope to compete against a market like that? Any individual who thinks he or she can out-trade the professionals from the comfort of his or her couch is likely in for a rude awakening, regardless of what the advertisements on talk radio and financial television shows promise about their winning trading strategies.

Even with my background in the investment management and investment banking industries, in the past I have bought plenty of individual stocks that turned out to have terrific returns over the years, but I have also bought a few that ceased to exist. Like most people, I tended to think about those great performers a lot more than the losers and thought that I could repeat my success again and again, only to find that I earned mixed results over long periods of time. One reason, probably the main reason, is that by the time I heard something on TV or saw something in the paper that made me want to buy an individual stock, I probably was not in the first ten thousand people to act on that information. From these hard lessons, I've learned to follow my own advice to my clients that asset allocation, disciplined investment and contribution strategies, and risk management have generated far better returns for me over the years than a few superior stock selections have when you net out the bad picks.

My advice to every investor is to avoid overconfidence and the accompanying losses that can result when you approach the markets with cockiness. It is highly unlikely that an individual investor—especially one that invests on a part-time basis, when they are not focusing on the very real demands of their job, marriage, family, and friends—can consistently outperform the market as a whole. On the other hand, you do have control over your asset allocation, your contributions, and your retirement plans. You can control when you buy a mutual fund, sell, and rebalance. You can control the level of active risk in your portfolio by selecting concentrated or diversified active managers, index funds, and ETFs. You can control your costs. Individual investors will be much better served by focusing on those things that are under their control and can directly benefit their results.

Changing Retirement Goals at the Top

Closely following my advice regarding avoiding overconfidence and focusing on a savings and investment strategy that you can control is my recommendation that you must keep a clear investment goal in mind. You should treat your retirement savings like you do the throttle in your car, adding more gas (savings) when the road gets steep, but making sure that there is always enough gas in the tank to get you where you need to go. As I discussed in Chapter 2, one of the greatest risks that any investor faces is changing their retirement goals without sufficient time or security to do so. It is okay to plan to retire in luxury, as long as you save accordingly. Extrapolating great short-term results to plan for the long run without sufficient contributions when times get tough can be very dangerous and leave you far short of your needs.

The Next Big Thing

In *Nerds on Wall Street*, David Leinweber described how he was able to replicate the returns of the S&P 500 over a period of several years with more than 99% accuracy based on butter production in the United States and Bangladesh, US cheese production, and the sheep population in the United States and Bangladesh.[7] Although you could certainly make the argument that when economic times are good, people buy more butter and fancy sweaters than they do when times are bad, that is a pretty loose connection—and the author's findings reflect this fact. As the author describes, these correlations, which were derived from an examination of the returns of hundreds of different types of assets to find the best match, are far more likely to be due to random chance than to result from a true economic relationship. In subsequent periods, the model's predictive ability was virtually zero, meaning that the relationships that worked on paper in the past had nothing to do with subsequent reality.

I would love to be able to simply laugh at Dr. Leinweber's story as an example of math gone mad. However, loads of actual investment products are just as much the result of spurious correlation (a random mathematical correlation with no true relationship) or a great deal of 20/20 hindsight as the butter, cheese, and wool example is. In fact, an entire industry seems to have sprung up over the last fe v years that is dedicated to offering clients strategies based on little more than past historical relationships. Using Dr. Leinweber's brand of mathematical analysis, many firms offer backtested investment products that they claim replicate the returns of the real estate market, hedge funds, or private equities using stocks, bonds, and other traditional assets. While some

[7]Nerds on Wall Street - Math, Machines and Wired Markets, David Leinweber, Wiley, 2009.

of these firms may have a unique insight into the market—and they may have even found a new way to do business—my fear is that many of these products look great on paper but really have no more substance than Dr. Leinweber's replication of S&P returns with Bangladeshi butter and sheep.

One common example of the Next Big Thing at the time of this writing is risk parity. Because stocks are more volatile than bonds, even a portfolio that is 60% stocks and 40% bonds normally will have more than 80% of its day-to-day risk tied to the stock market. It isn't until a portfolio has less than 35% of its assets in stocks that you will start to see the share of total risk from stocks fall below 50%. To offset the risk that stocks pose to the average portfolio, a large number of investment management companies have begun to offer risk parity products that increase the portfolio's total exposure to bond risk to the point where it becomes more comparable (on parity) with that of stocks. In many cases, this might mean holding 60% of your portfolio's assets in stocks and another 60% of assets in bonds, using leverage to make up the rest. Compared to those of a traditional 60% stocks and 40% bonds or 70% stocks and 30% bonds portfolio, the backtested and hypothetical returns for risk parity products look fantastic. As such, the products are being marketed as a panacea to pension plans that have less in assets than they do in promised benefits and need to find ways to close that gap quickly.

But are risk parity products as promising as they seem? Consider the following: Since about 1980, interest rates have been on a steady downward slide, and the last six years in particular have seen interest rates—especially short-term rates—fall to all-time lows[8]. As I discussed in Chapter 5, this rapid and large decline in rates has led to tremendous gains in price for bond investors. In retrospect, borrowing some money and buying bonds with leverage would have been a fantastic machine for printing money when rates fell to near zero. But what happens tomorrow? Rates cannot continue to drop as much as they already have because there is a floor at zero. When rates rise, a leveraged investment in bonds could have losses compounded by that leverage. In early 2013, for example, many risk parity portfolios suffered losses precisely as predicted when rates began to rise.

In fairness, some risk parity strategies have been adjusted to allow for this possibility in the future and now propose investing in other assets going forward. Consider, for example, so-called "All Weather" strategies, which invest in a wide variety of asset classes to prepare a portfolio for a variety of future economic environments. In addition, as interest in risk parity products grows, the market appears to be moving away from the fantastic hypothetical and simulated returns that were peddled to clients in the past. Nevertheless, when you are confronted with a simplistic leveraged fixed income strategy, you must

---

[8]See Figure 5-1 for more detail.

always question whether a strategy that worked so well on paper will generate as fantastic results in practice—even if the backtest looks fantastic. Hopefully the more diversified strategies will bear better results.

If the preceding paragraphs have not made my opinion on the matter clear, my advice to investors is to always be wary of the Next Big Thing, especially when it is driven by backtests. In every bull market, someone will try to sell a new idea that promises to get you all of the upside of the market but expose you to none of the downside. Then, when the next bear market inevitably rolls around, those optimistic bull market strategies will go the way of the dodo, and the new hot idea will promise to protect your money from any calamity. Rarely will those offering either of these ideas have any real performance history to show you, and it is unlikely that either will survive the next market cycle. If it truly was possible to capture all of the return and none of the risk in a given market, the world would be full of trillionaires. Use your best judgment and invest in strategies that you can understand and agree with—not just those that seem foolproof on paper.

Summary

Simply put, the best way to manage and reduce your risk is to take risk only when it is appropriate, well-considered, and consistent with your long-term investment plan. There is no magic way to generate the returns that you need, other than by following a steady and disciplined plan of consistent savings, sticking to your long-term asset allocation targets in good markets and bad, and maintaining a clear idea of your end investment goals. Refraining from chasing a fast trend, ignoring the Next Big Thing, and staying with a manager when performance lags might cause you to miss the occasional big win. However, doing so will also prevent you from falling into the trap of adding risk to your portfolio at precisely the wrong time and suffering the inevitable consequences.

Putting It All Together

Achieve your Financial Independence

Using the expert advice in this book, you have designed an asset allocation plan appropriate to your needs, worked your way through the question of whether you want indexed or active management (or some of both), determined which fixed income sectors you are willing to take risk in, and considered whether you can find alternative investments that are worth the high cost. Because you have worked your way through Chapter 7, you have also selected a diversified—yet not excessively large—stable of portfolio managers and mutual funds; examined your fees and expenses for places where you can reduce these drags on your long-term performance; and reviewed whether the risks you are taking in your investments have a reasonable chance of compensating you in excess of what they could cost you.

You are done, right? Now you can just ride off into the sunset?

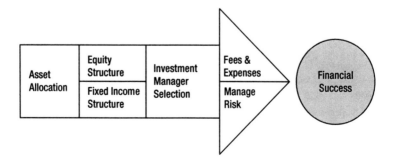

Not even close. Although the journey shown in the Road Map to Financial Success seems like a one-way trip, in practice it is a trip you must take over and over throughout your career, especially whenever your life's circumstances change. Managing your portfolio well requires you to take a combination of big steps, like those that are shown in the Road Map to Financial Success; little steps, like periodic rebalancing when one asset class generates meaningfully different returns; and continuous steps, like monitoring your investment managers for good or bad performance and organizational change on an ongoing basis. You never get to round the bases, jump on home plate, high-five your teammates, and go home. Managing your portfolio to maximize your chances of success is a lifelong challenge that entails a steadfast commitment to following closely the steps that I have outlined in this book. Instead of a baseball game, think of investing more like a 100-mile ultramarathon. You have an overall race strategy that you will need to adjust as your own progress and the external environment warrant; checkpoints at every mile to evaluate how you are doing; support when you need it from those closest to you; but, most unlike that baseball game, few adoring crowds to push you on your way. Your efforts and discipline to stay on the path must be almost entirely self-driven if you are going to have success.

As I have mentioned throughout this book, the world of investments is a competitive field. Millions of investors are looking at the same economic news, market returns, and multiple data points; and many of them have huge, dedicated, highly trained staffs of people to do so. Therefore, I urge you to focus on the real advantages that you bring to the table versus many of your peers and even large institutions like pension plans and endowments.

First, you can take a long-term, static, unemotional approach to asset allocation that is unbiased and uninfluenced by outside forces. Your contribution plan and your asset allocation plan can be determined with only your own interests in mind, with no need to compromise between the beliefs or values of a variety of interested parties. In the asset allocation, investment structure, and manager selection chapters, I have made some pension fund trustees and staffs sound like patient monks, always doing the best and smartest things they can with every single investment decision that they make. Ideally, they should be unemotional and long-term focused. In practice, however, many of their decisions are compromises that must balance a number of competing considerations, not all of them purely investment related, as I discussed in the section that outlined how you are free to act in your own best interests without outside influence or compromise.

Second, you can commit to making constant contributions to your portfolio, even when times are good, your returns are stellar, and extra dollars into the retirement plan seem unnecessary but will build up a rainy day surplus to protect you from a market downturn. In addition, unlike some pension plans, you can maintain a commitment to a constant level of benefits: your eventual retirement plan. When your returns are good, no one pressures you to reduce your contributions to your savings or increase your retirement goals. You can keep on a steady pace, exactly as you planned. Although this sounds simple, it is the single greatest benefit that your independence as an investor affords you. As I outlined in Chapter 2 on asset allocation, keeping yourself on that steady path is the surest way to get to your destination.

Third, although even small pension funds have massive scale and can negotiate cheaper investment manager fees than the average investor, if you devote yourself to reducing costs, you can significantly close that gap. Individual investors have no staff salaries to pay, investment or pension office overhead expenses, travel costs, and so on. In addition, whereas pension funds need to pay custodial banks and record keepers large fees to house their assets, audit their trades, and send out their benefit checks, with a little bit of shopping you can find a wide variety of banks, brokerages, and mutual fund companies who will provide you with no-fee IRA and brokerage accounts, interest-bearing cash sweep accounts, and no-commission ETF or mutual fund trades. For a large pension plan, the external costs of these banking and recordkeeping relationships can be anywhere from 0.20% to 0.50% a year, whereas all of this can be free for your personal account if you are willing to not only invest the time in doing a little comparison shopping but also undergo the headache of moving your assets from bank to bank or brokerage to brokerage when it is clear you have found a better deal. Though less than half a percentage point sounds like a small price to pay, it can add up to a difference of tens or even hundreds of thousands of dollars in final assets for a very long-term investor.

If you have taken the advice and guidance that I have presented in these pages to heart, I hope that you will be open to two more pieces of advice. First, please eradicate the language of Las Vegas from your discussions about investing. You are trying to build and secure your future. You are investing in the equity and debt of great corporations and profiting from their endeavors over meaningful periods of time. Investing should not be confused with blackjack or roulette. So, please, don't "double down" on a losing position. Buy a share of a company, don't place a "bet" on it. Invest in a company, don't gamble on something that you know as nothing more than a three- or four-letter ticker symbol. These are companies that make real products and employ real people; they are not "names" for you to place "bets" on.

The more that you can imagine that, even on a smaller scale, you are replicating the long-term, forward-looking work of great investors like Warren Buffett or Sir John Templeton, who have a deep understanding of what they are investing in and an eye toward a long time frame, the lower the churn, fees, expenses, and probably volatility in your portfolio will be. Pension plans invest to provide benefits to the old and the young, including recent hires in their 20s and dependents of their members who are still in their childhoods, which means that their financial obligation could last as long as

80–100 years. You build wealth over generations like these pension plans do through careful planning and a disciplined execution of a suitable investment plan—not by hoping that the stock CNBC is hyping today is worth more tomorrow.

The second thing I ask is that you simply turn off the financial investment talk shows. Stop making their contributors and guests richer by simply following the strategies they have already put in place and buying the stocks they already own, thereby bidding up the prices so they can sell at a profit. If you want to stay informed, read the *Financial Times* or *Wall Street Journal* to find out what is happening in the economy and markets. Better yet, read the *Economist* and start thinking in terms of decades and generations, not daily news cycles. Not only will you rest easier by not worrying about every investment decision you made that day, but you will give your wealth a chance to work for you and grow without interruption. When you reach the age that you need to finally draw on your resources, you can be certain that the patient, steady, disciplined, and lower-cost path will have served you better than a lifetime of risk, volatility, chasing fads, and second-guessing.

I

Index

value and growth investment
  cumulative record, 52–54
  DFA, 54
  potential client, 51
  prospective client's question, 51
  rolling three-year performance, 51
  style bias, 50
Synthetic equity strategies, 71–72

T, U

Three–five year
  planning period, 24–25
Top quartile funds, 139

V, W, X, Y, Z

Venture capital (VC), 135–136

Other Apress Business Titles You Will Find Useful

**Plan Your Financial
Future**
Fevurly
978-1-4302-6064-6

Financial Freedom
Advani
978-1-4302-4539-1

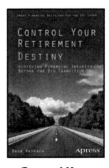

**Control Your
Retirement Destiny**
Anspach
978-1-4302-5022-7

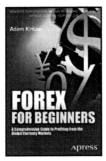

Forex for Beginners
Kritzer
978-1-4302-4050-1

Traders at Work
Bourquin/Mango
978-1-4302-4443-1

Tactical Trend Trading
Robbins
978-1-4302-4479-0

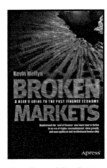

Broken Markets
Mellyn
978-1-4302-4221-5

**Investing in Emerging
Markets**
Gamble
978-1-4302-3825-6

**Protect Your Wealth from
the Ravages of Inflation**
King
978-1-4302-3822

Available at www.apress.com

CPSIA information can be obtained at www.ICGtesting.com
Printed in the USA
LVOW10s0310290813

350122LV00008B/218/P

9 781430 250593